GENDER TALES

Tensions in the Schools

GENDER

TALES

Tensions in the Schools

Judith S. Kleinfeld
University of Alaska Fairbanks

Suzanne Yerian
University of Washington

EDITORS

ST. MARTIN'S PRESS • New York

This book is dedicated to my double and opposite—my husband, Andrew Jay Kleinfeld—and to our children, Daniel, Rachel, and Joshua

JUDITH S. KLEINFELD

This book is dedicated to the people who have seen me through it all—my parents, Stan and Betty Pine; my brothers, Stan and Mike; and my daughter, Kelly

SUZANNE YERIAN

EDITOR: Naomi Silverman
MANAGER, PUBLISHING SERVICES: Emily Berleth
EDITOR, PUBLISHING SERVICES: Doug Bell
PROJECT MANAGEMENT: Richard Steins
PRODUCTION SUPERVISOR: Alan Fischer
ART DIRECTOR: Sheree Goodman
TEXT DESIGN: Gene Crofts
COVER DESIGN: Marek Antoniak

Library of Congress Catalog Card Number: 94-65157

Manufactured in the United States of America.
9 8 7 6 5
f e d c b a

For information, write:
St. Martin's Press, Inc.
175 Fifth Avenue
New York, NY 10010

ISBN: 0–312–10748–X

Preface

Most Americans believe that schools should develop the talents of all students, girls just as much as boys. We want all students, regardless of their sex or their race or their background, to have equal opportunity in our classrooms.

These are our ideals. Yet our classrooms usually mirror the same injustices we see in our culture. When we look at gender, the focus of this casebook, we see entrenched and upsetting patterns. Teachers give boys more attention than girls at every grade level. Boys get more of the intellectual jousting that develops a quick and lively mind. When researchers videotape their classrooms, even teachers strongly committed to women's issues are shocked to find that they, too, favor the boys. Why do they do so?

Some teachers take active steps to organize their classrooms in gender-fair ways. They emphasize group projects in which all students must take an active role. They rotate leadership positions so that girls as well as boys must learn to lead the group. All too often, these teachers find that the girls, as well as the boys, resist. The classroom slips back into old and comfortable ways. What should the teacher do then?

We may all believe that boys and girls should be treated equally. When we get down to cases, however, we find that we do not agree on what equal treatment means. Schools are complicated places, and in many situations we face competing values. We want equal opportunity for boys and girls, and we want all students to be free of sexual harassment, and we want all students to develop their physical abilities to the fullest and to play a sport at the peak of the game. Should we then allow girls on the wrestling team?

Teachers must be sensitive not only to gender but also to students' cultural and economic backgrounds. Many teachers may believe in gender equality, but many families give boys precedence. Suppose a Chinese girl pours out her troubles to her teacher—her parents favor her brother and threaten to spank her if she does not learn the multiplication tables over the weekend. Should the teacher do anything?

These are the kinds of real-world teaching dilemmas that teachers face when they set out to be fair and to develop the abilities of all their students,

girls as much as boys. We usually agree in principle. The problems come
when we turn to practice, when we get down to cases.

The Purpose of a Casebook on Gender Issues

We have developed this casebook because cases go beyond principles and
platitudes. Cases reveal the real world in all its complexity and ambiguity.
Cases show the kinds of dilemmas you, yourself, may face in the classroom.
Studying cases gives you the luxury of learning from others' experience.
You have time to think about these situations, to see what other people did,
and to learn from their successes and mistakes.

Although every situation is unique, you well may face the same kinds
of problems described in the cases in this book. The cases are particular
examples of general problems—how to deal with a classroom where a few
male stars dominate the discussion; what sexual harassment is (and what is
merely clumsy adolescent flirtation); how to recognize talent in young
women of color who do not display their abilities in the ways expected by a
teacher from a different background.

This casebook is intended to supplement textbooks and readings that
present theory and research findings on gender equity. The cases show you
what the problems look like in real classroom settings. The great advantage
of cases is that they ask you to figure out how to handle such problems not
in the abstract but in concrete situations complicated by particular personalities, competing values, cultural and class differences, and community conflicts. Cases go beyond prescriptions and lists of effective instructional strategies; they point out the importance of tone and nuance in what you do as a
teacher.

The study of cases does not substitute for classroom experience, but it
is a valuable supplement. Cases slow down the action. They give you the
chance to replay the tape—to view the scene again and see how other
people react. You may be surprised at how differently other people see the
same events. Talking with others about cases gives you insight into their
perspectives and helps you to see your own blind spots.

As a teacher, you will be working with cases—complicated human
situations. This book helps prepare you for them. Many are cautionary tales
that carry an implicit warning: This could happen to you.

Preparing for and Discussing a Case

Studying cases helps you acquire the art of learning from experience. Cases
let you practice thinking your way through troubling situations, rather than
dismissing them or rushing to careless action. You learn to frame your
personal experience as a case and to ask yourself the questions you would
ask in discussing a case: What are the issues here? Which matters demand

immediate action? Are there fundamental problems that drive this upsetting situation? What are the options? What is fair? What is at risk and what
is at stake?

Many of our students, after studying cases, tell us that these habits of
mind are helpful when they start to teach. When they run into trouble, they
have learned to say to themselves: "This situation would make a good case.
Keep calm. Think it through."

If you are asked to read a case to prepare for class discussion or to
write an analysis of a case, ask yourself questions like these:

1. *What happened? What is going on here?* You should be able to state the
   facts of the case, and you should be able to offer an interpretation
   of its events and what they mean.
2. *What perspectives might other people have?* You should be able to describe how the situation might appear to other people involved. If
   the case is told from the teacher's viewpoint, think about how students might interpret the same scene, how parents might react, and
   what the principal is likely to think.
3. *What are the issues?* You should be able to identify a number of
   problems in the situation. Look beyond the immediate crisis to the
   underlying problems that precipitated it. Consider not only the
   issue facing the teacher but also the underlying policy issues for
   the school as an institution.
4. *What are the strategies for action?* You should be able to identify a
   number of options for dealing with the situation. Try to describe
   the courses of action that the teacher might take and what their
   consequences might be.

In the case discussion, your professor will very likely try to elicit controversy in order to sharpen the issues and make you aware of your assumptions and the grounds for your opinions. In good case discussions, different
principles are pitted against each other—for example, the importance of
protecting people's feelings versus the importance of free speech. Expect
arguments and different viewpoints to arise.

Good case discussions can keep you on the edge of your seat. Like
stories, cases also give pleasure. They are full of the drama and interest of
human life.

Development of Casebook

This casebook began when a group of experienced elementary and secondary schoolteachers—the Gender Equity Project Teachers—met to discuss
the problems of nurturing the talents of young women, especially in mathematics and science. These teachers wrote many of the cases in this book in
order to prepare new teachers for the practical difficulties they had encoun-

tered when trying to put into practice what they had learned in university classes and in-service programs on gender equity.

We included many cases because they explore common problems in increasing the achievement of young women. We sought other cases not because they examine representative problems but because they capture in concrete and dramatic form great cultural conflicts and divides. Gender issues have become a flashpoint in our society. Some cases in this book have made headlines around the world; others have been debated in the courts, but their issues remain unsettled.

In presenting these cases, we have tried to leave room for alternative political perspectives. Some students hold radical feminist views. Others take liberal feminist positions. Some students have traditional views that are not considered "politically correct." We have found that many students sit silent in classroom discussions of gender issues because they hold unpopular views and fear personal attacks. We have seen students both with radical feminist views and with traditional views silenced by the weight of group opinion.

We want all students to be able to use case discussions to form and test their ideas, to see where alternative theoretical formulations lead in practical terms, and to consider with care positions different from their own. Change in attitudes, we believe, does not occur when people are backed up against the wall but when they feel safe enough to express their ideas—and to reconsider the problem from a new angle. We selected many cases precisely because they are not morality tales but instead raise troubling issues about which reasonable people of good will can disagree.

Good cases arise from conflicts, and good conflicts can be illuminating. We hope these cases create spirited debate and honest dialogue.

Organization of Casebook

We have organized the cases in this casebook into five parts:

= The Meaning of Gender Equality in the Schools
= Increasing Achievement among Young Women
= Establishing Professional Standing for Female Teachers
= Sexual Harassment in the Schools
= Sexual Slurs, Sexual Stereotypes, and the Marketplace of Ideas

The introduction to each of these parts highlights the fundamental issues explored by the cases.

Keep in mind that each case raises many issues. Learning how to spot the different issues in a messy situation is one of the central purposes of teaching by the case method. We have organized the cases according to their basic issues, but many cases also deal with issues that are highlighted in other sections of the casebook. "Jane, the Reluctant Mathlete," for example, focuses on what gender equity may mean in a mathematics classroom, but it also shows how a teacher can reorganize a classroom to improve the mathematics achievement of young women.

After each case, questions alert you to the major gender issues involved. With some questions, we play devil's advocate, challenging your beliefs in order to make you clarify and justify your views. Each case is also followed by a list of suggested readings that illuminate the issues raised by the case.

Some cases are followed by an epilogue that tells how the story ended. When we want you to think about the issues before you know how they were resolved, we raise the questions before giving the epilogue, and we place the readings and activities after the epilogue.

The activities after each case are intended to give you experience that brings the issues of the case to life. These interviews and observations will show you some of the ways that such issues may surface in your own school and community. Be aware, however, that any kind of data collection requires the permission of school administrators and the teachers involved. Most administrators have no objection to small, informal research projects if the goals are clear and if staff members are informed.

The Instructor's Manual that accompanies this casebook is valuable for students as well as for professors teaching the cases. The manual does not give "answers," of course, since cases have no right answers. Instead, the Instructor's Manual discusses the issues in the cases from different viewpoints, and it offers relevant research as well as expanded lists of readings and activities.

Acknowledgments

We especially want to thank the teachers who participated in the gender equity project: Deborah Reynolds, Pamela Randles, Leslie Gordon, Theresa Hall, Janine Lombardi, Betty McKinny, Stephanie Rudig, Michelle Saiz, and Gerry Young. We also thank the experienced teachers who wrote and reviewed cases: Elizabeth Horikowa, Paris Finley, and John Martin. Many teachers, because they were writing about politically sensitive issues, chose to present their cases anonymously. We appreciate their generous contribution to our profession.

We are grateful to the University of Alaska for providing financial support for this work. Susan Mitchell and Paula Elmes from the Center for Cross-Cultural Studies did valuable editing on many of these cases. Angie Sparks assisted with the typing of draft after draft as we struggled to make the cases both interesting and accurate.

Our editors at St. Martin's Press—Naomi Silverman, Carl Whithaus, and Sarah Picchi—were exceptionally helpful in providing advice, ideas, and assistance with this manuscript. We also appreciate the excellent advice of those who reviewed the casebook in draft form and alerted us to problems of omission and confusions of tone: Kathleen Bennett DeMarrais, University of Tennessee, Knoxville; Nona Lyons, University of Southern Maine; Wilma Miranda, Northern Illinois University; and several anonymous reviewers.

Contents

should drop the girl from the team or stick with her despite the risks to other students on the team.

---

*For reasons of confidentiality, the Gender Equity Project teachers prefer to be recognized for case authorship as a group. Participating teachers are Leslie Gordon, Theresa Hall, Janine Lombardi, Betty McKinny, Pamela Randles, Deborah Reynolds, Stephanie Rudig, Michelle Saiz, and Gerry Young, who teach in Fairbanks, Alaska, schools. Beth Horikowa, a teacher at Monroe Catholic High School in Fairbanks, Alaska, also contributed to these cases.

gifted girl who at adolescence resists conventions, gets pregnant, and drops out of school. Can the teacher help April find a way out?

Anna, a Mexican-American student with a rep as one of the school's toughest female gang members, crumples up her A papers and announces loudly to her friends, "Damn, another F!" Can her history teacher help Anna develop a different identity and go on to college?

Diane News can only recommend four students to the district's new gifted-and-talented program and is disturbed to find that her best candidates are all boys. The father of an African-American female student insists that the teacher recommend his daughter, but Diane News sees the girl as a "concrete thinker."

A Chinese third-grade girl is overwhelmed with emotional problems. Her parents favor her brother, threaten to spank her if she does not learn the multiplication tables by Monday, and have even given away her beloved dog. The teacher struggles to help her and to understand this Asian family.

Furious when her Jewish mother tells her that a foreign service career will interfere with marriage and children, Susan says her teachers are nothing but hypocrites for pushing achievement for women. Does a girl still have to compromise her dreams? she demands of her feminist English teacher.

Roberto, a Mexican-American student, has a good chance of getting into Stanford and going on to law school. An African-American teacher applies her own cultural and gender-based perspective to his decision: Don't go to a white rich kids' school where you'll be a minority face, cut off from your roots.

When the boys in Lisa's English class make sucking and moaning sounds behind her desk and push her up against her locker,
the assistant principal urges her to write a complaint, the first
step under the school's sexual-harassment policy. Lisa writes
the memo but refuses permission to deliver it to the boys. What
is going wrong?

Trying to persuade teen-age Rosa to learn to read, Mr. Wineburg attempts to establish a personal relationship. She tells the
school authorities the student teacher's interest in her is sexual.
Does he misunderstand her Hispanic cultural background, or
is street-wise Rosa setting him up?

In Mr. Monroe's view, he had done nothing wrong. He had just
ignored Shannon's flirtatious behavior, like the glamour photograph she gave him with a sexual invitation. How could he be
facing legal charges of sexual harassment and suspension of his
teaching license?

Mark had no intention of starting a court case when he wore to
school the *Co-Ed Naked Band* T-shirt that his parents gave him
for Christmas. But he and his parents see the school's banning
of his T-shirt as censorship of free speech and a pandering to
politics.

The Harvard Women's Law Association attacks Professor Macneil on the grounds that he is using sexist language and insulting sexual stereotypes. He accuses them of McCarthyism, of
using power politics to destroy the educational atmosphere necessary for the free expression of ideas in a university classroom.

>   José, who hates writing English, scratches down a few sentences
>   about girls and their nice behinds. Should Mr. Andrews encour-
>   age José to develop his ideas, even if where this teen-ager sees
>   beauty is in girls' bottoms?

>   College women read a John Updike story about a young gro-
>   cery clerk's sexual thoughts when he sees girls wearing only
>   bathing suits shopping at the A&P as nothing more than a
>   degrading sexist tract. The English teacher cannot bring the
>   students back to her analytic objectives. Should she?

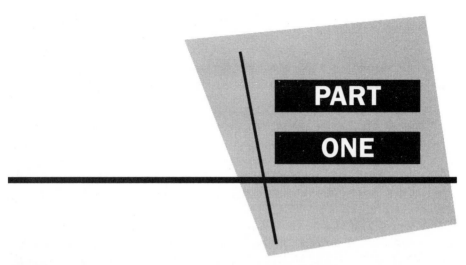

PART

ONE

The Meaning of Gender Equality in the Schools

Introduction

Most Americans think that people should be treated equally regardless of their sex. But we do not all agree on what that means. Nor do we agree on how to overcome inequalities that do exist between males and females in classrooms and activities. We do not always agree on what is effective and what is fair.

This excerpt from the teaching diary of the first author, Judith Kleinfeld, illustrates a classic dilemma:

> "You do not let the women in this class talk!" John informed me angrily after class.
>
> His accusation astonished me. We had just finished what I had thought was a particularly exciting class. John and another young man had started to debate an educational issue. Other students had joined the discussion. The intellectual momentum of the ideas was driving the class forward. I no longer had to call on students with raised hands.
>
> But few women in the class had joined the debate, I realized. John's accusation stung—I did not "let" the women talk. I "let" everyone talk, I told myself. The problem was that most of the women just sat there.
>
> Why were the women so often silent? As a female professor who de-lighted in debate, I was a living role model. I did *look* at the men more, I realized. Maybe the nonverbal eye contact encouraged them to talk. But then the men were more likely to look at me, especially in a quizzical, argumenta-tive way that encouraged me to challenge them. When I looked at the women, they were more often taking notes, their eyes down on the page.

I mentioned John's observations to a few of the quiet women in the class and asked what I could do to make the class more comfortable for women to talk.

"Oh, John's just one of those feminist men who are always pressuring women," one of the female students snapped. "Nothing's changed. Men always try to dominate us and tell us what to do. I like this class just fine. I don't always want to talk."

Think about this class from the standpoint of what equality means. From my perspective, I was providing equal opportunity. Everyone could talk. But the structure of the classroom—freewheeling debate in which students interrupted each other—favored the discussion style of men.

My class was hardly unusual. From grade school to graduate school, studies show, a few "star" males typically dominate class discussions (Sadker & Sadker, 1985a, 1985b). Male students tend to talk more in class and to call out answers more. Male students typically receive more attention from the teacher: praise, criticism, and, most important, specific responses to their ideas, which stimulates intellectual growth.

What, if anything, should or could I do about this situation in my own classroom? None of the women were complaining, and the spirited discussion was accomplishing just what I wanted—an analysis of different facets of complex educational issues. Did every student have to talk in order to learn?

I asked the advice of a male professor known for his conservative views. His reaction surprised me: "I don't think you should let the women get away with being quiet in class even if they want to," he said. "If women want positions of public authority, they have to learn how to take a position and argue for their views."

Maybe I should insist that the women—and the quiet men in the class—participate, even though discussions would be less lively and probably less interesting. For example, I could conduct a discussion by going around the group and asking for everyone to speak in turn. That would provide equal opportunities to speak, but it also might lead to a dull discussion.

I asked the advice of a female professor known for strong feminist views. She reminded me of the research on gender-based differences in styles of talk. Many females prefer collaborative conversations in which people build on each other's ideas, rather than debate and argument. She said that I should be sensitive to and support women's style of talk. When a woman suggests an idea, for example, I could ask other students to build on it, rather than encouraging students to argue the matter. But if I used this approach, I realized, I would not be teaching women to engage in debate. In addition, I wondered which speaking style actually brings results in the profession of teaching (which is what I was preparing students for): argumentative debate or collaborative talk?

This "case" of my own teaching illustrates the dilemmas in defining and achieving gender equity. What does equal educational opportunity mean? Is it enough to provide every student the same opportunities to talk, or does the underlying structure of the classroom favor males? Is the teacher's bias the problem, or is the problem the gender-based scripts that students bring into the classroom? Should educators insist that young women learn "male" styles, or should they support "female" styles?

The other cases in Part One present similar situations that raise subtle and complex teaching issues. Reasonable people of good will can disagree. We hope that discussing these cases will help you clarify your own ideas about gender equality. Class discussion may also introduce you to other experiences and viewpoints that you have not had the opportunity to consider.

Single Standards, Double Standards, New Standards

The first case, " 'Girlspeak' and 'Boyspeak': Gender Differences in Classroom Discussion," invites you to think through this widespread teaching dilemma. A social studies teacher struggles to understand the different ways that boys and girls talk in his class—and how he himself may be aiding and abetting negative patterns. Why do these differences arise, and what, if anything, can he do about them?

The next two cases ask you to consider how teachers' own families and cultural experiences shape their relationships with male and female students. Without realizing it, we play out practices from the past, including our own traumas and prejudices (Keating, 1990).

In "A Rare Commodity" a young African-American female teacher finds that African-American girls in her class first cling to her, demanding to know the details of her personal life and sucking up her identity as they try to use her as a model for achievement. Then the girls turn on her, charging that she discriminates against them and is easier on the African-American boys in their class. This case invites you to think about how different cultures shape gender problems and about equity when special relationships develop between teachers and students.

In "The Teacher Who Knew Too Much" a female teacher of chemistry and physics strongly identifies with a female student whose life parallels her own—including an alcoholic father, too many female family duties, and lack of parental support for a daughter's academic interests. The teacher has always had high standards; she strictly enforces science-project deadlines and has a policy of "no exceptions." But when Katie's family problems prevent her from meeting the deadline, the teacher wonders whether she should make an exception. What about being fair to other students in the class, who may have problems of their own? And what will help Katie most? "People have always made exceptions for me," the teacher poignantly observes. "The funny thing is that the ones who *didn't* are the ones I remember and respect the most."

"Jane, the Reluctant Mathlete" shows how a teacher can change a mathematics classroom to create an educational environment in which both boys and girls achieve. But how far should a teacher go in supporting and nurturing an underrepresented individual, a female math star, at the expense of other students? When Jane's interests at adolescence turn from mathematics to males, her behavior threatens the success of the team and the chances of other students for college scholarships. Jane is trying to deal with the classic dilemma facing bright girls: They want to do well in school, but they also want to be "feminine" and make themselves attractive to boys. As Jane's teacher, how would you approach this situation?

The issue of double standards is central in "Her Work Is Not Scholarly!" Department chair Bruce Gardiner decides against Audrey Mayles's tenure application because he sees her writing as "too soft" and "not scholarly." Audrey's flamboyant dress and lifestyle may have contributed to her tenure predicament. A woman on the tenure committee voted for Audrey on the grounds of "sisterhood," but privately she questions Audrey's professionalism. Does traditional research rest on a male-dominated system that privileges abstract, quantitative work and dismisses as less worthy the "softer" content areas with their rich, qualitative traditions?

Equal Treatment and Discrimination by Sex

The next group of cases ask you to consider the implications of the landmark legislation Title IX of the Education Amendments of 1972, which forbids discrimination on the basis of sex. Title IX and other federal and state legislation and regulations have become powerful weapons in forcing schools to promote equality for women. Bailey (1993) points out that in 1972, the year Title IX was passed, only 4 percent of high-school girls participated in sports; twenty years later, one-third participate. Still, twice as many boys as girls participate in sports, and boys' athletics are usually better funded and the focus of far more attention from teachers, students, and the community.

Title IX seems to state a clear and simple principle on which most Americans agree: Educational institutions that accept public funds should not discriminate on the basis of sex. But the meaning of nondiscrimination—as the cases in this section show—is not so simple.

Here is the actual language of Title IX:

(a) No person in the United States shall, on the basis of sex, be excluded from participation in, be denied the benefits of, or be subjected to discrimination under any educational program or activity receiving Federal financial assistance, except that:

[Congress here listed exceptions in which discrimination based on sex is allowed, such as religious organizations that hold contrary beliefs, colleges that historically have admitted only students of one gender, and such groups as the YMCA, YWCA, Girl Scouts, and Boy Scouts.]

Title IX and related statutes have been the subject of regulations, guidelines and policy statements by administrative agencies, decisions by federal courts, and applications by administrators. The law in this area is new, in flux, and evolving. To learn what the law requires in a particular case, a school district ordinarily would consult attorneys, who would research the law for the particular problem in that district's location. It is not prudent to guess what the law is on the basis of a few cases in the media or in a book like this. In fact, we offer a few cases involving the application of Title IX not to teach you "the law" but to help you think through the persistent issues that confront educators. The cases raise these issues in especially clear and interesting ways.

In "Girls on the Wrestling Team: A Community Fight" a small town explodes with controversy when the rookie wrestling coach admits to a reporter that he does not want girls on the wrestling team. Wrestling holds, he says, require sexual touchings that are not respectful to women. The coach, an American-Indian teacher, also wants male wrestling teams because of his cultural beliefs about gender-based social roles. Boys should be taught "some things about being a man in our society," he tells the reporter, "that are not what a woman should be taught." Males need to learn attitudes, behavior, and skills that will enable them to protect and cherish women. Some community members see these beliefs as paternalistic and oppressive, as well as a clear violation of Title IX, and they want the coach fired.

The last case in Part One, "The Venerable Tradition of Separate-Sex Schooling," invites you to consider a paradox: Could the principle of nondiscrimination by sex actually conflict with the goal of increasing achievement for females? Susan Vorcheimer's parents sue the school district when she is refused admission to Central High School in Philadelphia, a school for academically talented boys. Susan can attend Girls' High School, which is designated for academically talented girls. Although the research is not conclusive, some studies suggest that girls focus more on academic work and are better prepared for adult leadership positions when they attend all-girl schools. Should we consider "separate but equal" schools inherently discriminatory in the area of gender as we do in the area of race? Should actual effects on achievement be taken into account? This question has come up again with proposals for sexsegregated math and science classes on the grounds that such classes increase girls' achievement.

These are tough cases which invite you to think about difficult but interesting issues that actually arise in schools. It is easy to agree about generalities that advance gender equality and oppose discrimination, but it is hard to apply such generalities to the concrete problems that educators face. Discussing these hard cases, we hope, will help you develop clearer and richer views about gender equality and what it means for you as a teacher.

REFERENCES

Bailey, S. M. (1993). The current status of gender equity research in American schools. *Educational Psychologist* 28 (4): 321–339.

Keating, P. (1990). Striving for sex equity in schools. In *Access to knowledge: An agenda for our nation's schools,* ed. J. Goodlad and P. Keating, 91–106. New York: College Entrance Examination Board.

Sadker, D., and M. Sadker. (1985a). Is the ok classroom ok? *Phi Delta Kappan* 55: 358–367.

Sadker, D., and M. Sadker. (1985b). Sexism in the schoolroom of the 80s. *Psychology Today* 19: 54–57.

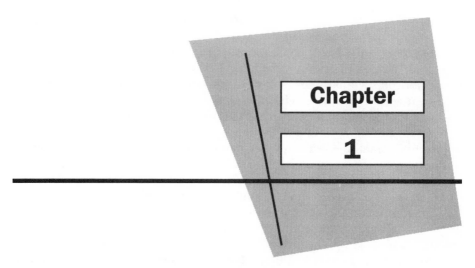

Chapter

1

"Girlspeak" and "Boyspeak": Gender Differences in Classroom Discussion

Brenda Weikel

The Problem

Greg was perplexed. As a social studies teacher, he believed strongly in the need for students to participate in discussions to help them understand important concepts. The problem was that his seventh-graders were not communicating well with him or with each other. The boys seemed to use talk one way, and the girls another. He was not sure about all the dynamics that were going on in the classroom, but he knew there was a problem. Greg decided to call on a friend who was studying social studies education in a graduate program at the local university. Perhaps Diane could help him figure out what was going wrong.

Diane was intrigued by Greg's request. She had been doing research on social studies discussion and was looking for a classroom to use for her study. This sounded ideal. The first step was to observe and tape a discussion for analysis. Greg agreed to arrange for a discussion of culture based on an archaeological activity the students had been working on for some time. Diane and Greg chose his first-period class for the study, since it seemed to exemplify the problems he was noticing.

The Discussion

The discussion began with Greg's asking a question: "Which will change less over time, the physical or the abstract aspects of culture?" Since the students had just created their own civilizations—including a variety of physical and abstract artifacts—they knew what Greg was talking about. As the talk began, Diane noticed several things. After Greg sat down, the students had chosen their own seats in the circle. The boys sat together with Greg in the middle of the boys' half of the circle; the girls sat in the other half of the circle. She also noticed that the girls raised their hands and waited to be called on in the discussion, sometimes leaving their hands up for a long time while other students were speaking. The boys were more likely to raise a hand when someone else stopped talking or to just speak out without being called on. Greg became confused at times trying to keep up with whom to call on next.

In addition to the way the students tried to get the floor to speak, Diane noticed that there were at least five girls and one boy who did everything they could to avoid talking. The girls spent most of the time looking at the floor, especially when Greg was selecting someone to answer a question. The boy had turned his chair a little so that he could look at something in his notebook. Despite several attempts, Greg was unable to bring these students into the discussion. Diane wondered what other issues the transcript would reveal.

Analysis

The analysis of the transcript brought several interesting patterns to light. The discussion itself had been quite lively. Greg had two objectives: (1) a content objective involving culture and (2) a process objective involving discussion strategy and critical thinking. About thirty identifiable topics were coded in the transcript of the discussion, which focused on how physical and abstract artifacts change over time, on religion as an abstract artifact, on fashion and culture, and on how artifacts are classified as abstract or physical. Greg introduced the discussion strategy of playing the devil's advocate to let the students know that he might argue a point he did not believe in, just to get them thinking.

The transcript showed that thirteen students spoke during the discussion. Eight students dominated the talk, taking fourteen or more turns each. Jamal, who spoke thirty-six times, had the most turns, but they were relatively short. Pam had the longest turns, with an average of thirty-eight words in her twenty-eight turns. Greg had used his turns in a variety of ways, trying to include more students, presenting an argument, and supporting students' efforts, to work out ideas. Diane was anxious to show him the coded transcript. She had found some differences in the ways boys and girls were using talk in this classroom. She also noticed some differences in the way Greg responded to boys and to girls.

The Meeting

"I am glad we could get together so soon," Diane said, as they settled down to work in the teacher's lounge. "There are some interesting points in this transcript that I would like to show you."

"Great," Greg responded. "How bad was it?"

Diane replied, "That's just it. When you told me that you were having trouble communicating with the students, I expected to see a disaster during the discussion. Actually, this is one of the best discussions I have observed, but there are some differences in the way the boys and girls use talk."

"Interesting. Show me what you mean."

Diane showed Greg her chart of speaking turns in the discussion. He had used almost half the turns, but mostly to call on students to speak. Greg was surprised that only thirteen students had participated. "How can that be true? I thought I had everybody talking that day." Diane assured him that it was not unusual for some students to remain quiet during a discussion. In fact, some students might learn more from listening than from talking, but there were more girls than boys who did not participate at all.

Of those students who did talk, the girls had the longest turns. They frequently used stories from their own experience to make a point. Pam talked about something she had learned in Hebrew school, Martha talked about an article she had read in a magazine, and Susan brought up a previous lesson from the social studies class. Greg stopped Pam several times when her story seemed to be getting long and he did not understand her point. The boys' turns were shorter, and their talk was more abstract. Walter and Barry both made up hypothetical situations with few details. Steve was trying to use logic to make his point.

Greg said, "I thought the girls were interrupting each other all the time in that discussion. They wouldn't let one person finish a sentence. Does that show up in the transcript?"

Diane flipped through the pages. "Is this what you mean?" she asked, pointing to a passage. "This is where Ellen and Betsy were working on an explanation of how religion changes over time."

Ellen: The basic ideas are the same but, um, but I mean if you look at, like, a lot of religions, they have lasted a whole long longer than that.
Greg: OK, OK.
Betsy: But they've changed a little.
Ellen: They've changed a little, but not as much as . . .
Betsy: Yeah, but their basic ideas are the same.
Ellen: Yeah.

"Right, that's what I was talking about," said Greg. "Why didn't Betsy just wait until Ellen was done to make her comments?"

Diane replied, "I think the two girls were using something called collaborative talk; working together to build an idea. Betsy was not trying to make a separate statement; she was just helping Ellen work out the idea."

"And you're saying that the boys didn't do the same thing?" Greg asked.

"Not really. They seemed to be talking to you more directly. You can see in the transcript that you talk before and after almost every boy's turn. There is at least one contrasting example where one boy interrupts another." She turned to a segment of the transcript where Barry and Steve were talking.

Barry: Well, I agree with you partly and partly not.
Greg: OK.
Barry: I think that part of it has to do with these people who think about what we will like and how they advertise so that people will like it. But part of it has to be that someone tries it out, and lots of other people like it, so they get it, too, and it . . .
Steve: That's still one person.
Barry: Well, not just one person, but *some* people try it out.
Steve: That's not what you said, though.

Steve's comment caused Barry to clarify what he was saying, but it was stated as a disagreement rather than support for an idea. After Barry clarified his thought, Steve challenged him again. Diane saw this interaction as different from the collaborative talk of the girls. Greg was not so sure, but he was willing to read the entire transcript to look for other examples. As he was reading, he noticed something he had missed during the actual discussion.

"Look how long I stayed with Jamal on that one topic."

"I was wondering if you would recognize that," Diane replied. "You and Jamal went on for about thirty turns with no one else talking. Do you think that was a good idea?"

Greg thought about it for a while. "I am concerned about that kid. I guess I stayed with his ideas because I wanted to draw him out. It seems like the girls don't need to be drawn out because they already talk a lot."

Diane reminded him that there were several girls who never said anything during the discussion and that he had interrupted Pam frequently rather than helping her get to the point by asking the kind of questions he had asked Jamal. "I don't mean to pick on you, Greg," she said. "In fact, studies have shown that the majority of teachers, male and female, give more classroom attention to the boys than to the girls. The difference is that you have noticed it and are willing to do something about it."

"That's just the problem," Greg replied. "I don't know what to do."

QUESTIONS TO CONSIDER

1. What are the particular issues that Greg and Diane have raised from their analysis of his discussion? Which are most important? Be sure to include issues evident in the observation as well as in the classroom.

2. Now that Greg has noticed a difference in the way he responds to boys and to girls, what, if anything, should he do about it?

3. Should Greg try to get the boys and girls to use talk in the same way? Should a teacher try to change gender-based styles of talk or try to support them?

4. Is it necessary for everyone to talk during a class discussion in order to learn? In this case, several girls and one boy did not participate in the discussion. How can a teacher know what these students are gaining from the discussion? When do students stay quiet because they do not want to talk and when have they been silenced in some way?

5. What roles can colleagues play in the analysis and improvement of teaching? What makes teaching such an isolated profession?

ACTIVITIES

1. Observe and record a class discussion. Look for patterns in the talk. How many students participated? Do boys and girls get different numbers of turns? Can you spot gender-based differences in the content of the talk? In the ways that teachers respond to boys and to girls?

2. Interview students about differences in styles of talk between girls and boys. You might try interviewing two girls together, two boys together, and then a boy and a girl together. Do you notice any differences in what they say or in how they talk that reflect the group's gender composition?

READINGS

Coates, J., and D. Cameron. (1989). *Women in their speech communities: New perspectives on language and sex.* London: Longman.

Freed, A. F. (1992). We understand perfectly: A critique of Tannen's view of cross-sex communication. In *Locating power: Proceedings of the second Berkeley women and language conference* 1: 144–152. Hall, K., M. Bucholtz, and B. Moonwoman, eds. Berkeley, Calif.: Berkeley Women and Language Group.

James, D., and S. Clarke. (1992). Interruptions, gender, and power: A critical review of the literature. In *Locating power: Proceedings of the second Berkeley women and language conference* 1:286–299. Hall, K., M. Bucholtz, and B. Moonwoman, eds. Berkeley, Calif.: Berkeley Women and Language Group.

Sadker, M., D. Sadker, and L. Long. (1989). Gender and educational equality. In *Multicultural education: Issues and perspectives,* ed. J. A. Banks and C. A. M. Banks, 105–123. Boston: Allyn & Bacon.

Tannen, D. (1990). *You just don't understand: Men and women in conversation.* New York: Ballantine Books.

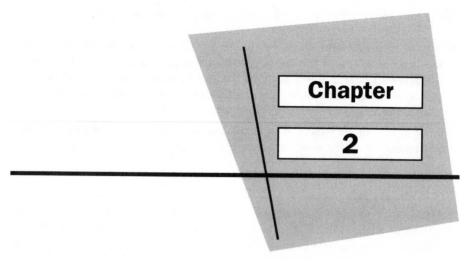

Chapter 2

A Rare Commodity

Joan Skolnick*

"I'm coming with you, Mrs. Jenkins!" Shequeta was in her face again as she exited the sixth-grade temporary building and headed for the office copying machine. Every time she took a trip somewhere, Shequeta wanted to go.

It seemed to Lisa Jenkins that she spent more time with this group of girls than doing anything else in her student teaching. Shequeta, LaTonya, Donna, and Tonesha—the "leaders" among the class girls—clung to her. They were always trying to get close to her outside of class, and they were persistent.

"How old are you, Mrs. Jenkins?"

"What made you decide to be a teacher?"

Lisa's dream of becoming a teacher had been born a few steps away from their classroom, at the child-care center where Shequeta and LaTonya had attended preschool.

They demanded to know where Lisa was *all* the time. And they were jealous.

"Where were *you* yesterday?" Shequeta shouted with that "little woman attitude" the morning after Lisa had been out sick for a day.

"What are you two talking about?" Tonesha demanded to know when Lisa was discussing a lesson with her master teacher at his desk one day. "You're flirting!"

Coming up through Lynnwood Elementary School—this predomi-

*This case is based on interviews with the student teacher and reflects her perceptions. Names and other identifying information have been changed. Special thanks to Dr. Flora Krasnovsky (University of California, San Francisco, and San Jose State University) for reviewing the case from her perspective as an African-American psychologist and educator.

12

nantly black Los Angeles school that Lisa had chosen for her student teaching—these girls hadn't been around many young African-American women in positions of authority. True, Lynnwood had other African-American teachers, but they were women in their fifties, and Lisa knew she was a rare commodity. She didn't sound or act like the other teachers, black or white. She didn't scream at the kids. And it was clear from her lessons that she cared about what they thought.

What had hooked Lisa into this group of girls was more perplexing to her. Somehow, they reminded her of herself. But why? They were the low achievers, whereas Lisa had always gotten good grades. She guessed it was their low self-esteem; she also had felt bad about herself during adolescence.

Shequeta, the leader, the persistent one, had a constant need to be included. LaTonya, the strongest student in the group, was willing to sacrifice the books she loved to the goddess of acceptance. And Donna, an often-teased "resource kid" on the fringes of the group, was a little more her own person (and the one Lisa admired most).

Cheryl Tiegs and the Dark Queen

Reaching adolescence in a white school during the 1970s, Lisa stood out. At the time, Cheryl Tiegs and Christie Brinkley were hot—stick-thin figures with perfect faces and perfect teeth. Lisa—not tall, not skinny—didn't fit this mold. And she certainly was not blond. Her face and hair were different, and she wore braces, to boot. A perfect speller, she made friends by proofreading all her classmates' papers before they gave them to the teacher.

Sixth grade and junior high were excruciating for Lisa. Her self-esteem took a dive, and her grades sunk with it. Finally, she switched schools. In her new, predominantly black high school, she developed a sense of self. In this setting, her dark eyes reflected an image of herself that she had never seen.

"I wish my hair was like yours."

"I wish I talked like you and could get your grades."

Lisa hated to see anybody else go through what she had. Now she found herself reliving those feelings through Shequeta and LaTonya. Embarrassed by her feelings as a girl, there had been times when she had wanted to talk about things, but couldn't. Shequeta's crowd really needed to talk.

Given her painful adolescence, Lisa came to Lynnwood with deeply held beliefs about what she wanted to do as a teacher. It wasn't just "producing" grades that counted. It was how the kids felt about themselves that would make them or break them. And these girls were growing up so fast, she was afraid they'd break. She was here to show them that they could get through school.

The girls had already faced a lot in their lives, and their grades were poor. Next year they would be in junior high, where one or another of them might end up pregnant, on drugs, or dropping out. They were growing up feeling bad about themselves. Worse, they were down on African Americans in general.

Lisa seized the chance to build self-esteem through her curriculum at Lynnwood. She introduced them to Zeely, the beautiful, dark, proud heroine of Virginia Hamilton's novel for children. Different from everyone else, Zeely is believed to be a queen, and she teaches her young black friend that royalty is "what's inside . . . when you dare swim in a dark lake."[1]

At first, Lisa didn't care if the kids in her class misspelled every word on their papers, if she could convince them that their thoughts counted and that what they knew about mattered.

"Are we going to do Magic Circle today, Mrs. Jenkins?" Shequeta asked her daily.[2] Several times a week, Lisa introduced a topic (like "my special place") and encouraged them to listen to one another talk about their thoughts and feelings. A leader was chosen to talk about a personal experience related to the topic. Then they went around the circle and took turns sharing what they heard the leader say, and the leader corroborated each response. For many of these kids, this was the first time in their schooling that their experience of the world was validated.

Shequeta listened, but she rarely spoke. When she didn't say anything, none of the other three girls would, either.

Sharing her own family's African heritage and recreating current events in the classroom, Lisa sought to show them the world through African eyes. They role-played the dilemmas of the Somalian war, dividing into small groups, each representing a different segment of Somalian society. They debated alternative solutions to the conflict. They were fascinated. Lisa was talking *to* them, not *at* them.

Sabotage

The first time Lisa noticed that Shequeta and her friends were sabotaging her lessons was during Magic Circle. At first, they just passed when it was their turn. But then they began to disrupt. They were beginning to give her a very hard time. They were trying to break her. When she gave them an assignment, they refused to do it. Someone had even gotten to LaTonya.

Shequeta's group deliberately decided to do no reading for the Somalian simulation, and in the final debate they couldn't play their roles. They sat there while everyone in the class waited for them to speak.

[1]Virginia Hamilton, *Zeely* (New York: Macmillan, 1967), 120–121. Hamilton has written many acclaimed children's books, including *M. C. Higgins the Great* and *The People Could Fly: American Black Folktales*.

[2]For information about Magic Circle strategies, see Uvaldo Palomares and Geraldine Ball, *Human Development Program* (LaMesa, Calif.: Human Development Training Institute, Inc., 1974).

When Lisa insisted that Tonesha get out her pencil and paper for her spelling test one day, Tonesha turned angrily on her, referring to her as "that white lady."

Outside the classroom, Shequeta and her friends still loved to talk. But once inside, they shifted to maintain a role among the other girls. Helplessly, Lisa worried that they were transferring to her their negative feelings about themselves. How could that happen? She was here to help them see that it was possible to feel good about themselves and to get through school.

As a teacher, Lisa felt rejected. Was it that the girls couldn't handle seeing an African-American woman in a position of authority? Did they think that she had "sold out" because she expected them to work? Was she supposed to do nothing but hang out with them? She refused to accept that role. And she began to wonder whether they would give a male teacher more of a chance. Were they arguing with her because it was like arguing with their mothers?

Benched

Shequeta didn't want to listen that day. Snickering about people during Magic Circle, she drew in the other girls and her boyfriend, Steve. She violated the "no put-downs" rule. Lisa gave her three reminders and even called on her to be a leader. But Shequeta wouldn't bite. She was afraid to talk. When Lisa picked on somebody else, the disruptions escalated. Finally, Lisa lost her temper.

"Get out! I'm not going to put up with this!" She shouted, banishing the girls to the playground bench.

Outside, the girls were furious! They paced about, screaming. They interrupted each other. Lisa couldn't get a word in edgewise. She felt overwhelmed—and distraught. "What did I do?" she asked herself. But she had broken her rule about not chastising them in front of their peers—the one thing she knew you *don't* do with students in this grade. They provoked, and she responded. "I should have known better," she thought.

"Why are you all becoming so negative toward me? Sabotaging. Not producing any work. I need some feedback."

That's when they let her have it. It was like dominoes falling.

"You play favorites with the boys." Donna shouted.

Now Shequeta screamed: "Steve did all the same stuff. But you never said anything to him. You just lay into us!"

They all felt that way. Lisa called on the boys more; she punished them less; she didn't expect the same things of them.

Lisa thought about it. Could they be *right*? Did she somehow just *expect* the boys to act out? Did she expect more of the girls? Especially *these* girls? And, if so, why was she so hard on them? What could she say to them now? How could she turn things around?

Epilogue

The benching incident cleared the air, and Lisa made a pact with the girls. She promised to watch what she was doing and to apply the same rules of fairness to the boys. In return, the girls would stop the sabotage. "At least," she thought, "I listened to them."

But in the weeks that followed, there was little improvement in the girls' work. By the end of the semester, their neediness had practically sucked the energy out of her. "Don't you know there aren't very many of us out here?" she'd shout at them in her dreams. "Don't run the rest of us out of the business!"

Deep inside, she knew they were responding to her. In the end, she believed they probably respected her more than they could voice. That's what scared them most, she supposed. Somebody was out there trying, maybe offering a flicker of hope they hadn't previously seen. But they found ways to fight it. Lisa would only be a student teacher at their school for so many weeks. After that, they knew it would be business as usual. If only she could become a stable person in their lives—*then* she'd see some changes! It was a lot of responsibility.

When Lisa left student teaching, she told the girls where she would be working and invited them to "Come by and say hi!"

All spring, three or four times a week, the girls showed up at work looking for her—sometimes, even before she arrived for work in the morning.

"What it's like to go past eigth grade, Mrs. Jenkins?"

"Will you come back and teach us again? We really liked your lessons."

That fall, the girls went on to Halsey Junior High. And Lisa became a teacher.

QUESTIONS TO CONSIDER

1. What are the issues in this case from Lisa's perspective? From the girls' perspective? From the boys' perspective? What might be the perspective of other teachers at the school?

2. What pressures do Shequeta and her friends face at school?

3. Is Lisa right about why the girls are sabotaging her? What other factors might affect their feelings and behaviors toward her? How is their reaction to Lisa related to gender? To culture? To her teaching strategies?

4. When the girls accuse Lisa of favoritism, how should she respond? Is Lisa being fair to both the boys and the girls in the class? What makes you think so? Why might Lisa expect "less" from the boys or be "harder" on the girls?

    In what ways are expectations related to success in schooling? How might differential expectations reproduce or counteract social inequities?

5. How do Lisa's own childhood experiences and identifications help and hinder her in responding to the African-American girls in her class? In responding to the boys?

6. Is Lisa correct in identifying low self-esteem as the fundamental problem she should be concerned about? How might differences in her own background (academic? class?) affect her perspective?

7. Why is adolescence a pivotal time for declining self-esteem and achievement in girls? Although some studies indicate that the self-esteem of black girls is more resilient than that of white girls in upper elementary grades and junior high school, their positive feelings about their teachers and school work plunge during these years.[3] What can schools do to reverse these patterns?

8. What, if anything, might have been different if the girls had been Caucasian, or if the teacher had been an African-American man? Why do you think so?

9. What factors help create resilient kids despite difficult life circumstances? What are the responsibilities and limits of a teacher and school in fostering resiliency and building self-esteem?

10. What do we know about the strengths of Shequeta, LaTonya, Donna, and Tonesha? In what ways do Lisa's innovative teaching strategies build on these strengths? In what ways, if any, are her strategies counterproductive?

11. What pressures do young teachers of color like Lisa face? What kind of support do they need? How could Lisa build that support? How can school districts and teacher preparation programs better support teachers working in inner-city schools?

ACTIVITIES

1. When you teach or observe in classrooms, you will probably find some students you particularly identify with. Who are these students? How do your own background and experiences influence which kinds of students you feel most drawn to and least drawn to? Do you treat such students in different ways—giving them special attention, making exceptions for them, being harder on them, talking with them more personally and more informally, offering them more suggestions and guidance? Teachers' responses to students with whom they identify can be subtle and complex.

   Try a Magic Circle activity with other education students, using the topic "a student I identify with." What do you learn about how a teacher's background influences behavior toward students? How are your reactions—and those of other students—related to gender, culture, and class?

2. Teachers of color often face special difficulties: expectations from administrators and colleagues that they serve as role models and advisors to students like themselves; pressure to serve as the "conscience" of the school; special committee and program responsibilities; unusual watchfulness on the part of students, parents, and teaching staff; obvious and subtle forms of discrimination.

   Discuss with your professors and other students how you might interview teachers of color in sensitive ways to develop a better understanding of their

[3]American Association of University Women Educational Foundation and Wellesley College Center for Research on Women, *How Schools Shortchange Girls: Executive Summary.* Washington, D.C.: AAUW Educational Foundation, 1992.

situations. Think about whom to interview—student teachers in different types of schools; experienced teachers; administrators; directors of equal-opportunity programs; directors of teacher placement services; officers of minority teacher organizations. Develop interview questions that will help you to appreciate the issues which teachers of color deal with and the strategies which they have found effective.

READINGS

American Association of University Women Educational Foundation and Wellesley College Center for Research on Women. (1992). *How schools shortchange girls: Executive summary.* Washington, D.C.: AAUW Educational Foundation.

Dorman, A. (1990). *Recruiting and retaining minority teachers: A national perspective.* Elmherst, Ill.: North Central Regional Educational Laboratory.

Hunter, L. (1992). *The diary of Latoya Hunter: My first year in junior high.* New York: Crown.

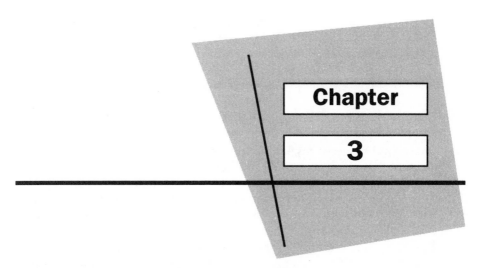

Chapter

3

The Teacher Who Knew Too Much

Deborah Reynolds

Katie

Katie was in my chemistry class during her sophomore year. She sat in the back of the room and didn't participate in class discussions very often. The only interaction I saw between her and her peers was with a girl who sat next to her and who later became her best friend. Academically, Katie was an A student earning a D. She had problems with any class that required outside work and constant attendance, mentally or physically. I sensed that she was conscientious, but I couldn't understand why she wasn't turning in her work or coming to class.

I found the answer a year later, when Katie was in my physics class. Little by little she began to see that I was trying to create a safe place so that students could trust each other and learn to work together. She saw that I cared, that I was interested not only in her academic performance but also in her. Eventually, she began to tell me about her life.

Both her parents worked. Her dad was almost always drunk at night. After work, her mother sat in a chair all evening and watched TV. Katie told me that her sister and her sister's two-year-old son lived with them. Her sister worked and went out a lot, and her parents had given Katie the responsibility of taking care of her nephew as well as taking care of the household chores. She told me that these things needed to be done and that she alone was responsible for them. She believed this sincerely. Occasionally she seemed resentful that she couldn't go out with friends or join a school activity. As I learned more and more about Katie and her home life, I felt sad and angry. I suppose a little sadness and anger was for myself, having grown up in similar circumstances.

The Teacher

I am the second oldest in my family, as was Katie. I, too, had to take care of the household chores and my little brothers. My sister, like Katie's, went out drinking and partying and took none of the responsibility for the family. My father drank constantly, and my mother was either yelling or watching TV. I got good grades in school and found some esteem in that. Katie, however, didn't do well academically.

I grew up with a lack of caring and consistency in my life, just as Katie had. I think I went into teaching so that I could provide a safe place, a class where teen-agers could get excited about science, where they could be loved for who they were, no matter how badly they performed. I wanted to provide students with a consistent environment where they had certain responsibilities and knew the consequences of their actions.

My classes are known for being hard but fun. For the most part, I teach upper-level science classes (chemistry and physics) to college-bound kids. I expect a lot from my students in terms of doing their own work and getting it in on time. I heavily penalize late work and in some cases will not accept it under any circumstances.

The School

Manning High School is considered the elite high school in town. It is relatively new and—in contrast to the other three high schools in the district—has carpeted floors, clean bathrooms, and unmarked halls. To visitors, Manning gives the appearance of being a well-rounded college preparatory school where students and faculty find spirit and pride in belonging. To an insider, however, it does not feel this way. After five years of teaching at Manning, I have never felt a cooperative spirit among staff or students.

I believe that the lack of cooperation is a result of the high percentage of Manning students who come from professional homes where parents have high standards for their children as well as for the Manning staff. The pressure from parents and administrators for teachers to perform above and beyond their colleagues creates an atmosphere of stress that no one acknowledges. This is the atmosphere in which I work and in which I met Katie.

The Project

Students in my physics classes are required to do two major experimental projects: (1) a group effort during fall semester and (2) an individual project during spring semester. The projects in the spring are displayed in the library for three days so that faculty and students can look at and play with them. This arrangement makes it necessary for projects to be turned in on time. I make no exceptions. I had devised a system by which the students had to give me a data update every two weeks for eight weeks before the project was due. This approach helped keep some students on course, but a few still chose to put their projects off. Katie was one of these.

Two weeks before the projects were due, I talked with Katie again about getting started. She had chosen the difficult task of setting up a holography lab at the university. Since my students had been using equipment and lab space there for four years, I knew that wouldn't be a problem. The problem was with the time it would take to set up the optics and find the correct laser exposure and developing times. Katie responded sheepishly that she had tried to go to the university lab two nights before. She had gone home from school first and was told by her mother that she had too much to do at home; it was more important for her to be at home, and who the hell cared about a stupid physics project anyway, because it certainly wasn't going to get her anywhere in life. I asked her if she wanted to do something else, a project she could work on at school or at home. Her response was a soft-spoken but emphatic no.

Two days later, Katie approached me. I rarely saw her so excited. She had been to the university, she said, and had talked with Don Maler, a professor of physics, and some of his graduate students about setting up the optics lab to do holography. Since they had never set up the holography lab before, they were eager to have the opportunity to assist Katie. Katie was to be the one in charge of the project. She was scared but enthusiastic. She went to the university two more times that week to look at equipment and go through catalogues to find film and developer. I heard from Don that Katie was doing a great job; both he and the grad students were impressed with her knowledge, enthusiasm, and sense of what needed to be done. He felt she would make a good physicist.

The next week Katie told me that she had ordered the film and chemicals but that they wouldn't arrive until the day the projects were to be displayed. Even when the materials arrived, I knew that there would be no way for Katie to get her project done before the end of the three-day display period in the library. This was agonizing news. Although Katie never specifically asked for an extension (she would never ask for special treatment), I felt that I had to make a decision. I had made a deadline. I had never made an exception to a deadline. Should I make an exception now, because I cared for this young woman and her success? I knew she could have started the project earlier. I also knew it was hard for her to get away from her family responsibilities and parents' attitudes. I could see a glimmer of self-esteem when she talked about her project. Did I have a right to squelch her feelings of worthiness for an arbitrary deadline that I had set?

But I also had an obligation to her and to the rest of my students to stick by my rules and deliver the consistent system that I promised them.

Would it be fair to the others to make an exception for Katie? Maybe one of them needed extra time just as much. It was a dilemma I wrestled with for many hours.

Epilogue

I allowed Katie to turn in her project late. Instead of displaying it in the library, however, she gave a presentation to the class. It was two weeks past the deadline before Katie finally completed all the project's requirements. Her presentation went well. The other students in the class saw a homemade hologram and learned about the concepts and process of laser photography.

As I look back, I don't know how the other students felt about my decision. I never asked. I know that Katie felt good about completing the project and about gaining the respect of Don Maler and the graduate students, but I don't know how she felt about my extending the deadline for her. I wonder if she felt it was fair. As for me, I still don't know what decision would have been more beneficial to her in the long run. In my life, people have made exceptions for me. The funny thing is that the ones who *didn't* are the ones I remember and respect the most.

QUESTIONS TO CONSIDER

1. Do you think this teacher went too far in her efforts to encourage a bright young woman in science, or didn't go far enough?

2. Katie's performance in this physics class is especially impressive, considering her background. Many bright science students do projects with help from their parents—who often work in scientific fields themselves. But Katie's achievement was her own. What else might a teacher do to encourage her now?

3. Consider the teacher's poignant observation at the end of the case: "People have made exceptions for me. The funny thing is that the ones who *didn't* are the ones I remember and respect the most." How do you interpret this observation? What implications can you find in it?

4. Was the teacher's decision to accept Katie's late project fair to the other students in the class? Possibly other students had problems as serious as Katie's but never brought them to the teacher's attention. Should she have offered the same opportunity to other students?

5. Consider the teacher's general policy of not allowing late projects under any circumstances. It is easy to say that the teacher should be more flexible, but such flexibility often results in late projects that are done haphazardly. Having a firm deadline and displaying the projects to the entire school sends important messages. Moreover, this teacher has 119 students. If students turn in projects at many different times, she will find it extremely difficult to keep track of them and grade them fairly.

On balance, do you believe this teacher's policy is right, or do you think she should change her policy to take into account students like Katie? If you argue that the policy should be changed, what policy would you establish in its place?

ACTIVITIES

1. Role-play the teacher talking to Katie about extending the deadline for the science project. What messages should the teacher give Katie?

2. Imagine variations of the way the case evolved, and role-play these situations. How would you address the following accusations?

   a. A student who turned her project in on time but failed finds out about the extra time given to Katie and takes her anger to the administration.

   b. A parent discovers that you have bent the rule for Katie and is angry that her child (an A student) only got a B because of time constraints.

   c. An African-American student calls you a racist because you made exceptions for Katie, who is white.

   d. A white student accuses you of reverse discrimination because Katie is an African American.

3. Create a list of rules that you will have for your classroom regarding deadlines for academic work. State your beliefs and assumptions about the nature of learning and the purpose of projects, assignments, and due dates. Role-play explaining your policy to your students. Have one of your peers, as a secondary student, challenge your policies and force you to justify them.

READINGS

American Association of University Women (1992). *How schools shortchange girls: Executive summary.* Washington, D.C.: AAUW.

Kahle, J. B. (1983). *Factors affecting the retention of girls in science courses and careers: Case studies of selected secondary schools.* Washington, D.C.: National Association of Biology Teachers.

Klein, C. A. (1989). What research says . . . about girls in science. *Science and Children* (October): 28–31.

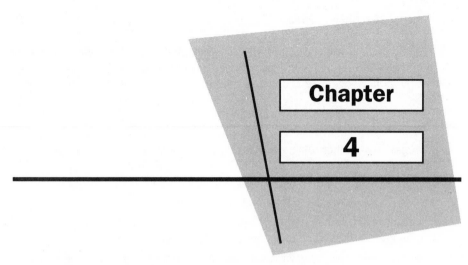

Jane, The Reluctant Mathlete

Suzanne Yerian

From Mathematics to Males

"No, you can't miss the state math championships, not for a stupid party!"

That's what I wanted to say to Jane when she asked me, the coach, if she could drop off the math team—but I didn't. It's true she had been frustrating me with her boy-crazy behavior in class for the past few months, but I was so pleased that her team had won the district competition two weeks before and made state. She and her three teammates would compete in Juneau against other district winners.

Imagine my shock when Jane stopped at my desk after class and announced she wasn't going to Juneau because she didn't want to miss her girlfriend's party that weekend. I felt Jane was making a bad choice—throwing away a chance to use her exceptional math talents.

I gave Jane my usual "You can do it" pep talk, even though I was fed up with her recent behavior: her boy craziness, poor attitude, unwillingness to work closely with her team, and disappearances at critical times during the district competition. I thought how easy it would be to coach the team without Jane, and how motivated John, the first alternate, was. I also thought about Sean, the only boy on the team. Sean, Jane, Kristy, and Deidre worked very well together. Each one had strengths that had contributed to the success of the team. Introducing a new student at this point would have disrupted that cohesiveness and jeopardized Sean's chances at winning a college scholarship, one of the prizes offered for winning at the state competition.

No one in Sean's family had gone beyond high school. Without financial help, he would never get to college. I felt committed to doing the right thing for both Sean and Jane. I wanted Sean to have the best chance at that scholarship, but I wanted to develop Jane's mathematics abilities and help her get the recognition and awards that she deserved. Jane had real potential and showed that women could be brilliant at math. By the end of my pep talk, Jane looked unhappy. I was confused and didn't know what to do: Should I encourage Jane to stay on the team or let her quit?

Jane's Background

Jane was in seventh grade at Fairview Junior High, a medium-sized suburban school of approximately eight hundred students. She was a year ahead of her peers mathematically and, as a result, placed in my eighth-grade Algebra I class. The math competition was one way students could complete the requirements for a math project that each student had to do by the end of the year. Practice for the school's math competition lasted from October through December. The school-level tests were held in January; the district tests were in February; and the state competition was in March. The four team members were chosen on the basis of scores on the school tests. These four students practiced together for the month before the district competition, and another month if they placed either first or second at the district level and went to state. Jane's algebra class had twenty-seven students, twenty-two of whom elected to enter the math competition.

Jane's test scores in all academic areas were superb—99th percentile on both achievement and aptitude—and she was a straight-A student. Jane's performance, comments, attitudes, and quick wit in class showed that she was an extremely bright girl. Her parents were very supportive (her mother was an engineer, and her father was self-employed), and they permitted Jane to make many of her own decisions about school courses.

In the beginning of the year, Jane was a model student. Her cheerfulness contributed to the overall positive atmosphere that existed in my class. Jane paid attention, was eager to take risks, and enjoyed learning. She was happy, outgoing, and friendly.

I began to notice a change in Jane around December. I was half way through the three months' worth of practice sheets for the math competition, and about one month short of the school competition that determines which students will form the team going to district. Jane was forgetting to do her assignments, seemed unconcerned about her grades, socialized more often, became more sophisticated in the way she dressed, daydreamed in class, and talked constantly about boys, clothes, and parties. She had become friends with a different group of students in my class who were more popular and less academically oriented. There were many kids in that class who wanted to be on the math team. Because it was a voluntary activity, most of the students who chose to do the competition were diligent about getting their work in on time and getting the right answers. I mentioned to Jane and her group that they would have to get their work done in order to have a chance to go to the district competition, but they would shrug, do their work for a day or two, and soon begin missing assignments.

My Background

I had spent three years developing and refining the math competition materials so that they were both fun and challenging. The first year I only had five students who wanted to participate. Now my students were begging to be allowed to compete; each fall they asked *when* they would start the practice sheets. Younger sisters and brothers told me they were eager to get to Fairview so that they could get into the program and have as much fun in math as their older siblings. I was especially pleased at the increase in the number of girls who entered the competition—one of my goals.

I have always felt that we needed to approach math teaching a little differently with girls. The boys seemed more competitive, enjoyed getting that one right answer, and were more self-assured. The girls preferred to work in groups and took wrong answers more personally. I tried to make the practice sheets fun, downplayed the focus on fast responses and right answers, played a lot of math games, let groups rather than individuals find answers, and held more after-school and lunch-time parties for mathletes only. It seemed to work. Each year in the competition, all my teams were very strong. And the girls were just as good as the boys.

The Competition

In January I gave the math students the three-day test that would determine who was to be on the official school team. Half the points would come from this test, and half would come from the grades on the practice sheets. I could usually tell ahead of time who would be on the team, based on the practice-sheet grades and a guess at the exam scores.

This year's results surprised me. I couldn't believe the totals. I calculated twice to make sure I had it right.

Sean had made it, as expected from the consistently high marks he had earned throughout the semester on both his practice papers and his tests. But three of the girls also had placed, and one of them was Jane.

I didn't think Deidre and Kristy had a chance because—although their practice papers were very good—they tended to score low on the tests. I thought they wouldn't be able to handle the time pressure. I thought Jane had blown her chance because of the lousy papers she had been handing in, but her test score was so extremely high that it brought her up. I thought she had made a tremendous final effort to join the team.

Jane's performance throughout the next month—practicing with her three teammates for the district test—was, at best, poor. This is the time when we build team spirit and camaraderie, and Jane just wasn't committed. She participated just enough, though, that I kept my hopes up.

At the district competition my team won a place in the state competitions. Although Jane had done well on her section of the test, she became enamored of one of the boys on another school's team and spent a good share of her practice time walking around with him or calling friends from a nearby phone. The team didn't do as well as they had expected, but they still won the opportunity to go to Juneau. This was an exciting moment for all of them, especially for Sean and his parents. Sean came from a large blue-collar family. His father, a carpenter, barely made enough to keep his family in the small trailer they rented near the school. They realized that Sean had a chance of winning the college scholarship, a prize at this meet. He had a good chance *if* his overall scores were high, but that would include the team round.

I started to drill the four students every day. I knew that a good place at state would open doors to other programs, trips, and prizes, and I wanted those opportunities for my girls and for Sean. After one of our practice sessions, Jane came up to my desk and asked to leave the team. I flashed back to a recent talk I had had with the school's wrestling coach about how I should handle my math team and Jane's superior ability but lackadaisical attitude. With no hesitation he had said: "Kick her off the team. Winning isn't as important as learning to work together. I don't care how good my wrestlers are; if they mess up, they're off." That made a lot of sense, but in my case the team wasn't just going for junior-high trophies and a little bit of glory. More was at stake. I decided to try to keep Jane on the team.

The State Competition

I gave Jane the weekend to think about continuing the competition. That night I called Jane's mother to let her know what was happening and hoped that she would have the good sense to convince her daughter to stay on the team. I felt that her mother should know that Jane might decline the honor of representing the region at the state contest. I would want to know, if my daughter won such an award and turned it down.

On Monday Jane announced that she would continue to participate. I had some doubts about how serious she was. I thought that her mother had persuaded her to continue and that maybe Jane wasn't as serious about it as I hoped she would be. But when I asked Jane about that, she happily insisted that she had made up her own mind. Knowing how often Jane was allowed to make these important school decisions by her family, I thought she had.

Jane joined the other students at a separate table near the side of the room. Their work was primarily self-directed group practice with periodic help from me. The other students in the class needed my help with their work. The math team consisted of very able, highly motivated students. They knew what they had to do, and they didn't need much direction.

I began noticing how quiet Jane had become. She sat back in her chair, rarely talked to her teammates, and daydreamed. I encouraged her as much as I could, but nothing worked. She didn't seem to associate with the two other girls. They were more academic and not as popular as Jane was, but they were friendly. Occasionally Jane would be drawn into an animated conversation with them.

By the time the team arrived in Juneau three weeks later, the girls were getting along again. That didn't last long. I began having trouble with Jane on the second day of the competition. She disappeared at critical times—generally to find a phone or "to find a store." I warned her to stick around. She spent lots of free time with the boy she liked from the other team. The boy stayed with his team, and so at least I could see her on the other side of the gym, talking to him.

I got very angry with Jane when the teams were called together by our hosts to do some practice drills that were designed to be fun. All the teams were busy—you looked out over the gym and saw the students' heads bent over the papers—that is, until you got to our table. There was Jane, sitting apart from her teammates reading a *Seventeen* magazine. I was furious! "Get busy," I hissed, and took the magazine away. Later, she did very poorly in the competition. That afternoon, while our team was shopping at the mall, she disappeared, and we had to look for her. She was shopping at another store and said that she had forgotten the time.

The last straw came at the awards banquet. Everyone sat with their own teams—except Jane, who sat with the team the boy belonged to. I could have forced her to sit with us but decided to let her enjoy the evening. I was kicking myself for not letting her leave the competition when she wanted to a month before. The worst part was that Sean didn't have a chance at winning the scholarship because Jane's scores were low and pulled down the group total. I felt I had let everyone down. Jane's past performance should have told me that her behavior was too erratic for her to be part of the team. She enjoyed her social life too much. I had tried to support her because of my commitment to helping girls in math; instead, I prevented Sean, the alternate boy, and the other two girls from doing their best. Though many years have passed since that competition, I still think about the decision I made and how it affected so many lives.

QUESTIONS TO CONSIDER

1. In the end, the teacher believes that she made a poor decision that hurt all the students on the math team. Do you agree or disagree with her? How would you have managed the math team and the problems with Jane?

2. Typically, girls lose interest in mathematics during adolescence, fall behind boys in math courses completed through high school, and give up opportunities for

future careers in math and science. This teacher has created an unusual class-room environment that encourages both boys and girls. Can you describe what this teacher does to attract students of both sexes?

3. The teacher noticed half way through the school year that Jane—previously a cheerful, attentive, and responsible student—had begun to neglect her school work. What dilemma is Jane facing, and how is she responding to it? What, if anything, might the teacher have done to help Jane at this point?

4. How far should the teacher go in supporting an underrepresented individual like Jane at the expense of opportunities for other students? What do you think of the wrestling coach's advice about removing Jane from the team? Why do you think the teacher ignored his advice?

ACTIVITIES

1. Observe math classrooms to discover gender-based differences. How do girls approach math problems? What about boys? How often do boys and girls collabo-rate with one another? How does the teacher respond to boys and to girls, and what might explain any differences you observe in the teacher's responses? Is emphasis in the class as great on competition as on collaboration and discussion?

2. Develop a lesson plan that you think will encourage both gender equity and academic excellence for the students you observed in the first activity.

3. Develop a survey that asks students to identify what they like and dislike about math classes including content, teaching strategies, teachers' characteristics, and the degree of competition. Analyze the results by gender, and discuss what your findings might mean for the organization of math teaching.

READINGS

Cohen, E. G. (1986). *Designing groupwork.* New York: Teachers College Press.

Reis, S. M., and C. M. Callahan. (1990). Gifted females. They've come a long way—or have they? *Journal for the Education of the Gifted* 12 (2): 99–117.

Seligman, R. (1990). A gifted ninth grader tells it like it is. *Gifted Child Today* 13 (4): 9–11.

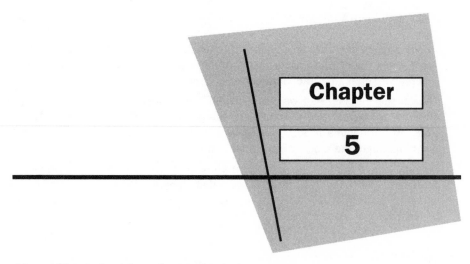

Chapter

5

Her Work Is Not Scholarly!

Selma Wassermann

The sultry southern air was an oppressive presence at the evening meeting, and the academics who had gathered for this learned professional colloquium were restless. When, at last, the panel concluded the debate and the doors of the auditorium were thrown open, Audrey Mayles felt that she could breathe again. As she worked her way through the crowd out to the large, open patio of the convention hotel, she felt an arm around her shoulder and a voice in her ear.

"How about a drink?"

"I'm a little tired, Bruce," she smiled at her department chairman. Audrey was one of the most recently hired faculty members in the School of Education and Social Services at State University, but she was not completely naïve about the social activities that took place above and beyond the obligatory conference sessions. She had heard much from other women in her department about the late-night drinking and partying that went on whenever a large group of her department met at out-of-town conferences, ostensibly to listen to academic papers and to learn about current research and development activities in the profession. Her office mate, Rita Anderson, had gone so far as to say that learned meetings were simply an excuse for the faculty to get off campus and have a good time. The meetings had nothing whatsoever to do with scholarship, as far as Rita was concerned. Audrey wondered if Rita was right. Well, this was her first off-campus conference with her new colleagues, and she'd find out for herself.

Audrey had been hired to teach English and humanities in the fall semester by the Department of Secondary Education. With a recent doctorate in secondary education from the University of Arizona, Audrey brought ten years' teaching experience in the public schools to her work in the department, as well as a two-year postdoctoral teaching assistantship from the University of Arizona. Her academic and professional credentials were excellent. She was considered an outstanding teacher, and her published book of poetry had received rave reviews. What she didn't know, however, was that during her interview for the position at State, the Appointments Committee had engaged in lengthy debate about her appearance. Specifically, they remarked on Audrey's flamboyant style, her plunging necklines, and her "Marilyn Monroe" curves. One woman on the committee noted that Audrey "did not exactly give the appearance of a scholar." Nonetheless, the committee recommended that Audrey be offered the rank of assistant professor, by a vote of 6 to 1. At that rank, Audrey would have five years before she came up for tenure.

Audrey, with her extroverted enthusiasms, quickly fell into pace with life in the department. Divorced, with no children, she had few demands on her time outside of professional work, and it was easy to get caught up with teaching, program development for the new Humanities major, committee work, and writing. In her first year, she received modest funding to conduct a two-year research project examining evaluative practices in secondary English classes. When she had a chance to sit down and take stock of how she was spending her time, she found that she was giving more than ten hours a day, six days a week to her job. "I hate this," she told Rita. "I'm a social person. I want to have a life outside this university. I need romance!"

Rita smiled. She was getting used to Audrey's "flair for the dramatic," and she appreciated the breath of fresh air that Audrey had brought into the stuffy department of academics.

"Yeah, I know what you mean," Rita winked. "But be careful, Aud. Remember what I've been telling you: You have to play the game here, and do what's expected. The operative word is *tenure*. When you've got that, you can relax. In the meanwhile, you must keep grinding out the stuff."

Audrey looked past Rita, out the window, onto the pastoral scene below. With spring in the air, it was hard for students to concentrate on studies. They were walking hand in hand, lounging on the grass, or throwing Frisbees. Audrey became wistful. "Look at what I'm missing," she said sadly. "Tenure or no tenure, Rita, I need a romance. I'm thirty-four years old, and pretty soon I'll have tenure—maybe—but I'll be past my prime."

Two months later, when Audrey became romantically involved with a construction worker who was ten years younger, it became the talk of the department. Not that Audrey felt she had anything to hide; on the contrary, she invited her live-in lover, Vic, to all departmental functions that included couples, and she talked of their relationship openly. But once again, Audrey was being out of step with the scholarly ambience of academia.

In June, after her first academic year at State University, Audrey's paper on "Teaching the Gifted Writer" was accepted for presentation at the Association for Academic Studies in Teacher Education, a national conference being held in Atlanta. On acceptance of her paper, she quickly informed the department chair, Bruce Gardiner.

"Congratulations, Audrey," Bruce smiled. "It's not easy to have a paper accepted by this group, so this is indeed an honor for you. This means a very prestigious line on your c.v., you know. There will be quite a few of us going down to Atlanta, of course, and so I'll be seeing you there."

Audrey noticed Bruce's smile as he said this. Was he leering, or was she imagining something that was not there? Were his eyes shifting from her face to her breasts? Was she going crazy? She had heard rumors about Bruce ever since coming to the department, but so far the stories were only rumors. What did she care if he *had* slept with every secretary in the office? If true, it was not her concern; that was strictly between him and his wife. In his role as department chair, Bruce so far had been very supportive of her as a new faculty member. He had gone out of his way to see that she got a computer for her research, and he had asked her to represent the department at a writers conference in San Francisco, paying her conference fees and trip expenses from departmental funds. As department chairs went, Bruce Gardiner was a strong supporter of his faculty, and he made sure that the department was recognized and valued in the university community.

"Of course, I'll see you in Atlanta," Audrey said. "I hope you'll have time to attend my presentation. I'd be interested in your reaction to my paper." Audrey tried to wipe out thoughts of his possible sexual interest in her.

"I'll try, Audrey, but I'll also be involved in recruiting some new faculty, and so my time is not entirely open to attend regular sessions. I'm sure you'll understand if I don't get to hear your paper. But, you know, we *will* be getting together for the social evenings, and I'm sure I'll see you then."

"Of course," Audrey said, as she opened the door to leave. "See you in Atlanta."

Now, here she was in Atlanta, with his hand around her waist and his mouth at her ear.

"You're not too tired for one drink?" he said, with a parody of an astonished face. "The evening is young. And do I detect the aroma of magnolias in the air? I just love the south, don't you? It's filled with such romance, such history."

"I am quite tired, Bruce," Audrey confessed, as she eased away from his arm. Had he been drinking? She thought she detected a strong smell of gin on his breath. She might be a new and naïve member of this department, but she was neither new nor naïve in the arena of men-women relationships. Bruce Gardiner was coming on to her. The last thing she needed was a behind-the-scenes tussle with the chair of the department.

"Are you rejecting me?" he said with mock seriousness. Was he going to trap her into consent?

"I hope not, Bruce. But please remember, I have a paper to give tomorrow. I need to do a good job. I need my concentration." She picked up his hand, held it, and looked directly into his face. "I'm sure you'll understand."

She thought she saw his eyes turn cold as he stepped back, searching, she thought, for a graceful exit. His words sounded mean: "If you don't want a man's attention, Audrey," he said in a heavy parental tone, "don't show so much white meat." His finger reached out and traced the edge of her neckline, from one side of the V down, and up the other, and then he walked away without a backward glance.

Sol Stone caught her elbow. "You look like a lady who could use a drink."

"Sol! Yeah, I sure could use one, but *only* one. I'm definitely going to bed early. I give my paper first thing in the morning."

As Audrey walked to the bar with Sol, she couldn't help noticing Bruce watching them. Would there be a price to pay? Audrey wondered later, when she entered the elevator to return to her room. Would Bruce's pride be hurt enough to make him vindictive toward her later? Was her refusal bad departmental politics? Or would the entire incident just blow over, like another leaf torn from a magnolia blossom in the warm spring breeze?

"Rita, I need your help with this!" Audrey shouted, as she raced into their office, hair flying and papers scattering in testimony to her mental state. "I couldn't imagine that it would be anything like this, Rita. Getting the paperwork together should, in itself, be proof of my scholarship! I've never done so much organizing, collating, writing, and rewriting! They may give me tenure, but not before I have a nervous breakdown."

"Look, Aud," Rita said, trying to reassure her friend and colleague. "Stop worrying. For Pete's sake, look at what you've done in this department during the last five years."

Audrey sat down with a small explosive sigh, the back of her swivel chair collapsing under the pressure, tilting her backward unexpectedly. Both women laughed. "Just what I need," smirked Audrey. "A broken neck." The women laughed again, releasing some of the tension that had been building over the last two months. Audrey was coming up for tenure, the life-and-death decision of an assistant professor's career. The stakes were high, and the variables in the decision-making process were full of unknowns.

On the face of it, the three academic criteria were clear: teaching ability, scholarship, and contributions to the university. If a professor met these criteria to the satisfaction of the Tenure Committee, tenure was assured. But there also were many ambiguities about the decision, and judgments about eligibility depended—as they said in the old Indian story—on "where one sat on the medicine wheel." Professionals differed with respect to how they judged scholarship; different people valued different aspects of scholarly work. As much as academics liked to think that the process was fair and equitable, those around the university for a long time believed that satisfying the criteria for tenure lay very much in the eye of the beholder. Judgments about scholarship were intimately connected with the membership of the committee, itself. For example, were the majority of committee members sympathetic to the candidate's orientation? Were they sympathetic to the kind of scholarship the candidate was producing? Were they flexible in their orientation? Did they consider that only quantitative, empirical studies were relevant? The nature of what constituted scholarship might be perceived differently by different committee members. And since a new tenure committee was elected each year, standards could vary from year to year. To what extent did a professor's persona enter into the committee's deliberations? Although no professor would openly admit that "certain candidates were not of academic caliber," how would bias and favoritism influence a member's judgment? All these variables, and others, would affect the committee's deliberations. Meanwhile, Audrey had to wait an interminable four weeks to learn her fate. Until then, she was sure she would not be able to draw an easy breath.

"Look at the data," Rita told her. "I mean, just look at what you've done in the last five years. First of all, you've developed a humanities major that is the envy of three other universities. Your teaching evaluation forms show that students think you are one of the best teachers in the department. I wish *I* had such evaluations! It's true that you've had only one grant, and a small one; but the research you produced on evaluative practices in English is very sound. You've been on a zillion committees. You've given papers at conferences. You've worked tirelessly in the field, doing staff development in many schools. And look at the quality of your writing. You've won awards for it from two educational journals. You've published over ten articles in respectable journals. I can't believe that you've got anything to worry about. How can they deny you tenure, given your record?"

"In my heart, I know you're right, Rita," Audrey said with a small sigh. "But you know who's on the committee this time around. Do you think that Roger Bailey is going to look at my writing and call it scholarly? For him, if it doesn't have fifty thousand numbers in it, it's not research. My writing is definitely what he would call, 'soft.' But, that's how I write."

"Audrey, you are a writer—a real writer. Not just an academic; not just a scholar; but a *writer*. I mean, like a Hemingway. I say this with no exaggeration, and with more than a trace of envy. I wish I could write like you. You are truly gifted, and if that isn't scholarship, I don't know what scholarship is. You have the unique ability to take educational principles and weave them into narrative writing, so that readers can understand what the principles are, in the context of beautifully written prose. That's a gift that very few academics possess. Most of us write in stultifying, academic prose. You bring beauty and style to your manuscripts, while giving us the important messages as well."

Rita was just getting warmed up. "I mean, can't we, in our department, find room for the kind of scholarship produced by the Audrey Mayles as well as the Roger Baileys? Are we so narrow and stupid that we can only point to one form of scholarship as legitimate? For Pete's sake, listen to this. Just listen to your own stuff, and don't lose your perspective." Rita pulled out a manuscript from the stack of publications strewn about on the floor. She cleared her throat and read aloud the opening paragraph of the article:

If You Can Read This, Thank a Teacher

He was an enormously appealing boy—freckle-faced, with impish eyes and a smile that would light up a teacher's heart. Courteous and well behaved, he knew all the social forms, and never—not once—did he commit an indiscretion worthy of a reprimand. Smart without being smart-alecky, he seemed to have an intelligent grasp of everything going on. A model fifth-grade kid, right? There was only one flaw. He couldn't read. Not a single word, except for his own name, and I'm not even sure about that. Social promotion had allowed him to move through the grades with his age mates. Was this good? I didn't know. His ability to compute—add, subtract, multiply—was excellent. Yet, give him a word, any word, and within a space of five seconds he'd forget he'd ever seen it before in his life. The school psychologist assured me that he was a bright, healthy boy, with a high-measured intelligence, who had "an emotional block." I was the reading teacher. My job: Teach Daniel to read.

The two women sat, echoes of Audrey's written words resonating in the small office. At last, Audrey broke the silence: "If I don't get it, maybe I just don't deserve it. Maybe I don't deserve to be a tenured professor at a university. I just don't know anymore."

It was a week before Christmas that the formal notice arrived. The Tenure Committee had voted in favor of Dr. Mayles's tenure. The last obstacle in the process was the formal vote of approval from the department chair, Bruce Gardiner. It was all over but the shouting. A chair rarely, if ever, cast a vote in opposition to what the committee had decided.

Rita was in the office when Audrey came in, tears streaming down her face. "You won't believe this," she said, her face red with fury. "Bruce has voted against my tenure. I have a two-page letter from him outlining his reasons. You just won't believe it."

Rita sat down in her chair, stunned. This couldn't be happening. Bruce wouldn't take such an action. What could have motivated him? She took the document from Audrey's hands and began to read. She could not make too much sense of his argument, but it came up looking odd. Gardiner felt that Dr. Mayles had not demonstrated her scholarship in any way that he could consider satisfactory to meet the standards of this department. Her writing was "soft." She did not use the language of a scholar or even of an academic. Gardiner granted that Mayles was an excellent teacher and that her contributions to the university were above standard. But on the criterion of scholarship, he was adamant. Mayles did not measure up.

"I went to see him, too, Rita. After I read his statement, I went to see him, and I can't even believe what he said: that my writing was too clear; that such clarity was not a hallmark of scholarship. I'm *so* upset, I can't really believe that he said that. I don't even know if he was serious or was mocking me. But he is *not* prepared to change his mind. He even told me that one of the women members of the Tenure Committee came to him privately and said that, although she had voted in favor of my tenure, she did so primarily because I was a 'sister'—that, in fact, she believes my work is worthless.

"This means that the case will now go before the University Review Committee to be adjudicated. Another long process; another bunch of hearings; another several months before anything is decided. While I wait, I have anxiety dreams, and my life is upside down. What I'd like to do is just go to that SOB and hand in my resignation right now."

QUESTIONS TO CONSIDER

1. How would you describe Audrey Mayles? Write a profile that would describe her to another university, to which she had applied for a position.

2. How would you describe Bruce Gardiner? How do you interpret his behavior toward Audrey at the conference in Atlanta?

3. How would you respond to the female member of the Appointments Committee who was concerned that Audrey "did not give the appearance of a scholar?" What, in your view, should a scholar look like? How should a woman behave if she wants to be accepted by an academic community of scholars?

4. Does Audrey deserve tenure based on her performance at State University? To what extent do you agree with Gardiner's view of her scholarly writing? Do men and women tend to write in different styles? Should universities have double standards? Expanded standards? One scholarly standard?

5. What is your view of the female member of the Tenure Committee who voted for Audrey but privately scorned her work as "worthless"? To what extent should women support each other because they are "sisters"? What forms should their support take?

6. What should Audrey do next? If you were her office mate, how would you advise her? What specific suggestions would you make?

7. Does this case relate to any events in your own professional experience? If you want to discuss these events, describe the specific actions you took to resolve the dilemma and tell what happened.

ACTIVITIES

1. Some scholars claim that the logical and numerical basis of traditional quantitative research is a product of a male-dominated system that gives little value to the "soft" content areas and to the equally valuable, rich qualitative traditions characteristic of women's ways of knowing. Look at the example of Audrey's work. In your opinion, is her work too anecdotal and too informal to be considered scholarly?

   In small groups, identify the readings and research you have found most useful in preparing for a teaching career. Do these readings and research come from a quantitative or a qualitative tradition? What criteria would you propose for scholarly productivity in the education profession?

2. Imagine that your group is the University Review Committee considering Audrey Mayles's tenure application and the conflict between the Tenure Committee and

the department chair. Discuss her case. What issues are legitimate to debate? What would your decision be in Audrey's case? Would you take other action?

READINGS

Baker, M. A., and P. Goubil-Gambrell. (1991). Scholarly writing: The myth of gender performance. *Journal of Business and Technical Communication* 5 (4): 412–443.

Belenky, M. F., B. M. Clinchy, N. R. Goldberger, and J. Tarule. (1986). *Women's ways of knowing.* New York: Basic Books.

Farrell, W. *The myth of male power.* New York: Simon & Schuster.

Spender, D. (1980). *Man-made language.* London: Routledge & Kegan Paul.

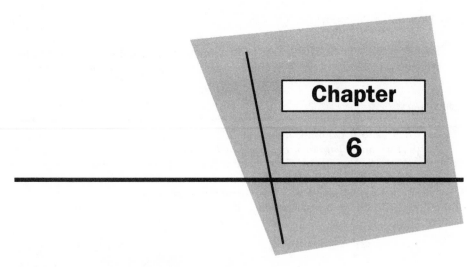

Chapter

6

Girls on the Wrestling Team:
A Community Fight

Judith S. Kleinfeld

The strong community reaction to the wrestling coach's remarks surprised even Superintendent Jack Paulsen, a veteran of small-town school wars. Some community residents were urging him to fire Mike Williams, the new wrestling coach and a first-year science teacher at Jackson High. A few even urged that Paulsen himself be removed, since he had hired a person with Williams's views about gender roles.

The controversy erupted when a young female reporter, in a routine preseason article about the high school's wrestling team, published comments Coach Williams supposedly had made. The reporter quoted Mike Williams as saying he "had a problem with [girls] wrestling." The coach went on to say: "There are a lot of things about the team that I'd like to teach that has to do with being a man in our society. What I want to teach to men is not what a woman should be taught."

When furor erupted over his remarks, Williams said that he had been misquoted and misinterpreted. But the editor defended his reporter and refused to budge. His paper had quoted Williams accurately, he insisted.

In a later interview, Williams tried to explain his views about boys' wrestling with girls: "I would like to see men respect women, and to handle women in that way would go against the values of treating women with respect. The holds that you can put people in—it doesn't present women in the proper way."

Two girls on the high-school wrestling team, junior Janet Lake and sophomore Karen Collins, said they were not quitting the team, even though Williams had tried to discourage them and other young women from joining the team at the start of the season. But another girl who originally was on the team had quit.

"Did Williams's behavior amount to discrimination against women, prohibited by Title IX of the Civil Rights Law?" Superintendent Paulsen asked himself. As he read the passionate letters to the editor that filled the town newspaper, Paulsen realized that the issue of girls on the wrestling team had touched a nerve. Feminism, freedom of speech, Christian views of family relationships, sexual touchings in wrestling holds, sexual discrimination against women, violence against women, indoctrination in the classroom—all the hot-button issues were threatening to overwhelm his showcase school.

And then there was Mike Williams himself—a Native American in his first year of teaching at age twenty-four. Williams had a family to support. He was a home-town boy and a nice guy, besides. His relatives were furious at the character assassinations appearing in the newspapers. His views, they said, reflected their cultural values concerning gender roles and respect for women.

Paulsen thought about the letters in last night's paper:

> I have serious questions about the hiring procedures which allow a teacher with ideals such as Mr. Williams's to be hired from a field of many highly qualified individuals whose personal philosophies fall more in line with current educational goals. . . . Did the committee purposely select someone who chooses to withhold his skills from his students based on their gender? . . . I respectfully request that Mr. Williams's employment status be reviewed and his appointment terminated.

Whatever he was going to do, he had better do it quickly, Paulsen realized. Community sentiment was rising to a fever pitch, and the wrestlers' first regulation meet was only two weeks away.

Background

The state School Activities Association considered wrestling and volleyball to be equivalent winter sports that complied with the Title IX requirement for equal emphasis and access in publicly funded girls' and boys' sports.

The small high schools in the region typically offered wrestling for boys and volleyball for girls as varsity sports during the winter season. Girls were allowed to go out for wrestling, and most small schools in the region had one girl or so on the wrestling team. But boys were never allowed to go out for volleyball because their typically greater musculature would result in unfair competition and drive girls from the team.

"Although girls can't be denied the opportunity to go out for wrestling, schools are not required to open volleyball to boys," explained the director of the School Activities Association. "Separate but equal" wrestling and volleyball teams for both girls and boys had been suggested. But historically the small schools in the region did not have enough girls interested in wrestling to make up a team and to justify the expense of paying a coach.

Girls on the Wrestling Team: Sexual Equality or Sexual Harrassment?

The wrestling coaches in the region were divided about the issue of coeducational wrestling teams. The coaches at the four other high schools in the region went on record as disagreeing with Williams's opinion that girls should not participate in wrestling. "Athletes who can endure the rigors of this sport learn valuable lessons whether they are male or female," the coaches maintained in a public statement. "We support all wrestlers equally."

A parent who was a booster of the wrestling team explained how his initial concerns about girls' wrestling had changed with experience. He invited people from the community to come to a "Meet the Teams" exhibition and a tutorial on "how to watch and understand wrestling."

"I was very uncomfortable the first couple of times I watched a young man wrestle a young woman," the parent explained. "I have watched young women compete against young men in a middle-school tournament and have been in the gym at numerous practices where young men and women wrestled. While there are special challenges associated with young women moving into wrestling, there is no question in my mind that denying opportunities to anyone interested in participating in this great sport would be wrong."

Others took the opposite view: Wrestling involves holds in the groin and chest areas, and these wrestlers are adolescents. In the honky-tonk district of New Orleans, people pay to watch men and women wrestle while covered with oil. The whole idea is unseemly, they argued.

A former coach expressed the following concerns with delicate understatement:

> One of the main objectives in wrestling is to pin your opponent, which requires wrestlers to get their opponent on their back, get chest to chest for good balance, and keep the head low in the chest so the opponent being pinned will not be able to use the head for leverage to escape. How will it be perceived by other athletes, moms and dads, and classmates when a member of the opposite gender is placed in this position? Will the athletes be forced to make decisions about what moves they will or will not use because they don't wish to be made fun of or embarrassed by the position of their body parts in mixed-gender situations?

The coach raised a host of other questions. If we are concerned for the quality of male and female relationships and violence against women, should the school support activities in which males attempt to use their strength and aggressiveness to pin down and defeat females? What if a young man refused to wrestle a girl because of his personal beliefs or religious convictions, should he be denied the chance to advance in meets and tournaments? At least one wrestler, the coach remembered, had refused to wrestle a girl at the regional meet because of his personal convictions. It cost him the opportunity to make it to the state wrestling tournament.

Coaches demonstrate wrestling holds during teaching. Could a wrestling coach be charged with improper touching if he demonstrated certain holds with a girl? If he did not do such a demonstration, could he be charged with sexual discrimination because he denied the young women the same educational opportunities?

Compromises could be worked out, the former coach reflected. But in wrestling, actions and reactions are tested in seconds with everyone striving for peak performance and glorying in the freedom of movement. "Can this freedom be attained if we force our athletes to be placed in situations where their minds will be muddled with decisions that have no place in the joy of the sport?" he asked.

"Freedom of movement—what nonsense!" snapped another participant. "All athletics require movement according to rules. That's what makes athletics a sport."

Joining the Fight

The most vehement participants in the fight saw the question of girls on the wrestling team as a peripheral matter. The basic issue was different— teachers' attitudes toward women and what public school teachers told children about women's roles and appropriate family relationships.

"The issue here is Mike Williams's *reasons* for not allowing girls on the team and his treatment of these girls," said one woman in the community. What were the grounds for saying that boys should be learning something about life that girls should not? The notion of special training for manhood was absurd. That kind of nineteenth-century thinking savored of Sir Baden-Powell and the Boy Scouts. It had no place in the contemporary world and especially in the schools.

Athletics did teach important lessons useful in life—how to win, how to lose, how to work together as a team. Life is filled with ups and downs, and sports prepare you for the rough-and-tumble world. "Where is it written that lessons like these are 'wasted' on girls?" fumed a female coach. "The 'things about the team' that can be taught are not about being a man, they are about being a person."

Others raised broader questions about the role of the schools and teachers like Mike Williams in perpetuating male patriarchy and oppressive stereotypes about women. Violence toward women, battering and rape, were rooted in the very attitudes Mike Williams had expressed, they insisted. Such attitudes were intolerable in an educational institution supported by public funds.

Others saw the kind of attitudes Mike Williams had expressed as demonstrating just how schools "shortchanged" girls. Citing the report "Shortchanging Girls: Shortchanging America," they pointed out that girls begin schools with the same skills and ambitions as boys, but they learn that they should aim lower. America needs the contributions of women. Jackson School, they insisted, should immediately examine its approach to gender equity and make sure that female students get equal treatment.

One letter writer spotted the religious foundation of Mike Williams's views about the relationships of men and women. His attitudes, she pointed out, were rooted in Christian teachings about authority and submission. She wrote: "I grew up attending a church that taught these same hierarchical values. First in authority is God, the Father; then Christ, the Son; then men; then women; then children; then animals; and so on. But dominating all else were *men*. I no longer believe these teachings. The philosophy that any person possesses the authority or right to require submission from another has not brought us peace and never will."

The issue of whether girls should be on the wrestling team was turning into a debate about Christian family relationships. Some letters to the local newspapers attempted to explain that "domination" was not what Christ taught at all. Biblical teachings emphasized treating others with respect and recognizing the need for order in a society and obligations in relationships. The Bible does tell women to be submissive to their husbands, but it also admonishes husbands to love their wives, to nourish and protect them. It is not Christian teachings that are at the root of wife abuse or any violence toward women, these writers argued, but the modern emphasis on personal freedom that recognizes no restraint and honors no commitment.

A Native-American leader wrote a letter to explain the cultural values with which Mike Williams had been raised: "I believe you would understand him better if you knew more about our culture. We have grown up being taught by our parents in the ways that some describe as traditional Christian family values. Others might label us as 'old-fashioned' or 'out of touch,' but nevertheless this is still our cultural heritage. From Mike's cultural perspective, women are viewed as people to be treated with respect, honor, and dignity. We were taught as little boys not to hurt girls, nor to use our natural physical advantage in any way other than to help them or protect them from harm. Our concept of male leadership in the home has been badly misunderstood. Our whole concept of loving our wives and daughters involves mutual respect and using our strength sacrificially to provide, protect, and enable them to fulfill all the potential that God has placed in them."

In a culturally diverse community, said a few voices, we need tolerance toward each other's values and ways of creating families. It is hypocritical to say that everyone should be free to "do their own thing" and then savage someone whose thinking does not conform to modern orthodoxies. If schools are to be intellectual communities, a marketplace of ideas, then students should be exposed to a range of views about desirable patterns for family life and proper relationships between men and women.

"If domineering feminists are allowed to preach their beliefs in the classroom, then traditional teachers like Mike Williams are entitled to tell kids the other side of the story," asserted one writer to the newspaper.

"Sexual discrimination is against the law, and that is the bottom line," said another.

Refereeing the Fight

Superintendent Paulsen considered the emotions gripping the community because of the remarks of his young wrestling teacher. The reporter had asked few questions about the boys on the team. She kept pressing and possibly baiting the rookie coach.

In dealing with Mike Williams and the wrestling issue, Paulsen realized that he was dealing with a lot more. He had not missed the letter to the editor asking whether he, himself—not just Mike Williams—"should be teaching our children." Furthermore, he was sympathetic to Mike Williams's views on the wrestling issue itself. Girls should be able to wrestle against each other, he thought, but wrestling against boys involved too much close physical contact. Could he express his own view, or should he keep quiet?

Superintendent Paulsen had built a school known throughout the state for its high standards and innovative educational programs. This controversy could swiftly undermine the school's reputation. But besides the future of the school, there were individuals to think about—namely, Mike Williams and his family. Mike may have been dumped into a political shark tank in his first year of teaching. But Jack Paulsen was an old hand. He should be able to swim out. But how?

QUESTIONS TO CONSIDER

1. A prominent citizen of the town argued that the wrestling issue should be the subject of public hearings. This is the resolution he proposed for debate: "High-school wrestling is a gender-specific sport. Because of anatomical and physical differences between males and females, wrestling is not a sport in which women can safely and effectively participate along with men." If you were at this hearing, would you testify for or against this resolution? Explain your reasoning.

2. Suppose that the School Activities Association did adopt this resolution and created gender-specific wrestling teams but that too few girls went out for wrestling. The school could not form teams to participate in competitive meets. Is this situation a form of gender discrimination against girls?

3. The policy at Jackson High School is to allow girls to participate on the wrestling team but not to allow boys to participate on the volleyball team. What reasoning do you think lies behind this policy? Is this situation a form of gender discrimination against boys?

4. Should teachers be free to present their personal views about family patterns and appropriate relationships between men and women to high-school students? If not, what views should be presented, and who should make such decisions? Should teachers present both sides?

5. If you were Superintendent Paulsen, how would you handle this controversy?

Epilogue

Superintendent Paulsen chose to handle the controversy in the following way. He consulted the state attorney general's office, the state department of education, and the state School Activities Association for recommendations regarding proper procedures, and he kept all these agencies informed. He also reported that an infraction of gender equity had taken place.

Paulsen was advised to investigate the charge of sexual discrimination against Mike Williams and to conduct a further investigation into possible sex discrimination more generally at Jackson High School. Paulsen found that Williams had, indeed, discouraged girls from participating on the team at the start of the season.

Mike Williams resigned as wrestling coach. Students from his science classes were questioned to determine if he had discriminated against girls in any way. No discrimination was found. "In fact, it has even been the other way," Paulsen said in a press interview.

A schoolwide investigation of gender equity was launched. "We want to make every program available to all students regardless of gender," Superintendent Paulsen told the newspapers. In addition to finding violations of Title IX, the investigation was intended to teach students and staff what "gender equity" means and how to report violations. Students were interviewed in groups and could also come forth individually. They were asked such questions as: "Do you feel that attitudes at Jackson High School in any way treat males and females differently?" "Do you personally feel that activities or resources at Jackson High School are unavailable to you because you are a boy or a girl?"

Students raised no instance of gender equity, except that boys could not play volleyball. Paulsen stated that he would look into forming gender-specific volleyball and wrestling teams and said that he himself felt uncomfortable with girls' wrestling boys. Nevertheless, since his investigation had determined that girls at Jackson High School had, indeed, been discouraged from participating in the wrestling team, Jackson High would make a fresh effort to encourage girls to join the team. As a result, three more girls did join.

Superintendent Paulsen brought a consulting group to the school to educate both students and staff about gender issues. Mike Williams was reinstated as wrestling coach for the following school year, but he was required to get special training in gender equity. Nothing came of the effort to establish gender-specific wrestling and volleyball teams at Jackson High School.

ACTIVITIES

1. Interview coaches at the local junior and senior high schools. Find out how many girls participate in wrestling teams and how these girls are integrated into the overall program. Do the coaches make any allowances for gender differences? What kinds of allowances? Observe wrestling practice sessions that include girls. Do you see differences in how boys wrestle with boys and with girls? In how girls wrestle with girls and with boys?

2. Interview girls who wrestle on school teams. Determine why they decided to wrestle; what their initial experiences on the team were like; the reactions of their friends, families, and teammates; the nature of public competitions with other teams; and their personal feelings about the sport. Interview boys on the same teams, and analyze any gender differences you find in the results. How do the boys feel about having female teammates?

3. Look through the local school district's policy manual for guidelines on who is eligible to play specific sports in local schools. Another controversial issue is whether girls should be allowed to play with boys on football teams. This issue centers on physical safety—gender differences in body weight and musculature of athletes.

   Investigate and evaluate the medical evidence that supports each side of the safety argument. In examining these studies, consider such issues as whether girls are using equipment that is appropriate for them rather than equipment designed for boys. What conclusions do you reach about gender differences in the potential for injuries when males and females play coeducational football and other contact sports?

READINGS

Dyment, P. G. (1989). Controversies in pediatric sports medicine. *Physician and Sports Medicine* (July): 17 (7), 57 (7). [Girls being allowed to play football or wrestle in high school]

Neff, C. (1989). Hold the mud, please. *Sports Illustrated* (September): 71 (13), 12 (2). [World Wrestling Championships include women for the first time]

Whiteside, K. (1993). Lauren Wolfe. *Sports Illustrated* (February): 78 (7), 158 (1). [A woman wrestler]

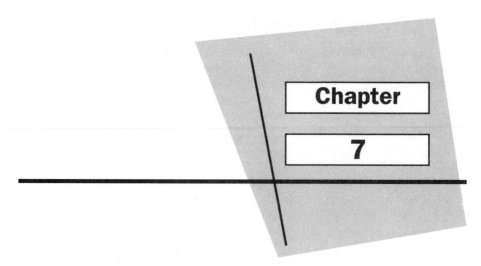

Chapter

7

The Venerable Tradition of Separate-Sex Schooling

Judith S. Kleinfeld*

Susan Vorcheimer graduated with honors from an academic junior high school. Her scholastic standing made her eligible to attend an academic high school for excellent students. The Philadelphia School District had established two such high schools for academically superior students, Central High School, which admitted only boys, and Girls' High, which admitted only girls.

Susan looked at the high-school options available in the Philadelphia School District and decided that she wanted to go to Central High School, not to Girls' High. "I liked it there," she said of Central High. "I liked the atmosphere and also what I heard about it, and its academic excellence."

Since Susan was female, she was refused admission to Central High. Her parents sued the school district to admit her. An admission requirement based on gender, they argued, was unconstitutional. It denied equal opportunity to girls solely because of their sex.

About Girls' High, Susan said during her lawsuit: "I just didn't like the impression it gave me. I didn't think I would be able to go there for three years and not be harmed in any way."

While her case was in the courts, Susan chose to go to a comprehensive coeducational high school, George Washington. But she was dissatisfied with the quality of education at this school, because she felt the teachers did not set sufficiently high standards for the students.

The Philadelphia School District had established four different kinds

*This case is a summary of *Vorcheimer v. School District of Philadelphia*, 532 F.2d 880 (3rd Cir. 1976), aff'd., 430 U.S. 703 (1977). All quotations are from the majority opinion of the Third Circuit, written by Judge Joseph F. Weis.

of high schools: academic, comprehensive, technical, and magnet. The academic high schools draw students from the entire city, and they offer only college-preparatory standards. The comprehensive high schools—mostly neighborhood schools—provide a wide range of courses including advanced placement.

Both Central High and Girls' High offer similar academic courses and are widely considered to be of equal quality. The one exception is that Central High—open only to boys—offers better courses in science. Graduates from both schools are accepted at prestigious colleges and universities and have distinguished records of achievement.

Separate education for girls and boys at both high-school and college levels has a venerable history. Research on the effects of separating students by gender is not conclusive. Still, many studies suggest that girls do better academically in single-sex institutions. The judge considered two such studies, for example, in deciding this case. In New Zealand, where separating students by gender is common, Dr. Charles Jones found that students in single-sex high schools placed more value on achievement and spent more time on homework. Studies of women's colleges have found that women who attend single-sex colleges tend to achieve more than women who attend coeducational institutions. Dr. M. Elizabeth Tidball, for example, found that more women who attend women's colleges are listed in *Who's Who of American Women.*

Susan McGee Bailey (1993) of the Wellesley College Center for Research on Women, however, cautions that girls' schools can show a lack of "academic vigor." She also points out that the same drop in self-confidence that occurs generally among young adolescent girls occurs in selective girls' schools as well.

If you were deciding this case, would you allow Susan Vorcheimer to attend Central High School? Would you bring an end to single-sex public high schools?

QUESTIONS TO CONSIDER

1. Think about the policy of separate-but-equal schooling from the standpoint of gender rather than race. Do you see any justifiable differences? Recall the Supreme Court case *Plessy v. Ferguson,* which upheld "separate but equal" segregated schools for African-American students. The landmark Supreme Court case *Brown v. Board of Education of Topeka* reversed this earlier decision and pointed to the inherently stigmatizing nature of racially separate schools. Does this same reasoning apply to single-sex schools, or should we take into account the different histories and purposes of school segregation by race and gender?

   Are separate educational experiences for boys and girls desirable in some circumstances? Explain.

2. Although research about the effects of single-sex schooling is not conclusive, a reasonable case can be made that girls do better academically in single-sex

schools. According to this view, girls in a single-sex school will occupy 100 percent of the leadership positions and will spend more time on academic pursuits. Should the actual achievement of girls and boys in separate-sex high schools be taken into account in deciding whether these schools discriminate by gender?

3. Some school districts have proposed all-male high schools for African-American students as a way of providing an educational atmosphere that supports achievement and pride among African-American males. Do you support this policy? What is your reasoning?

4. If Girls' High offered science courses that were equivalent to the courses at Central High, would your opinion about this case be the same? What if Central's better science courses were balanced at Girls' High by better courses in literature, art, and dance? Should boys then be entitled to enroll in Girls' High?

5. Some school districts give adolescent girls the option of taking sex-separate math and science classes in an effort to increase their interest and skills in math and science. What are the benefits and drawbacks of such a program? What if the boys' math and science classes move ahead at a much faster rate than the girls' classes? Should girls be admitted to the boys' classes?

The Court Decision

[Keep in mind that gender equity is an area of the law that is in a state of flux and evolving. The court decisions in such cases will be based on many different considerations—the relevant federal legislation, the laws of the particular state, the particular facts of the case, precedents in the particular circuit, and so forth. The Vorcheimer decision should not be regarded as "the law" on the matter of separate schools for girls and boys but rather as the decision a particular court made in one set of circumstances.]

Susan Vorcheimer and her family won in federal district court. The judge ruled that she and other qualified female students must be admitted to Central High, the all-male academic school.

The school district appealed this result and the Third Circuit Court of Appeals reversed the district court. The circuit court reasoned that the educational opportunities offered at both high schools were essentially equal and that attendance was voluntary. According to the majority opinion:

> Equal educational opportunities should be available to both sexes in any intellectual field. However, the special emotional problems of the adolescent years are matters of human experience and have led some educational experts to opt for one-sex high schools. While this policy has limited acceptance on its merits, it does have its basis in a theory of equal benefit and not discriminatory denial.

The court pointed out that this decision did not bear on the wisdom of segregating boys and girls during adolescence, only on whether this practice was constitutional. It also pointed out that Congress could pass legislation prohibiting single-sex schools but had not yet chosen to do so.

Although race is a suspect classification and raises immediate concern that distinctions made by race are unconstitutional, gender is not in the same category. According to the majority opinion:

> We are committed to the concept that there is no fundamental difference between the races and therefore, in justice, there can be no dissimilar treatment. But there are differences between the sexes which may, in limited circumstances, justify disparity in law.

Susan Vorcheimer's case was appealed to the Supreme Court. In an equally divided opinion, the Supreme Court affirmed the decision of the appeals court. In 1993, two public schools for girls were in existence in the United States, one in Philadelphia and the other in Baltimore (Bailey, 1993).

ACTIVITIES

1. Research the history of gender- and race-segregated schools and the achievement of students in both kinds of segregated schools. What can you conclude about the effects of segregation by race compared with segregation by gender?

2. Collect articles about schools, classes, and programs that have segregated on the basis of race or gender. Stage a debate among individuals with widely different views about issues arising from such segregation.

3. Interview youth leaders from gender-separate organizations like the YMCA, the YWCA, the Boy Scouts, and the Girl Scouts. What are their views about the benefits and drawbacks of gender-separate educational programs?

READINGS

Bailey, S. M. (1993). The current status of gender equity research in American schools. *Educational Psychologist* 28 (4): 321–339.

Gross, J. (1993). To help girls keep up: Math class without boys. *New York Times* (November 24): A1 (2).

Eaton, S. (1994). Forty years after *Brown*, cities and suburbs face a rising tide of racial isolation. *The Harvard Education Letter* X (1):1–15.

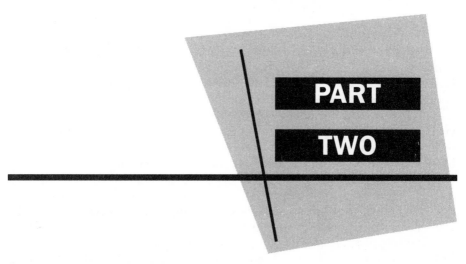

Increasing Achievement among Young Women

Introduction

Why do men so vastly outstrip women in achievement? Whether we are talking about occupational status or earnings, renown in music or in literature, power in public office or in the corporate world, men greatly surpass women. Even in the schools themselves, where female teachers outnumber male teachers—a place where we might most expect females, in the ordinary course of events, to advance to management positions—the person in the principal's office is more likely to be male.

We argue about the real reasons for this state of affairs with our families and our friends and in the pages of political magazines and scholarly journals. What is going on is complicated, and, with the increasing emphasis on gender equity, it is also changing.

Consider as an example the area of mathematics and science achievement. Girls start school with standardized test scores higher than boys, but they leave school with scores trailing far behind them (Sadker, Sadker, and Steindam, 1989). Scholars hold conflicting views about the origins of gender-based achievement differences—whether innate differences exist in cognitive abilities, and boys simply have a higher aptitude for math; whether tests are biased against females; whether achievement differences result from girls' adaptation to the subordinate status of women; whether parents develop the mathematical and scientific abilities of sons more than daughters by the kinds of toys they purchase and the more independent experiences they allow; and whether girls see mathematics and science as male-dominated fields at which they are not good, fields they do not enjoy and where they do not belong.

Whatever the origins of gender differences in mathematics and science achievement, children's experiences in schools typically amplify the differences that already exist. Upon graduation from high school, males outperform females on standardized tests of mathematics partly for the obvious reason that more males take advanced mathematics courses, such as calculus (Kimball, 1989). Even when girls and boys enroll in the same classes, they do not necessarily have the same experiences in them. In science classes, where boys and girls work together on laboratory projects, for example, boys are more apt to take leadership roles and to work actively with the materials, while girls are more apt to watch on the sidelines and to make halfhearted stabs at participation (Kahle, Parker, Rennie, and Riley, 1993).

The first case in Part Two, "The Square Parachute: Science in Gender-mixed Groups"—along with "Jane, the Reluctant Mathlete" in Part One—offers you real-world examples of teachers who are trying to combat gender-based patterns of mathematics and science achievement in their own classrooms. These cases offer concrete models of how to organize classrooms in ways that encourage girls as well as boys to take leadership roles in group laboratory work, to plan and conduct experiments, and to enjoy scientific and mathematical problem solving instead of anxiously avoiding such work. But these cases also show the power of cultural scripts that girls and boys have learned outside the classroom to sabotage a teacher's efforts at reform. The teachers must figure out what to do when girls, as well as boys, resist. In "The Square Parachute" the students know their roles like actors in a situation comedy. The boys dangle fish eggs in the girls' faces, the girls scream and run away, and the classroom careens out of control.

From birth onward, girls and boys learn from their parents, their peers, the media, and their textbooks just how males and females are expected to behave in their particular cultural setting. The age of adolescence, however, marks a turning point. At puberty, bright girls confront a dilemma and often think it through quite consciously: Should they attempt to achieve in school, or will conspicuous achievement make them unpopular and unfeminine? Girls who are bright, confident, and assertive during their elementary years often lose spirit and retreat at adolescence (Brown and Gilligan, 1992). Adolescent boys also decline in self-confidence, but the drop for girls is far more dramatic and long-lasting (American Association of University Women, 1991).

"Burn Schools to the Ground" offers an extreme example of the downward spiral that can occur at adolescence in girls who have seemed to be emotionally stable and academically successful. April, gifted in music and writing, refuses to attend her high-school classes. She announces to Joan

Adams, her gifted-and-talented teacher from her middle-school days, that she is going to drop out of school. Adams tries to figure out what is going so terribly wrong. Could April have been sexually abused? Are the school district's programs and requirements simply misconceived for a nonconformist like April? Adams has seen this pattern too many times before: a bright girl who stops going to classes, eventually gets pregnant, and drops out of school. She struggles to prevent it from happening to April.

The next group of cases asks you to think about the ways in which culture and class, in combination with gender, influence achievement. Most teachers are white, middle-class females with a perspective that arises from their own cultural values and background experiences. Despite the best of intentions, they do not always know how to interpret the behavior, attitudes, dress, and dilemmas of minority students and their families. These cases alert you to the kinds of issues that experienced teachers have faced, often wishing in retrospect that they had understood better.

"Tough Anna" and "Diane News: The Choice" ask you to consider how to spot and develop talent among young women when it appears in culturally different forms. Anna is a tough-looking Mexican-American girl with a habit of crumpling up her A papers, throwing them into the wastebasket, and announcing loudly to her friends that she has failed again. Her eleventh-grade history teacher, Judy Baur, comes to realize that her own cultural stereotypes have prevented her from recognizing just how bright and ambitious Anna is. The case traces Judy's efforts to get Anna interested in going to college and to show her that she can have friends, an identity, and a voice in the unfamiliar college world.

Diane News confronts a distasteful choice: Which students should she recommend for the new gifted-and-talented program? Despite her concern about women's issues, she is leaning toward recommending four boys. Three of the boys are white and have the best grades, test scores, and class work. Diane thinks another boy, Stuart—with his off-beat sense of humor and insightful comments—is truly gifted, although his test scores don't show it. On the other hand, Margie, an African-American girl, has slightly higher test scores than Stuart. But Diane sees Margie as a "concrete thinker" who lacks Stuart's flash and brilliance. Diane's ability to make the right choice is not helped when Margie's father hints at racism and criticizes her creative classroom. Still, if Margie's family emphasizes strictness, structure, and one right answer, perhaps it is her cultural milieu that explains Margie's habits of mind.

Culture and class also influence what families expect from sons and daughters and what opportunities they provide. Parents typically place more emphasis on the achievement of sons, and they favor boys when making hard economic choices (Flanagan, 1993). Girls are more often required to help at home with younger children and family chores, at the expense of their other interests. When a family lacks enough money to send all children to college, they are more likely to invest in boys.

"Opening Pandora's Box: The Mystery behind an 'Ideal Student' " offers you a case where a teacher works with a third-grade Chinese girl who is experiencing such family favoritism. Connie appears to be a model student but is actually an emotional volcano. She passionately wants to be best friends with Mai Ling, who rejects her. She resents her parents for favoring her brother and for giving away her pet dog without even telling her. Connie's teacher finds it hard to understand these Chinese parents' emotional remoteness, their threats to spank Connie if she doesn't learn her multiplication tables over the weekend, and their insistance that Connie apologize to the teacher when Connie is the one who is upset.

The last two cases in Part Two ask you to think about a philosophical question that different people and different cultures answer differently: What does "achievement" actually mean? We do not all see success in the same way.

From a libertarian perspective, the central gender issue is not equality but freedom. In this view, we should take action when girls receive stereotyped messages about what occupations are available to them. We should take action when employment criteria, biased testing, or any other institutional barriers hold women back. Men and women should have the same opportunities to make their own choices. But when people are free to make choices, they may well make different choices. Some women may choose to invest themselves in family life, more than in occupational success. "Inequality"—outcomes that are not the same—does not mean "inequity"—unfairness.

"Going to the Oracle: Susan Consults the 'Big Feminist' " offers you a case example of this issue. Susan, a high-school senior from a child-centered Jewish family, is enraged when she talks to her parents about her dream of a career in international relations. Her father encourages her, even though Susan realizes he himself gets upset if her mother leaves on business travel even for a few days. Susan's mother urges her to choose a career that won't take her constantly away from home, a career that lets her combine the joys of satisfying work with the joys of raising children. Susan is furious at the hypocrisy she suddenly sees. Her teachers have always told her that a girl as bright as she can be whatever she wants to be. She decides to consult her English teacher, known to be a "big feminist."

"You'll Be Washing Dishes" asks whether "achievement" for a minority student means entering an elite college and succeeding in mainstream society or making something of yourself while staying connected to your own community. Roberto, a gifted Mexican-American male, is filling out his college application to Stanford. Kathleen, a white teacher and his Quiz Bowl coach, believes he has a good chance of making it and going on to one of the best law schools in the country. An African-American feminist teacher sees Roberto filling out his application and urges him to forget Stanford and to go to a local college instead. She tells him he will feel alienated and alone at an elite "white" school, just as she did. Is her cultural and gender-based perspective any more valid for Roberto than Kathleen's.

The cases in Part Two ask you to think about why gender differences in achievement exist and what you as a teacher can do about them. The cases alert you to biases in schools and in yourselves that you may not have had the opportunity to think about. But the cases also caution you to keep in mind individual and cultural differences. Not all people define success and a good life in the same way.

REFERENCES

American Association of University Women. (1991). *Shortchanging girls, shortchanging America: A nationwide poll to assess self-esteem, educational experiences, interest in math and science, and career aspirations of girls and boys ages 9–15.* Washington: D.C.

Brown, L. M., and C. Gilligan. (1992). *Meeting at the crossroads: Women's psychology and girls' development.* Cambridge, Mass.: Harvard University Press.

Flanagan, C. (1993). Gender and social class: Intersecting issues in women's achievement. *Educational Psychologist* 28 (4): 357–378.

Kahle, J. B., L. H. Parker, L. J. Rennie, and D. Riley. (1993). Gender differences in science education: Building a model. *Educational Psychologist* 28 (4): 379–404.

Kimball, M. (1989). A new perspective on women's math achievement. *Psychological Bulletin* 105: 198–213.

Sadker, M., D. Sadker, and S. Steindam. (1989). Gender equity and educational reform. *Educational Leadership,* 44–47.

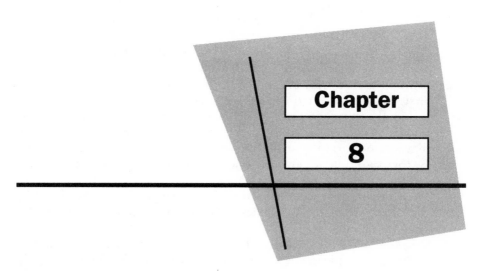

The Square Parachute:
Science in Gender-mixed Groups

Gender Equity Project Teachers

The Fish Lab Is a Bust

"Eeeeeeeeeeee!" Marilyn screamed. She was one of the younger girls, pretty and very feminine. (She spent a lot of time working on that.)

Teddy was smart and smart-mouthed. He understood the fish lab and had completed the tasks; and when he was done, he wanted to do something fun, like take a skein of fish eggs, sneak up on one of the girls, wave it in her face, and yell, "Yaaaaaaaaaah!" Predictably, Marilyn screamed and sent the fish eggs flying. Immediately, all the girls were screeching, and all the boys were laughing and grabbing fish guts.

The fish lab, thought Meg Eliot, the new science teacher in this rural Indian community, had been a bust. The kids had been loud and rowdy. The room was a mess. In an effort to control her rising anger, Meg calmly asked the kids about the lesson. The students didn't have the foggiest idea what part of the fish was the stomach, liver, or brain—let alone what any of these parts did for the fish.

"If I had a brain, I would stick with my tightly structured activities," Meg thought. When the kids were in their seats talking about fish anatomy and fishing in Beluga Bay, things went all right. They could handle observing the fish in the classroom aquarium. But they had never dissected anything before. They had only watched her. The dissection lab was falling apart.

Meg had set up the dissection lab with clear objectives. Students would come to know the names and functions of the parts of the fish. They were also supposed to investigate the age of the fish through observing the scales. They were to weigh, measure, and determine the sex of the fish as well. Meg set up dissection trays and broke the students into groups.

First she demonstrated what she wanted the students to do, and what she wanted them to find out. "This is how you cut open the fish. Be careful to be gentle so that nothing gets cut that you don't want cut. Open the fish and look carefully at the internal organs. See how many you can identify, then carefully remove the ones on top so that you can see what is underneath."

The students were clearly interested and delighted at the opportunity to do this dissection themselves. They all set to work diligently until Teddy's group got done first.

Meg reminded the kids that they had promised not to be rowdy. To her surprise, Teddy pleaded with her. "We were just having a little fun, Ms. Eliot," Ted said. Meg just looked at him. This fish lab was their second chance. Indeed, it was their umpteenth chance at doing active learning in science labs. The principal had warned her to keep things under control. He would have her hide.

Background

Meg Eliot loved teaching science. Since her first year of teaching, she had taken summer courses in science education—especially if the courses were held outdoors. She had come to the conclusion that science could best be presented to students as something one does, rather than something one reads about. She had a strong bias toward showing students how to do science rather than telling them what scientists had learned over the centuries.

When Meg accepted the job of teaching a middle-school class at Beluga Bay, she decided this was an opportunity to try out some new ideas about teaching science. She wanted to try to teach science in such a way that, at the end of the year, students could independently arrive at a question to be studied, state the question as a hypothesis, design and implement an experiment to test the hypothesis, collect and interpret data, draw conclusions, and apply the understanding gained. She felt it could be done, but she had nagging doubts about whether it could be done in a year and whether she could do it.

Beluga Bay was a small fishing town. She had been told that her class, consisting of fourteen students, was difficult, especially the older boys. Junior-high-school students, she realized, could indeed be difficult. She was also told that three of the students had "moderate to severe problems learning at school," whatever that meant.

When Meg arrived, the principal told her that the students were three to four years behind academically, and he expected her to make them work quietly and diligently. While he wanted them to achieve at grade level, he really didn't expect that to happen. Their former teacher, he said, had "burnt out" and had found these students difficult to cope with. The former teacher spent his energies getting the students to behave and felt, according to the principal, that bringing them to grade level academically could not happen until they learned to behave in school and have respect for learning. The previous year the students had all used the fifth-grade text, regardless of grade level.

The principal also informed Meg that she would teach girls' physical education and shop, and that the male high-school teacher would instruct the boys. The shop teacher, he explained, had felt that the boys needed a real shop class, while the girls really needed crafts more. "The girls make all those knickknacks," he said, "but the boys really need to *know* this stuff."

The First Semester

The first week of school was the honeymoon period. The students were docile and well behaved. Meg established a classroom routine, outlined the year, and got to know the students. Yes, indeed, there were fourteen distinct personalities there, few of them weak. More than half the students were outspoken to the point of being disruptive; they had a negative attitude toward school and enjoyed trying to get the teacher's goat. One student, Clint, was described by the principal as very bright but lazy and prone to throwing temper tantrums. Apparently, he regularly staged great outbursts. The principal said that Clint would threaten the tantrums and then carry them out. Another student, Mark, was thought to have alcohol-related birth defects and was classified by the principal as emotionally disturbed. Mark had difficulty concentrating. Another student, Joe, read at a second-grade level but was as large as a professional wrestler. Then there was Mike, who came from out of town and was picked on by the other students until he blew up. Several students took delight in making obscene remarks. Throwing objects, spitting, and slugging each other were common practices. It truly was "the class from hell." The principal encouraged Meg to "run a tight ship." She tried to do that. She established strict behavioral guidelines based on rewards and punishments.

In science, Meg tried to establish an atmosphere of questioning. She asked students about the local animals, plants, and weather. On weekends, she walked over the tundra, trying to get to know the area. She brought plants and small tundra critters into class to look at. She asked about the traditional names of things. When students asked questions, she asked them how they could find out the answers. When she was able, she told them what she knew about the permafrost, the caribou, the willow, and the small water creatures.

Students started to bring things from their environment to class—lemmings, a wounded kittiwake. They began to show a strong interest in these things. Meg got an aquarium and planned a unit on fish and fisheries for later in the year.

Meg decided it was time to find out where these kids were in science. Had they done labs? No. She would try a lab that was straightforward, and that would give her an idea of the skill levels of the kids: Could they devise ways of finding out? Did they know about controlling variables? Could they interpret data? Did they know the necessity of accurate measurements? Could they make these measurements?

The lab emphasized a fairly simple observation. Students were asked to make observations about a burning candle. All she wanted to learn was where the students were in science. She discussed observation. How does one observe? What are the senses? How does one use the senses? How do tools extend the senses? Students were asked to observe a candle mounted in clay before, during, and after it burned.

Meg discovered that the students saw the less tightly controlled lab as a time to play, an opportunity to get out of their seats and have fun. They looked at the candles and described them as being red or blue-striped; they lit them and burned them until they were gone; and then they launched into their favorite topic of late: farting.

"Eeeuuu! Mark farted!"

"I did not!"

"You did too!" (Gales of laughter)

"Well, at least I don't fart as much as Tina!" Mark snarled at his sister. (Gales of laughter)

Meg told the students to settle down, commenting that farting wasn't a topic for school. They did settle down, sort of. Meg tried to find out if they had made any observations at all. She discovered that the observations were very few, and the measurements none. Meg was dismayed. Was this a result of assigning a lab that the students considered silly? Was it a result of poor directions? Or was it a result of the students' lack of experience with labs? She tried to probe to find out. The students said that they had never done any labs before. It never occurred to them to measure anything, even though she had talked with them about using tools to extend the senses.

Meg felt she would have to teach the basic process skills of scientific inquiry one at a time before they could design anything. They needed to learn how to observe, measure, classify, predict, infer, hypothesize, design experiments, and interpret data. She decided to try a controlled demonstration with the whole class. She would do a unit about air pressure, and all the labs would be demonstrations, with one student at a time trying the experiments. This approach was not perfect. The experiments would not be as accessible to all students, but air-pressure experiments could be straightforward: They had clear variables, results that were easy to see, and data that were easy to measure and interpret. She could model behavior, she hoped, that would foster inquiry and elicit questions that could be tested. The demonstrations went well, but the students were observers and not participants. When they sat in their rows, with their eyes front and no one talking, the lesson proceeded smoothly. But if they were allowed to do something themselves or work in groups, they went berserk.

Meg did acknowledge that some progress was being made in the students' abilities to work in mixed-gender groups. Meg chose working groups on the basis of several criteria. The first was who would get along with whom without friction. She had discovered that the social relationships of the students were extremely important. At the beginning of the year, she could not mix boys and girls in groups. Some of the boys took over at the expense of the girls. The girls were always the recorders and never the leaders, even if she designated them to be leaders. Some of the students were socially so self-conscious that they simply opted out of participation when the groups were mixed. She had spoken to the kids about this and said that in the real world men and women had to work together, and so she wanted them to learn how to do that and to practice it. The class had finally gotten to the point of being able to work in mixed-gender groups if she was very careful about which girls worked with which boys.

The second criterion had to do with the various strengths of the kids. Some were better leaders, some were better writers, some were sick of always being the better writers, and some had language difficulties and needed to be placed in roles that let them participate successfully and contribute positively to the effort. Grouping the students was an ongoing effort that led to changes every other week. Meg accepted it as a personal challenge to try to keep a finger on the collective pulse of the students and choose groups that worked. Sometimes she managed the task, and other times she didn't.

She noticed, with a shred of hope, that more students asked questions. They asked "What if?" more often, and they tried things at home. She also noticed that they became impatient with peers who were disruptive, but the disruptions didn't decrease.

By Christmas Meg was thoroughly dismayed. Never in her career had she felt so discouraged. She decided to take the holiday break to sort things out. She considered breaking her contract. She found a place to house-sit that was quiet, where she could think. Despite all evidence to the contrary, she still believed that she could provide a learning environment that not only would allow but would encourage the kids to learn and think independently. But the kids went out of control whenever the activities allowed them to get out of their desks. They had been unable to have a class council, although she still wanted to try that. They were interested when she talked about or demonstrated scientific principles. She wanted to empower the kids and teach them to think for themselves; but every time she undid the ball and chain, things fell apart.

Over the Christmas break, Meg made several decisions. She would back up and teach the basic process skills necessary to scientific inquiry. She would clearly and overtly state what she wanted students to learn during the rest of the year, and she would relate that to the district curriculum. She would tell the students that she wanted to have labs but felt that she couldn't because they got out of hand and didn't learn anything. She would tell them that she wanted them to make decisions and think for themselves but that she could not allow anyone to hurt anyone else or interfere with any other student's learning. She would tell them that she had to keep the classroom a place where *all* students could learn in comfort. She would ask them how they felt about that. She would offer them a choice: the existing system of extreme structure and control or a system where they could have more freedom if they respected the rights of others to learn.

When she returned after the holiday, she discussed these matters with her students. Of course, they wanted the freedom; of course, they were willing to behave to get it. One girl asked, "Last year, Frank used to give us gum and pop so we would be quiet and get our work done. Why don't you try that?"

Meg was appalled. She knew there was a school rule against gum and pop in the building. How could he give it to them? Why would he set himself up like that? More important, why was he trying to buy learning?

Meg said that she wouldn't do what Frank had done. She told the class that she thought learning was important, that it was reward enough. The students argued with her, but only a little. Finally, it was agreed that all would try. Meg was unsure about all of this, but she would try, too.

Then came the fish lab. The kids were out of control; they had learned nothing. It seemed that all her ideas and plans were going down the tubes.

Teddy looked at her, "It was only a joke, Ms. Eliot."

"Now what?" she thought.

Losing It and Gaining It

Meg looked at Teddy. He looked contrite. For reasons unknown to her, she began to laugh. It was so absurd! Now she was sure she had lost it completely.

"Teddy, it may have been only a joke," Meg said, "but what about learning? I'm here so that you can learn. I already know this stuff. It's for you, not me. Yeah, I know, you've heard all that before, and it sounds like a bunch of garbage to you. But it's true. If I'm not here for that, what am I here for?"

"The money. You're here for the money," someone shouted. Well, she had heard that one before, too. She looked right at the kid and said, "There is no amount of money that could pay me for this job. Your parents make more than I do and don't have nearly the grief. You know that. Wages here are very high. I would do better painting the community center."

There was a silence. She surveyed the class—all with downcast eyes and showing what looked like remorse. She felt something very tender.

Sherry, one of the "good" kids, said, "We could try it again, Ms. Eliot. We'll get it this time. Promise."

"I don't know if I have enough fish. We'll see." She felt skeptical. Should she pounce on this moment of apparent contrition and risk another fiasco? "Well, what the heck," she thought; "You never know."

She had enough fish, and so the next day she tried the lab again. The cooperative learning book said to keep small groups together for a time before changing them. So she tried to create effective working groups. She put a natural leader in each group. She divided up the kids who had reading and writing problems into different groups. All groups were of mixed gender except one. In that group she put a boy who was overcome with bashfulness when he had to work with the girls. She asked one member of each group to keep track of how well everyone in the group listened; one member was in charge, one was the artist, and one was the researcher. She told them that they would remain in these groups for a while and that they would change jobs for each activity. She also reminded them that their purpose in the lab was to get to know what the inside of a fish looked like and what each part did, as well as to make some measurements of the fish.

Meg mentally crossed her fingers and handed out the fish. She wandered from group to group, talking to students. They were doing what she had asked them to do. They were even asking intelligent questions. Occasionally, students would look up something in the biology reference books or wash their hands so they could draw. There was a gentle murmur. At one point, one student picked up a skein of eggs and asked what it was and why all the fish didn't have it. A discussion ensued about male and female fish. One student shot a knowing glance at Marilyn and waved the eggs. Teddy told him to knock it off.

A question was asked: Are males bigger than females? Meg didn't know. The students had weighed the fish at the beginning. Meg made a data chart for the fish, recording each one's weight, sex, age, and length. When the students were done, one asked if they could take the dismembered fish home. Meg gave them plastic bags and—with a knowing glare—told them not to take them out of the bags until they were off school grounds at the end of the day. She had learned from a previous event not to throw an enticing gross object into the school trash. It had a way of returning from the dead to be thrown about in the hallway.

The discussion of the chart of data went extremely well. All the students were attentive, asked intelligent questions, and offered ideas that showed thought. The discussion of size and gender couldn't be resolved, given the small sample of nine fish. She asked the students how they could find out if females were smaller among herring of all ages. They understood sample size. They understood the need to control for both age and gender. They wondered if a different species would show gender differences. Then they discussed how they had listened to each other in their groups. They had worked well. They had enjoyed working well and learning something. They said it was interesting. All the students participated in the discussion. ("This is too good to be true," Meg thought. "I wonder if we can actually get on to experimental design and controlling variables!")

Meg finished the day in a daze. She had told the students how pleasant it had been to work so well that day. They had agreed. She didn't want to get saccharine for fear of breaking the spell. But she felt like weeping; it was wonderful. They were wonderful. In the days and weeks that followed, they did more group activities. Some Rubicon had been crossed, but Meg didn't know what it was. The kids were great—not perfect, but vastly improved.

Several physics labs and a few biology and chemistry labs went fairly well. Little by little Meg let up on the strict rules in the classroom. She let the students move their desks occasionally. She let them listen to their stereo headsets when they were done with their work, if they didn't disturb anyone. In turn, they were more inquisitive, more interested, and more self-policing.

Whenever they started a new project, Meg asked each group member to change roles: Leaders became artists or expediters, then reporters, and then observers. That way, everyone practiced each set of skills. At first, when she had shifted the jobs in the groups, there was some dissent. The students wanted the natural classroom leaders to be leaders. All these leaders were boys. Sometimes, when the girls were leaders, they abdicated the job to a boy in the group. Meg made sure she expected the girls to be leaders and to report when it was their turn. She encouraged them to stand up and make reports. She required more oral presentations. She waited for the girls to talk when it was their turn. She waited past the uncomfortable point. She also made a point to praise them. Little by little, the class changed. The girls began to insist on being leaders when it was their turn. Classroom talk was more often about classroom subjects. The topic of farting rarely came up anymore.

One day, in the middle of a social studies lesson about transportation, Teddy asked, "Which kind of parachute is better? A round one or those square ones?" Meg didn't have a clue. She asked, "What do you mean by better?" The class discussed whether better meant faster, slower, more maneuverable, prettier, or cooler. Consensus developed that "better" meant that the person using the parachute fell to the ground more slowly. Someone mentioned that the difference in a chute's size might make a difference, rather than its shape. Meg pulled out her well-worn question, "How could we find out?"

It was one of those magic days. The kids all were intensely involved in the discussion, which evolved into the planning of an experiment to determine which shape made a better parachute. Meg hardly spoke at all. The kids just went on with their ideas. She could almost stand back and watch. This is what she had wanted back in August and thought she would never see. These kids were defining a question, discussing the variables, setting up the experiment, discussing the design of the parachutes and the methods of recording data, and making sure the discussion was fair and that it involved everyone in a positive way. They were even using the right vocabulary in an unselfconscious way:

> "What is your hypothesis, Mike—that the chute's shape won't make a difference, but that its area will?
> "We'll have to take turns practicing the timing of dropping the parachute so that we all do it the same way."

"But Tim is taller than Marcia. We'll have to measure the height of the drop so that it will always be the same. Height can't become another variable; it won't be fair."

"We could go to the ledge of the gym and drop the chutes from there; then we won't have to worry about wind messing up the fall."

"*I* get to drop from the ledge. *You* can time."

Well, nothing is perfect. But they were working together as a group, fair and square, boys and girls, enemies and friends; and they were planning a well-designed experiment.

Planning an experiment wasn't part of the curriculum, but that didn't matter to Meg. What was important to her was that the kids were working together to plan a well-designed experiment to solve a problem. And they were behaving like the best of adults.

They built and tested their parachutes. They practiced their timing. They discussed the ramifications. Two days later, they were ready for the test. Meg found a time when the gym was empty. The droppers had to go up through the storage room to get to the ledge. All the other students were at the bottom, timing, observing, and recording. The students held several trials to perfect their technique, and then several drops were recorded. It was getting close to lunch time, and the tables had to be set up in the gym. They returned to the classroom and made up a chart of data. Mike had taken a tennis ball from the storage room on his way down from the ledge. Meg sent him to return it. The principal found him in the halls and sternly started to return him to class. Mike showed his pass, returned the ball, and returned to class. The kids decided they needed more trials because their results weren't clear enough. Then they went to lunch, and the rest of the day went according to schedule.

Meg was delighted. "It isn't such a big deal," she said to herself; "but, damn it, they did it. All by themselves, they did it, and they knew what they were doing! These kids—who couldn't weigh a pencil or measure a string at the beginning of the year—can design and implement a real experiment!" She felt giddy all day.

After the students had left for the day, the principal came in to speak to her. "What were you doing in the gym today?" She went on excitedly about the experiment and how well the kids behaved. She said that they were going to repeat it tomorrow. The principal said no. No repeats. Don't go into the gym and use it for those purposes. He had caught Mike with a tennis ball. Students shouldn't be in the storage room.

"But . . . it went so well." She was astonished. "How about if I go upstairs with them and. . . ." But his "no" was final. He turned on his heel and left the room.

Meg was deflated and angry. She wanted badly to encourage the students' efforts and praise their achievements, but now she couldn't. If she openly defied the principal, he would make her life miserable, and her students would suffer. If she told the kids that they couldn't continue the experiment and gave some lame excuse, they would feel cheated and angry, and she would be lying. It would compromise all the progress she had made. She decided to be truthful. There are many ways to be truthful. She needn't do it so as to anger the principal. Yet she felt she could not be the one who took away their project, because she had worked so hard to help them get there. She didn't want to betray them.

The next day she told the kids that they would not be able to continue the experiment. The principal had told her that students were not allowed in the storage room. He had been firm about it. She turned to the table of data and discussed what they had learned. She praised them for their experimental method. She asked them if they liked this type of project and would like to do this again. They discussed other projects they might do. They were not happy about it, but they accepted it. She knew they were angry at the principal, but so be it. When she was asked why the principal had decided this, Meg shrugged and said he hadn't told her more than what she had said. When they said it wasn't fair, she said that sometimes things aren't fair and that she understood their disappointment. She said that they could do other experiments that were just as much fun, and then she moved on.

Epilogue

For the rest of the year, Meg's class went well. The kids devised several more projects (which Meg related more closely to the curriculum). They came up with a recycling project for the whole community. They collected beverage cans, flattened them, and found an air carrier to ship them out for sale. They did acid-snow studies and discovered that some toxic substances had been spilled. Meg found her classroom an exciting place to be. Her kids were motivated and interested and were learning faster than ever. They liked school; in fact, attendance in her class was the best in the school. They published a literary journal. They finally got the class council off the ground and running.

Clint didn't have one temper tantrum that year and actually took a hand at class government. Gradually, over the year, he lessened his harrassment of Mike. Mike learned to take time-outs instead of exploding in anger. The students functioned more as a group, and Mike wasn't picked on as much. He became part of the group. Meg worked with Joe on his reading, and he gradually gained confidence and skill. At the end of the year he was beginning to read sixth-grade books: still a year behind, but that was better than four years behind. Mark continued to have difficulty concentrating. He was easily distracted by any noise, but he became more interested in learning the material. Meg tried giving him awards for good days. He said that he put them on his wall at home and was proud to get them. He acted out much less. He really tried to get along and learn, particularly in math. The class had become a team.

But the principal continued to disapprove of the activities. Students were out of the classroom. They were not always working at their desks. Relations between Meg and the principal became more and more tense. She left the following year.

QUESTIONS TO CONSIDER

1. Meg Eliot encountered problems common when teachers first try organizing students into cooperative groups. At the same time, Meg was trying to transform the curriculum from a textbook-centered one to an experiential, inquiry approach. Furthermore, she was a new teacher and hadn't yet established rapport with the students.

   Many new teachers, fired up with new approaches to science teaching, want to make radical changes in the science curriculum. What problems arise in changing from a structured curriculum to an inquiry approach? What gender issues might arise?

2. This case is essentially a success story. By the end of the year most of Meg's students were able to work effectively in mixed-gender groups and in an inquiry-based curriculum. They learned how to make measurements, develop hypotheses, and test their scientific hunches. How did this transformation occur? Meg used a number of highly effective techniques. What, exactly, are these strategies?

3. Note that Meg talks about "crossing a Rubicon," making some transition to when the students began supporting her approach. Can you identify anything Meg did that created this change? Consider her personal relationships with the students as well as her instructional techniques.

4. An important theme of this case is the conflict between Meg and the principal, who insists on running a tight ship and does not support the goal of gender equity. Some of Meg's problems with the principal may stem from gender-based differences in their management styles. Meg believes in group decision making and cooperative teamwork, while the principal seems to favor a top-down, hierarchical structure of authority.

   Teachers can forget that teaching is a political activity. Should Meg have been more direct with the principal about her teaching philosophy and expectations from the start? Could she have negotiated a better situation for herself and her students? How?

ACTIVITIES

1. Observe several different science laboratories taught by excellent teachers who favor an inquiry-based teaching environment. Note how the class is organized; how students are grouped; the ways in which the teacher expresses authority; how the teacher interacts with boys and girls; how boys and girls interact; the kinds of activities in which each gender is engaged; which students dominate; the kinds of behavior the teacher tolerates or does not tolerate; and how innovation is introduced.

2. Talk to science teachers—particularly to those who have taught in culturally different environments—and learn about their first two years of teaching. What unexpected difficulties did they face, and how did they resolve them? How did the teachers adapt their classrooms to the cultural setting and to the needs of young women in their classes?

READINGS

Cohen, E. G. (1986). *Designing groupwork*. New York: Teachers College Press.

Heath, S. B. (1983). *Ways with words: Language, life and work in communities and classrooms*. Cambridge, England: Cambridge University Press.

Kleinfeld, J. (1975). Effective teachers of Indian and Eskimo students. *School Review* 83 (2): 301–344.

Madhok, J. J. (1992). The effect of gender composition on group interaction. In *Locating power: Proceedings of the second Berkeley women and language conference* 2: 371–385. Hall, K., M. Bucholtz, and B. Moonwoman, eds. Berkeley, Calif.: Berkeley Women and Language Group.

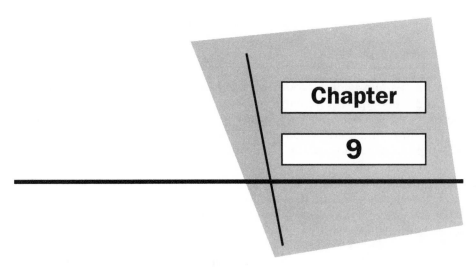

Chapter

9

Burn Schools to the Ground

Betty McKinny

Introduction

"Your mom tells me you are thinking about dropping out of high school."

Joan Adams looked at the fifteen-year-old high-school sophomore slumped into a chair in the gifted-and-talented room. She recalled the exuberant April of two years ago, when April was a superstar in her middle school's gifted-and-talented program. She could picture April hunched over the page layout for *Writers' Cramp,* the literary magazine she and her friends published.

"It's the people, they're just so immature. They don't like anyone who is different," April replied.

"Is it the teachers?" Joan probed.

"They're OK. They're not that bad," April shrugged.

"Is it the curriculum?"

"That's OK. But it's just so boring. Why do we have to learn all that stuff? It doesn't make any sense."

I'm not getting straight answers, Joan thought. April wasn't the first girl she had known who had done brilliantly in school only to fall apart when she hit adolescence. April was genuinely talented. She had won literary prizes for her creative writing. She was passionate about music, played the saxophone and the piano, and composed and arranged her own songs. Was she going to be another girl who dropped out of school, got pregnant, and threw away her chances? Joan had seen the pattern before.

Joan and April

Joan's gifted-and-talented room was filled with half-completed student projects and videotape equipment for the media projects she encouraged. An experienced teacher who had earned her educational specialist degree in gifted-and-talented education, Joan favored an individualized approach in which students wrote contracts to do creative, independent projects.

In both seventh and eighth grade April had been in Joan's room for two courses—Advanced Reading and Gifted and Talented (a course elective). Joan and April's mother also cosponsored the literary magazine. The student staff met after school and on some Saturdays. April had never missed a meeting. April's mother came as well, but April hadn't seemed to resent her mother's presence.

When April entered high school, Joan no longer saw her. But she had run into the wife of a fellow teacher in the grocery store who told her April was in trouble. Later, April's mother called and asked if she could bring April in to see her. Her daughter had run away with a friend, she said, but explained that she was just trying to help out the other girl, who had been sexually abused. April's mother had paid the $70 cab fare and had driven to a neighboring town to get the girls.

April was not going to her high-school classes. Her mother would drop her off at the front door, and she would leave through the back. April wouldn't even work in her favorite literature course. She had failed Introduction to Literature three times because she refused to read *The Iliad*. She wanted to drop out and take correspondence courses.

April's School Career

April's teachers had oddly different perceptions of her. Most of her elementary schoolteachers saw her as a child exceptionally talented in creative writing and music but not especially gifted intellectually. April was an overachiever, they said, whose mother pushed her very hard to succeed. April's sixth-grade teacher said that her mother questioned any poor grade her daughter received, and the teacher had to justify the grade by showing her mother each entry in her grade book.

April's middle-grade teachers took the opposite view. They saw her as an underachiever—a gifted student who did not use her capabilities. Given her high language abilities, April had been placed with the gifted-and-talented teacher for English to work on special projects.

April did very well in social studies, Joan found, if she could personalize the projects. For example, April wrote a first-person journal about what it was like to be a member of the first explorations in the Americas. She wrote a play about the Holocaust. But April did not do well on objective tests or even on essay tests. Even though she wrote well, she did not have good general background knowledge, and she lacked detailed information.

April's test scores had started out high but had declined upon adolescence, especially in mathematics. At age five she had scored in the superior range (IQ = 125) on the Slossen Intelligence Test, and she had received a similar score (IQ = 127) when tested again at age seven. But her achievement tests showed a pattern of decline beginning at adolescence.

Grade Level	Grade Equivalent Reading	Grade Equivalent Mathematics
Kindergarten	4.2	3.2
Fifth Grade	12.9	11.1
Eighth Grade	12.8	9.0

When April entered high school, a comprehensive secondary school of about two thousand students, she had to leave the personalized gifted-and-talented program offered at the middle-school level. Other than honors courses, the high school had no special programming for gifted students. Of the forty-six days of school during the fall of her sophomore year, April had only attended twenty-eight days. She told the counseling office that she was sick and that she didn't like what was happening in school.

Joan called the high-school counselor to talk about April and also tried to reach her high-school teachers. April had been absent so much that none of her teachers remembered her very well. Even her high-school counselor was vague about April. He did not know how old she was and seemed to think she was a junior or senior. The reason April was doing badly, the counselor said, was that she had poor attendance and wouldn't do what was required of her. With the exception of a D− in Elementary Algebra, she was failing all her high-school classes.

"April is living in the sixties," the high-school counselor remarked. "She is just rebelling because it is the thing to do. When you get to high school, students really don't have a lot of choices. There are required courses they have to take, and many students don't understand that."

April in Her Family

April was nine weeks old when she was adopted by her present family. She was the second adopted child. Her brother Robert, three years older, was also in the gifted-and-talented program, but he started using drugs and then drifted out of school. April never got along well with Robert, and she had cut off communication with him.

April's mother adopted two other children, both from a mixed racial background and with disabilities. The first child arrived when April was three years old, and the second came when she was a fifth-grader. April resented the adoption of these children. She asked her mother why they had to take in misfits and why they had to adopt all these kids. According to her mother, April sees herself as a premium baby because she is Caucasian, and she doesn't like the fact that she has to wait for things and make the money stretch.

April's father, an electronics technician who works out of town every other week, doesn't have what he calls a "one-on-one relationship" with his daughter. April's problems with school, he said, come from her being unable to handle the pressure to conform. At times, he felt, the pressure to conform was so hard on her that she would explode.

April's mother calls herself a professional volunteer—active in all her children's school activities, Boy Scouts, Girl Scouts, and community organizations. She adopted all the kids, she said, because all she wanted to do was to be a nurturer and raise a family. In her view, she and April had a good relationship until the eighth grade. But April is now pushing the limits. Her mother had to go down to the police station when April and two soldiers were picked up in a parking lot at 1 A.M. The soldiers had helped April crawl out of her bedroom window. She insisted she had done nothing wrong. "All we were doing was talking."

April's closest friend, said her mother, was a disturbed child. But the friend shared April's passion for music and poetry. In elementary and middle school, April had friends from stable families, children involved in scouting activities. Now she was forming what her mother termed "addictive relationships" with one friend at a time. She and her friend had been picked up for shoplifting, and April was seeing a probation officer. Her mother feared that April would just disappear one day. When she finally does get to leave, April said, she would never come back.

Joan and April in the Gifted-and-Talented Room

As she looked at April's stubborn face, Joan searched for what to say. It would be such a waste—a disaster—if April dropped out of high school. Well, at least the problem wasn't drugs. Her mother said that she had taken April to a drug-and-alcohol assessment center, which reported that the girl was not using drugs.

Could April have been sexually abused? Dramatic behavior change was one of the signs. The music teacher at her high school had been convicted of sexually abusing students. But April's name had not come up, and April refused to talk about the subject.

Joan remembered a disturbing story that April had written for her two years earlier, when she was an eighth-grader. Although it was a work of fiction, it described the suicide of a young girl who seemed a duplicate of April:

April's Story

But Jessie, I'm so confused. I don't know what to do. Everything keeps getting worse and worse. I've finally realized that I *do* love my brother, but it's too late. He hates me. And my mom, my mom is constantly hovering over me, checking up on me. I'm trying real hard to get my grades up, but it's so hard with all this pressure. She just isn't being fair. And then there's my music. It isn't going anywhere. I've got a strong feeling that music isn't going to play any part in my future. It's just not fair! And to top it all off, the guy I really care for, the guy I know I could never live without, the guy I would die to be a part of, only likes me as a friend! I just can't take the pressure anymore, Jessie! I feel like screaming my head off, or better yet, blowing my head off. Yes! That's it! I'll *kill* myself! Oh, Jessie, it's so easy! Don't you see how *easy* it is? I'll never have to worry about any of my problems ever again! And it won't hurt many people at all. You know, I can't think of more than a handful of people that would shed a tear at my funeral. . . . And look at how much hurt their unfairness has bestowed on me! Jessie, please don't be mad at me. This is the only way out. I'm tired of caring, worrying, or trying to solve my problems. Can't you understand, this is the only way? You know I'll always love you, so do me one favor. Don't cry for me. I'll finally have conquered my problems forever, if forever is for real. I know this is for the better. Goodbye.

> Love,
>
> Alex

That letter to Jessie was the first many people had heard of Alex's problems, and, unfortunately, the last they heard from *her*. Alex did kill herself, like many teens do, and she was right; it did solve her problems. She didn't have to put up with anything anymore. No more naggy, concerned parents, no more sibling rivalry, no more problems in school, no more worrying about her music, no more talking to her friends, no more wild Friday nights with the guys, no more tomorrows to wonder about, no more changes to hope for, and no more love to long after. Alex had, without realizing it, thrown away a lifetime full of tomorrows, hopes, and satisfactions. For what? What did she get in return? Nothing.

That is not fair.

April's favorite remark, said her mother, was, "Who cares? We're all going to die anyway." But her mother also told the story of April at age ten, when she had been pushed off the monkey bars and had broken her hand. She had convinced the doctor not to put a full cast on her hand so that she could play her saxophone for the Christmas pageant. She had learned to write with her left hand so that she could do all her homework, even though most of it had been excused.

"If it were up to me," April said to Joan, "there wouldn't be school. I'd do everything on my own. We should burn schools, burn them to the ground!"

Finding the Right Road

"April," Joan said, looking at the girl slumped before her, eyes fastened on the table. "Have you checked out your options?"

Joan asked April if she had talked to her high-school teachers about modifying the curriculum. She asked if April had looked into the alternative high school. Had she thought about transferring to another high school?

What about university classes? April said no, she hadn't done anything; she hadn't checked out anything.

Drawing on the contracts April had done for her years before in the gifted-and-talented classroom, Joan asked her to do a standard contract now. The contract lists goals, steps, resources, roadblocks, and rewards. April returned with the following contract filled out:

I. Goals

To be able to attend a school in which I can
  A. Work somewhat at my own pace
  B. Use my creativity for credit
  C. Use my music for credit
  D. Get along with the teachers and students
  E. Take the courses I'll really need in my career
  F. Improve my attitude (toward every aspect of school)
  G. Graduate
  H. Get a scholarship (maybe)

II. Steps

I'm planning to
  A. Withdraw from high school
  B. Enroll somewhere else
  C. Become more self-motivated and self-confident
  D. Live up to everyone's, including my own, expectations of me

III. Resources

To reach my goal, I'll need
  A. My teachers' support
  B. A good attitude
  C. My family's support
  D. Some quiet time at home
  E. My friends' support
  F. A flat-out miracle

IV. Roadblocks

Things that might get in my way are
  A. My laziness
  B. My self-doubt and self-criticism
  C. Not getting enough praise and support for my work
  D. Not getting along with the teachers and students wherever I end up

V. Rewards

If I reach my goal, I expect
  A. A better attitude toward school and learning
  B. A diploma
  C. A scholarship (possibly)
  D. To be prepared for a musical career
  E. A few new friends
  F. At least one letter from a teacher recommending me for college

April promised that she would check out the options before she made her decision, and Joan swung into action. She called over to the high school, but none of April's teachers remembered much about her or wanted to meet with Joan. The guidance counselor was no help either. She then spent three days on the telephone trying to find out what April's options really were.

She took a day of personal leave, picked April up, and went with her to check out the possibilities. April wouldn't consider staying at her present high school, no matter what. She didn't even want to walk inside the building.

They went to a different high school. The counselor was negative about the idea of arranging a flexible curriculum for April.

They drove to the university. The head of the music department said April could take music courses while still in high school.

They swung back to the school district's central office and reviewed the correspondence courses. The material was not challenging.

After taking April out for lunch, Joan ended with a visit to the Alternative High School, which she had spotted all along as the best choice. The students worked on individual projects and had a lot of freedom to combine school with work and other activities. April commented that the students looked tough, like they were involved with drugs, or might be. But she seemed to like the approach at Alternative High.

Joan dropped April off at home and told her mother what she needed to do to get April into Alternative High School. Two months later she ran into April's mother at the grocery store. "What happened with April?" she asked.

QUESTIONS TO CONSIDER

1. Teachers rarely have sufficient information to understand students' behavior. April could be seen as having some but not all of the characteristics common among girls known to have been sexually abused: dramatic behavioral changes, self-mutilation, drug and alcohol abuse, a sudden lack of interest in school, declining grades, and thoughts of suicide. Should Joan Adams have developed suspicions that April had been abused? If so, what should she have done about them?

   April's difficulties could be interpreted as an extreme example of the drop in confidence and achievement common among girls as they reach adolescence. April could be viewed as the female counterpart of Holden Caulfield in *The Catcher in the Rye*—an adolescent searching in a tinsel world for what is true and authentic. What do you see as the basic sources of April's problems? What responsibility does Joan Adams have in this matter? What responsibility does the school district have?

2. April has been absent from class so often that her teachers do not remember her clearly. Even her assigned counselor does not recall who she is, but he offers a reason for her poor performance: poor attendance and not doing what is required. "She is just rebelling," the counselor states. "Students really don't have a lot of choices."

   Has the counseling system failed April? Keep in mind that a secondary counselor may have five hundred or more students to keep track of during the school year. Given budget constraints, how else might counseling be organized?

3. Joan Adams tried to find the right type of high-school program for April but could not locate an option that April would accept. What type of high school might be right for a young woman like April?

Epilogue

April refused to enroll at Alternative High School, saying that "most of the kids were druggies and really weird." She was speeding through correspondence courses. Her mother had tried to enroll her in music courses at the university, but April was skipping out of them.

At sixteen, April met a soldier and had a baby. Her parents encouraged her not to get married, and so she is now living at home with the baby. April recently enrolled in a vocational program in which young mothers can bring their babies and leave them in a day-care program at the school.

"I was so frustrated," Joan concluded. "I was frustrated because I couldn't fix things. In retrospect, I should have followed up with Alternative High School."

Joan now is looking into correspondence schools for the performing arts for April to consider.

ACTIVITIES

1. Interview a high-school counselor about the particular problems girls face upon entering secondary school. How many girls are at risk for dropping out? Can you develop a profile for the girls most likely to be at risk?

   What school or community resources and alternatives are available for young women who are beginning to opt out of the educational system, or for those who are involved in substance abuse, or those who become pregnant? What options are available outside your community?

2. Form small groups, and have each group design an effective program for April. How would your programs fit, or not fit, your school district's approach to educational alternatives?

3. Imagine a team meeting in which April, her mother, the school counselor, Joan Adams, the alternative school principal, one of April's high-school teachers, and a school psychologist try to work out a plan for April's education. Role-play what might happen in such a meeting. What issues emerge?

READINGS

Bell, L. A. (1989). Something's wrong here and it's not me: Challenging the dilemmas that block girls' success. *Journal for the Education of the Gifted* 12 (2): 118–130.

Gilligan, C., N. P. Lyons, and T. J. Hammer (eds.). (1990). *Making connections: The relational worlds of adolescent girls at Emma Willard School*. Cambridge Mass.: Harvard University Press.

Seligman, R. (1990). A gifted ninth grader tells it like it is. *Gifted Child Today* 13 (4): 9–11.

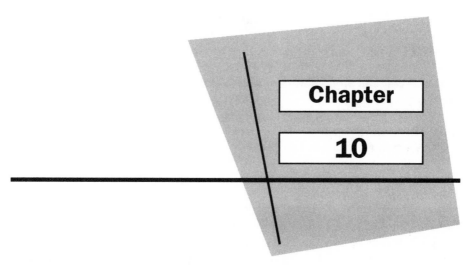

Chapter

10

Tough Anna

Brenda Weikel
Suzanne Yerian

"Anna Fernandez? Come get your paper."

Judy Baur, an eleventh-grade U.S. History teacher at Garfield High, a predominantly Mexican-American school in a large urban area, watched as Anna, an excellent student who had a "rep" as one of the school's toughest female gang members, sauntered up the aisle toward her desk and toward the A paper Judy held in her hands. Judy planned to whisper her congratulations—part of her usual class routine of saying a few words to her students as they came up for their work. But Anna had other ideas.

"Damn, another F!" she said, loudly enough for everyone in the class to hear. She snatched the paper away from Judy and dramatically ripped it apart on her way back to her seat. Judy wasn't surprised. Anna did not want other students to know that she received good grades. She usually made a big show of "flunking," when, in fact, she usually got the highest grades in the class. Anna had other ways of hiding her achievement, Judy had noticed. She occasionally sent her papers to the front of the class via another row. Judy suspected that Anna liked Carlos, a gang member and a D and F student, who sat a couple of seats in front of her.

Although Anna hid her achievement from the other students, she appeared to pay attention to the lessons. She never spoke in class or caused a disruption. Except for her ganglike look, she didn't attract much of Judy's attention. Anna was taller and heavier than most young Mexican-American women. She wore her hair long in the back and teased high and wide in the front. She dressed in the current gang style of men's jeans or cords, and everything she wore—pants, shirts, and shoes—was black. Her makeup was extreme, even by students' standards. She circled her eyes in black eyeliner. Her cheeks were heavily rouged. Her lipstick and nails were a dark, blood red. She covered herself with jewelry—lots of metal necklaces, big hoop earrings, and rings.

"Anna came across as a student you wouldn't want to mess with," said Judy. "Even though she seemed relatively quiet, other students got out of her way when they saw her in the hall. She looked mean."

The Future Teachers Club

Judy decided to start a club for students who wanted to become teachers, thinking that she might have something to contribute, after her own teaching career of seven years, to students who wanted professional advice. She contacted the local university and arranged to offer her students one college credit that would fulfill an Introduction to Education requirement. Students would come to discussion meetings held each week in Judy's classroom after school, and they would tutor students who were in the English as a Second Language (ESL) program.

Judy recalled the first meeting. "Anna came into my room about ten minutes before the meeting was to start. She had always looked so outrageous that I had never associated her with a career or with teaching, or with anything other than being a tough gang member. So I asked her what she wanted. She said, 'Well, isn't this where the meeting is?' I was embarrassed. It was obvious to both of us that I hadn't anticipated her being there. I couldn't believe that I—who take credit for open-mindedness—had put her in a mental 'not college material' category, in spite of knowing how capable she was in her class work. I was stunned that she was there, and stunned that I hadn't considered that she would be!

"About eighteen girls showed up. Anna sat in the front row. She pulled out thick glasses that I had never seen before and put them on. She attended all the meetings over the course of the semester. I paired her for tutoring with an ESL student who was a younger version of herself—tough looking. After a few weeks of tutoring, Anna made a remark about the girl's 'bad attitude toward school.' I filed the comment in my head, still trying to revise my mental picture of this student I knew as Anna. In time, she even started participating in my history class and wearing her glasses. Her reputation was such that no one dared to make fun of her."

The Field Trip

The last activity of the club for the semester was an all-day field trip to the university. Judy arranged for the students to meet with the dean of the school of education and with some financial-aid advisors, and they were to have lunch with some student teachers. The trip took place on Cinco de

Mayo, a Hispanic holiday, so that the students could see some of the out-
door festivities and look over the information in the booths sponsored by
the campus Hispanic clubs. At the end of the day, Judy thought the field
trip had been a big success. The students particularly mentioned how much
they enjoyed seeing their own culture represented on campus.

But something was wrong with Anna. She had almost missed the
group's bus that morning. She seemed distracted and seldom talked during
the entire day. When the group returned to the school that afternoon, Anna
hid behind Judy as they got off the bus and walked into the building. Anna's
gang friends were hanging out by the school's front entrance, and it was
obvious that she was desperate not to be seen by them. But why? Judy and
Anna hurried upstairs to Judy's room.

"OK, Anna," Judy said when they were alone, "What's the problem?"

Anna told Judy that she had been invited that day to a "ditching
party"—meaning that a group of students would "ditch" school and go
somewhere to drink. The goal was to get into enough trouble so that someone called the police. The police would then bring the students back to
school. Anna had gone on the field trip instead of ditching with the gang,
and she was afraid that some of her friends had seen her getting off the bus.
Now, she would have to come up with a good excuse for not having gone
ditching. Maybe she would have to fight somebody to defend herself.

A Second Trip

"I drove Anna home after our talk that day. I discovered that Anna lived in
the worst part of the city and walked through these neighborhoods every
day in order to get to and from school. It was clear that she dressed the way
she did and ran with a gang for protection, to avoid getting hurt. She told
me she was trying to get money for a car so that she wouldn't have to walk to
school, and that her sister had planned to sell Anna her car just as soon as
she could afford another one. There seemed to be so many obstacles against
Anna getting away from her neighborhood and gang friends that I decided
then and there to take her back to campus to reinforce the idea that she
belonged there."

Judy got permission from the principal to have a day off if she could
get other teachers to cover her classes. With a great deal of effort, Judy
arranged for six teachers to teach her classes the day she was gone. She
contacted a Mexican-American woman in the university's education department and arranged to have lunch. She also made plans for Anna to talk to a
Mexican-American advisor and to sit in on a U.S. History class taught by
one of Judy's former professors. Anna had trouble believing that a teacher
would go to such trouble for her.

On the day of the trip, Judy picked Anna up at her home. Although
she wore her usual makeup and jewelry, she had on a pink sweater and her
nicest black cords. Anna put on her glasses as soon as they drove onto the

campus. As they were walking to the education department, she tapped Judy on the arm and pointed to another Hispanic girl. "Hey, there's a girl who looks like me."

Connections

The advising meeting with the Mexican-American professor didn't work. Anna refused to meet the woman's eyes. The advisor would ask Anna questions, such as what she was interested in studying or what she wanted to do, and Anna would mumble, "I don't know."

"I thought I had made a big mistake," Judy said. "I wondered if this whole day was going to be a waste of time." Lunch, however, turned out to be a success. "Gloria, the Mexican-American education professor, spoke to Anna in an English-Spanish mix that I couldn't follow easily because of the slang. She talked to Anna about high school, and about the university dorms, and the cafeteria food, and what their respective mothers wanted them to be. Because I was cut out of the conversation much of the time, they seemed to become closer—as if they had some secret they were sharing that didn't include me." Judy paused. "In retrospect, it was good that they cut me out and shared what they had in common. It gave Anna a personal contact on campus without me as the intermediary.

"At the end of the lunch, Gloria pulled Anna aside and said something to her privately. I later asked her what Gloria had said, but Anna just smiled and wouldn't tell me. I think it was something encouraging—something Anna could hold onto as an image of what was possible.

"When we got to the classroom, my former history professor was teaching a topic I had just covered with Anna's class," Judy said. "So Anna came away from that observation feeling that college classes weren't that much different from what she already knew. I could tell she was feeling much more confident about her ability to handle college life."

The last stop on Judy's agenda was the bookstore. Anna bought herself a key chain with the university's logo and name. When they returned to the car, Judy presented Anna with a university sweatshirt that she had purchased earlier. Anna began to cry. "I'm not going to let you down, Ms. Baur. I'm going to college. I'm going to do this."

Epilogue

In her senior year, Anna got a paying job in the school's front office. All the office staff were Mexican-American women, who took Anna under their wing and advised her over time about softening her clothes, hair, and makeup. Anna saved her money, and eventually she bought her sister's car.

At this time, Anna is completing her second year of junior college. She has been accepted at the university next year. She continues to live at home.

"I have a photograph taken the day of the group field trip," Judy recalls. "Anna is hiding behind us. You couldn't even see her." She paused, "Anna has come a very long way."

QUESTIONS TO CONSIDER

1. Judy is surprised to see Anna at the meeting of the Future Teachers Club and is surprised at her own surprise. How might teachers like Judy determine whether they hold lower expectations for certain students in their classrooms?

2. During adolescence, students make decisions about their identities, and these choices are often quite conscious. Are they going to be "wavers," "dopers," "brains," "jocks," "sluts"? What identities does Anna choose at various points in this case? What influences the choices she makes? What creates change?

3. What specific role did Judy, a white teacher, play in helping Anna choose her identity? What roles did the Mexican-American models play? How does this case affect your views about the importance of minority and nonminority role models?

ACTIVITIES

1. Sometimes it is hard to visualize how intimidating "tough" high-school girls can appear. Share in class your experiences with "tough" girls and the way teachers and other students respond to them.

2. Develop questions that can be asked of girls who are members of gangs. Interview some of these girls about their daily lives, gang organization, academic work, and thoughts about the future.

3. Identify conscious identity choices that you and others you know made at adolescence. What influences shaped these choices?

4. Identify programs in your community designed to help students, especially students of color, make the transition to college. How are students recruited into these programs? How successful are these efforts for young men and young women?

READINGS

Anzaluda, G. (1990). *Making face, making soul: Haciendo caras—Creative and critical perspectives by women of color.* San Francisco: Aunt Lute Foundation.

Jankowski, M. S. (1991). *Islands in the street: Gangs and American urban society.* Berkeley: University of California Press.

McKenna, T., and F. J. Ortiz (eds.). (1988). *The broken web: The educational experiences of Hispanic American women.* Berkeley, Calif.: Tomas Rivera Center and Floricanto Press.

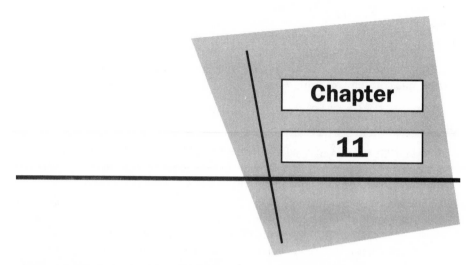

Chapter

11

Diane News: The Choice

From R. Silverman, W. M. Welty, and S. Lyon
Case Studies for Teacher Problem Solving

Diane News sat at her desk watching the first gold and orange leaves falling onto the Talner Elementary School playground. "It's time to take down the 'Welcome Back to School' display," she thought. As she pulled a pad of paper toward her to begin sketching ideas for a new social studies bulletin board, she glanced around her room with pride. Diane had been teaching part-time for two years; this fifth-grade class was her first full-time position. Her room reflected her love of the arts and her understanding of enrichment materials. A science table invited exploration. Books and magazines in a well-stocked library in the back could be checked out by her students. A bulletin board labeled "Where in the World?" contained a map and photographs. Originally, Diane brought in the photos for the display, but now her students were bringing in pictures, putting them up, and connecting them with yarn to places on the map. The room was bright and colorful. It looked like the kind of place where students could be active and involved learners.

Diane, 27 years old, was married and had recently completed a master's program in arts and education. Prior to her current position, she taught at an alternative school in the district, where she helped to develop after-school enrichment programs for gifted and talented students. She had become interested in gifted education when she took a course on creativity, and she had taken several more courses in the area as part of her master's program.

*This case has been reprinted from R. S. Silverman, W. M. Welty, and S. Lyon. *Case Studies for Teacher Problem Solving.* New York: McGraw-Hill, 1992. Reproduced with permission of McGraw-Hill, Inc.

As Diane sketched ideas, she began to think about a more immediate problem. She was faced with an issue that she did not know how to resolve. On the surface, the situation appeared straightforward: She had to recommend no more than four students from her classroom for a new gifted and talented program (called "G&T" by everyone) for students in the second through sixth grades. Students were being chosen from each grade level since the program was in a start-up year. The students would be taken from classes to another school twice a week for half a day. Each grade-level teacher was asked to recommend no more than four students because class size would be limited. The G&T coordinator was urging each teacher to pick the maximum number of students, but no one was allowed to exceed four. Of her twenty-seven students, three were obvious choices, but her selection of the fourth was complicated by other factors. However, this decision was only part of Diane's dilemma.

Diane had to choose the four students using criteria that she considered unacceptable. The district required a score at the 90th percentile or above on the Iowa Test of Basic Skills (ITBS) as the primary consideration for admission to the program. Class grades and group-administered IQ scores also had to be high. There was room for a brief personal evaluation of each student recommended by the teacher, but the form stated that this opinion was of less consequence than IQ and achievement-test scores and class grades.

Diane's standards for choosing students had little in common with those of the district. She felt that individual creativity in a variety of areas had to be evaluated when assessing children for placement in a gifted and talented program. For example, creativity in problem solving, choices of imagery in writing, and analytic thinking skills in a variety of subjects all needed to be considered. Diane also thought that some students who did not fit a standard profile and who met only some of the criteria often flourished in the challenge of such a program. She was troubled that she had to ignore these factors as she made decisions about her students.

In addition to having doubts about whether she would be able to make her recommendations according to the district's standards, Diane had other concerns about her decision. While in graduate school, she had taken a number of courses in women's studies. She had read enough in the field to know that girls scored lower than boys on standardized tests and that they were underrepresented in programs for the gifted and in other advanced courses, especially in math and science. Diane was aware that young girls were not sufficiently encouraged to participate in these programs. Yet she was considering recommending four boys.

The dissonance that this created in her was not helped by another recent event. The father of one of the students in her class had called to pressure Diane into including his daughter in the gifted program. Even now, Diane was furious as she recalled the conversation.

George James, a high school teacher and football coach in the district, had called the previous evening. James, who was black, had a reputation for being critical of other staff. Diane knew from other teachers that he was quick to call whenever he thought that they were not providing sufficient challenges for his daughter. When James called Diane, the conversation began calmly enough but escalated quickly to an unpleasant pitch.

"Hello, Mrs. News, this is George James, Margie's father. I've heard about the start-up of the G&T program, and I wanted to make sure that Margie will be included in it."

"Mr. James, I'm glad that you're so interested in Margie's progress, and. . ."

"Progress? I'm not calling about her progress. My daughter is smart enough to be in the program, and I intend to see that she gets there."

"Go on."

James was only too happy to continue. "I know she's gifted, and she deserves a lot more than she's been getting in your class. If she's having any school problems, *you* have got to be the cause. How can you let her get away with such sloppy writing and careless spelling on her papers? Don't you ever take time to look at the assignments these kids turn in? I have to go over every single thing she's written in class—everything she's done in there! What kind of teacher lets kids do such work? It's not my job to be on her case every night, correcting her, seeing that she does her work neatly and properly. You should be setting those standards, and I'm warning you now, I'm giving you notice that I'm going to be watching your teaching very carefully. You have an obligation to teach my daughter well and to recommend her for G&T. If Margie isn't in it, you better have some good reasons why a bright black girl was excluded."

Diane hardly knew how to respond to George James's tirade. She muttered something about the doorbell ringing and hung up. Diane was both upset and angry as she replaced the receiver. She felt that James had practically threatened her. And she was angry that he hadn't given her a chance to tell him about the creative writing assignments she gave. They allowed for inventing spelling and sloppiness in early drafts so that students could concentrate first on the creative process of writing stories and poems.

But Diane recognized that she could not discuss certain aspects of Margie's classroom performance with her father. How could she tell him that although Margie's test scores were at the 91st percentile, the girl was what the literature called a "concrete thinker"? When class discussions veered away from straight recall of text material, Margie would not participate; slouching low in her seat, she would rest her head on her desk as if exhausted. Diane tried to encourage Margie to think more analytically, but her responses always remained at the level of concrete thought. She never brought new insights to the group. She did not seem to be a prime candidate for the G&T program.

The obvious choices were Mark Sullivan, Seth Cohen, and Josh Arnold, all of whom scored in the 99th percentile on the ITBS; they were the only three in the class to do so. Their daily homework and quiz grades were equally high, their classwork was consistently excellent, and they were lively participants in class projects and discussions. But all three were white and male.

Diane thought about the other student she wanted to recommend. Stuart Johnson's offbeat humor and easygoing manner had won him many friends in the class. He was genuinely funny and could easily have become the class clown, but he never called out jokes or disrupted the class. Diane believed that he was truly gifted. She smiled as she remembered her original impressions of him.

Stuart was a 10-year-old slob. His lank, black hair was rarely combed. His clothes looked as if he dressed in the dark; everything was clean but rumpled and mismatched. Diane often had trouble reading Stuart's scrawled handwriting, but once she could decipher it, she found that his work was consistently accurate. His creative writing seemed beyond his years, and he always completed the bonus critical-thinking questions she included on worksheets.

When Diane began a new topic, Stuart was the student who made insightful connections to related material. Last week Diane introduced the topic of Eskimos in Canada. Stuart was the one to notice the closeness of Alaska to Siberia and to speculate about the existence of an ice bridge between the two regions. Students enjoyed having Stuart in their group for class projects because he often provided a creative edge.

Stuart was new to the area, but he quickly became friends with Seth, Mark, and Josh. Diane would hear them cheerfully arguing with each other at lunch time, with Stuart often defending his more unusual views. His friends also loved challenging Stuart's math ability. Diane once overheard a problem the boys had given Stuart.

"C'mon, Stuart," said Josh. "You'll never get this one. What's 32 times 67—and no paper!"

Stuart paused for only a moment. "2144," he replied.

His friends quickly took out paper and pencils to check him.

"Tell us your trick," said Mark. "There's no way I can do that stuff in my head. Are you a pen pal of Blackstone or something?"

Stuart grinned and shook his head. "I don't know how I do it. I can just see the answers." The boys were then off arguing about some new topic, and Diane walked away, amazed.

While Stuart's skills were outstanding, his test scores didn't reflect his ability. Diane had checked Stuart's records from his former school. His grades were just above average, and he scored in the 88th percentile on the standardized achievement test. Even so, there was no question in Diane's mind that Stuart was gifted.

Diane decided to ask Bob Garrett, the principal, for advice. Garrett was in his first year as principal of Talner Elementary School. He had been a teacher in the district for several years and then an assistant principal. Diane was the first teacher he hired, and she knew that he liked her teaching style so far. He seemed to be the appropriate person to talk to about her concerns.

"Mr. Garrett, I'm in a bind. I received the district memo about the gifted and talented program, and the limits on four students per classroom sound absolute. But I have five possible candidates and several questions about two of them."

"Who are the five?" he asked.

"Well, Mark Sullivan, Seth Cohen, and Josh Arnold are clear choices because of their scores and class performance. The other two are Margie James and Stuart Johnson. Their test scores are fairly close, but there are some other issues that concern me."

Mr. Garrett said, "If those two seem about equal, I'd say that you really need to consider the issue of racial balance. All our programs, and especially this one, need to reflect the diversity of our student population."

"I realize that," said Diane. "But they are both black."

Mr. Garrett looked puzzled. "Stuart? Really?"

Diane nodded. "I know. I met Stuart's dad when he came to a parent conference. He's black."

Garrett shook his head. "Look, Diane, you've got a tough problem. You're a good teacher, and I certainly trust your judgment. I'll back you up on your decision, but at this point I can't tell you whom to pick. You know the kids, so it's your call."

Diane appreciated the vote of confidence, but her meeting with the principal hadn't been much help. While her background and experience should have made the decision process an easy one, she was faced with a set of unfair criteria, an angry parent, and two students who were competing for one slot. Diane again turned her thoughts to Margie. Using district criteria only, Margie should be her choice. But Margie did not show the brilliance and thinking skills that Stuart displayed, skills that flourish in a gifted and talented program. However, Margie was a girl. Perhaps in a more intimate setting, Margie's skills might develop. So much of Diane's energy had gone into the study of women's issues. How could she choose four boys from her class? And it would look as if she had chosen four white students, since no one seemed to know that Stuart Johnson was black. George James would be furious. Diane had picked up his implication that she was a racist, but she was so angry at his demands that it was just one more unreasonable piece of her conversation with him.

"Why can't the district's standards be more flexible?" Diane thought. "Why must I choose only four students?" Diane stared at the five names on her list, wondering what to tell Mr. Garrett tomorrow.

QUESTIONS TO CONSIDER

1. Describe each of the five students Diane News is considering for the gifted-and-talented program. How does the school district define giftedness? How does Diane News depart from this definition?

2. Both Stuart and Margie are African American, but one of them—the male—doesn't look black. Should Diane choose Margie, to give the appearance of fairer representation by gender and race? Or should she choose Stuart and face accusations (her own included) that she is discriminating by gender and race? Although

Diane does not appear to be required to choose students by race or gender, should she take the politically correct course of action?

3. Describe Margie's father and his expectations for high-quality education. What kind of academic support and standards is he likely to have given Margie? Could Margie's tendency toward "concrete thinking" have come from the educational environment of her home? How could Diane News determine if Margie might have intellectual talent that she is not displaying in the classroom?

4. Like many parents of gifted students, George James is a strong advocate for his daughter. Often parents such as George are equally adept at going over the teacher's head and pulling political strings if they believe that their children are treated unfairly. Faced with this kind of parental pressure, would you choose Margie? If Diane does not chose Margie, George James is likely to publicly attack her teaching. If you were Diane, what justification would you give for not choosing Margie? How would you defend your style of teaching?

ACTIVITIES

1. Interview the director of your school district's gifted-and-talented program. Ask about the entry requirements for the program; problems with standardized tests; the number of boys, girls, and minorities; parental pressure; and the ways in which different people define giftedness.

2. Do research into the creation and norms of standardized tests like the Iowa Test of Basic Skills. How do test makers handle issues of gender and cultural fairness? What judgmental and statistical procedures are used to deal with problems of bias? Look at a copy of the test for different grade levels. Do the questions seem culturally fair to you? Would such questions identify unusually talented students?

   Do research into the methods of identifying intellectually superior minority children. Ryan (1983) finds, for example, that the Leiter International Performance Scale and parents' opinions may be better measures than more commonly used methods. On the basis of your research, what methods of identifying intellectually talented children would you recommend?

3. In small groups, identify men and women of color whom you consider especially gifted and talented. In what ways are their abilities expressed? How might cultural differences mask their giftedness? How might you as a teacher spot them?

READINGS

Clarke, B. (1988). *Growing up gifted*. Columbus: Merrill.

Delpit, L. (1988). The silenced dialogue: Power and pedagogy in educating other people's children. *Harvard Educational Review* 58 (3): 280–297.

Gardner, H. (1993). *Frames of mind*. New York: Basic Books.

Guskin, S. L. (1992). Do teachers react to "multiple intelligences?" Effects of teachers' stereotypes on judgments and expectances for students with diverse patterns of giftedness/talent. *Gifted Child Quarterly* 36 (1): 32–37.

Ryan, J. S. (1983). Identifying intellectually superior black children. *Journal of Educational Research* 76 (3): 153–156.

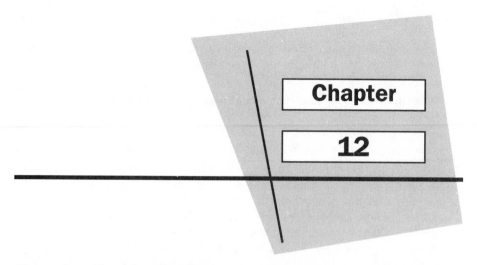

Chapter

12

Opening Pandora's Box:
The Mystery behind an "Ideal Student"

From Judith Shulman and Amalia Mesa-Bains, Editors
Diversity in the Classroom*

The summer I changed schools and was unpacking in my new classroom, I suddenly noticed a very thin Asian girl with shoulder-length hair peeking in. She looked as if she were about to run away, so I said hello and invited her to join me. "Are you the new third grade teacher?" she whispered. When I said yes, she shyly looked down and said, "I'm going to be in your class." She didn't make a move to go so I began asking her questions. Her name, she said, was Connie. Born in Hong Kong, she had come to the United States when she was three. She had one brother who was going into the first grade. Connie spent from 7:30 a.m. to 5:30 p.m. at the childcare center on the school site since both her parents worked. In addition, she attended Chinese school three days a week, which was taught on site. She spoke Chinese at home and had been to Hong Kong three times to visit relatives.

When school started, Connie proved to be an ideal student. She was cooperative, self-disciplined, motivated, artistic, and above grade level in every area. She loved to help and would often appear in my classroom after school. Given a choice, Connie preferred to work alone. However, she worked well in groups or in paired projects.

Her parents did not come to Back-to-School Night, and I told Connie I

*This case has been reprinted from *Diversity in the Classroom*, edited by Judith Shulman and Amalia Mesa-Bains, pages 93–96. Copyright © 1993, Lawrence Erlbaum Associates, Inc. Reprinted by permission of Lawrence Erlbaum Associates, Inc., and Far West Laboratory for Educational Research and Development.

was eager to meet them. I met her father very briefly one evening when Connie brought him down to the classroom to introduce me. He appeared to be in a hurry and left quickly. The same thing occurred with her mother about a week later.

I began to notice that Connie would often play with a classmate named Mai Ling. If not with Mai Ling, she would usually be alone. She always asked to stay in at recess to help, and I often allowed her this.

All went well until October. I change seats randomly on the first school day of every month, and by chance Connie and Mai Ling were seated together for October. Everything seemed fine. I noticed that Connie would often bring things to Mai Ling in the morning—letters, origami, and other handmade paper things. Connie would also bring these kinds of things to me. Then one day another student told me Connie was crying. Connie had her head down, and Mai Ling was as physically apart from her as possible at the table. This behavior continued off and on for about two weeks. Any attempts I made at talking to the girls either individually or together were fruitless. Both would withdraw or cry, but would not talk.

Seat changing time came again and the two girls were no longer together. They were no longer playing together as far as I knew. One morning I saw Connie give Mai Ling a letter. I asked Connie how things were going. She started to cry and I noticed she would bite her lower lip continuously as I talked to her. She told me Mai Ling would not be her friend and would not even talk to her.

The tears had escalated, so I decided to speak with the principal. When I explained my difficulty getting a response, she volunteered to speak with the girls. I carefully explained to Connie and Mai Ling that the principal was trying to help solve the problems they were having. She spoke to them at the end of the school day. When they left school, both looked very unhappy. The principal, I learned, had been unable to get much response from either girl. About an hour after school, Mai Ling's mother called me to find out what was happening. Mai Ling's sister had called her at work, saying that Mai Ling was in tears. She thought she was in serious trouble because she had been sent to the principal.

Mai Ling's mother explained that it was difficult to get Mai Ling to express her feelings. She would withdraw at home in the same way she would withdraw at school. I explained the situation with Connie, and Mai Ling's mother said she would make every attempt to talk with Mai Ling and let me know if she could supply any more information. The following day she called back. Between coaxing Mai Ling and talking with her sister, she had gathered that Connie wanted Mai Ling to be her best friend and not play with anyone else. Mai Ling liked to play with Connie, but she also wanted to play with other girls. When Mai Ling played with other friends, Connie would cry and go off by herself.

The following week was parent conferencing time. Mai Ling and Connie seemed friendly again. In my conference with Mai Ling's mother, I reported that all seemed to be going smoothly again. By chance, a new student arrived before school had begun, and Connie was helping me in the classroom. I felt this might be a good opportunity for Connie to make a new friendship. I introduced the two girls and asked Connie if she would sit next to Annie and show her the routines. She moved her things, and then the bell rang. I brought my class up to the room and when I looked over to Connie and Annie, Connie had her back to Annie and was as far away from her as she could possibly be without being at the next table. I went over to see what was happening and overheard Connie say to another student in a very angry voice with her arms folded tightly across her body, "Ms. Johnson made me move over here." Annie was looking quite bewildered so I took Connie aside and asked her quietly if she wanted to go back to her old seat. She nodded her head. She moved back, and I asked for volunteers to sit at Annie's table. Every other girl in the class and a few boys raised their hands. I spoke with Connie at recess and tried to explain to her how a new student would feel. She bit her lip continuously and did not respond. She spent the rest of the day extremely sullen and withdrawn.

On Friday, Connie's mother came in for her conference. She mentioned the situation with Mai Ling immediately. Lowering her voice, she explained that she was very worried about Connie's friendship. She said Connie was obsessed with Mai Ling and it wasn't natural. She had intercepted a letter Connie had written expressing how much she liked Mai Ling and how unhappy she was that Mai Ling would not be her friend. She told me that Connie talked about Mai Ling constantly, wrote about her and made her gifts, and she was worried that this was not normal behavior for a third grade girl.

In fact, she kept repeating, "This is not normal." It seemed to me that she feared sexual implications, but I didn't pursue it. I explained to her what I had observed. When I asked if this had been a problem before, her response took me completely aback: Connie, she said, had threatened to cut her wrists when she was five years old because a friend wouldn't play with her anymore. "I really gave her a hard lesson that time," the mother went on. "I spanked her, and explained to her what suicide really means." A red flag went up in my mind.

Remaining composed, I described Connie's behavior with Annie that morning. Her mother was upset. At that point Connie happened to come into the room—she had a recess break from Chinese school. I invited her to join us, and explained what we were discussing. I told Connie I wasn't angry with her; I merely wanted her to understand how she had hurt another child's feelings. I asked her to think of how she would have felt in that situation. Connie began to bite her lip and not respond. Her mother said, "You have to make new friends." All of a sudden, Connie started crying. "I don't want new friends. I just want to be Mai Ling's friend."

"You need more than one friend," said her mother.

Connie started to sob. "You gave away Sparky," she said. "He was my friend, and you didn't even tell me. You did it while I was in school."

While her mother interjected that the landlord wouldn't allow dogs,

Connie kept on repeating, "You didn't even tell me you were going to do it." Sobbing and gasping for breath, she railed, "You never let me put anything on my bedroom walls. You always let Martin do what he wants to do, but you don't even let me talk on the telephone. Now you also stole my letters to Mai Ling!"

I was witnessing anger and resentment that I'd never seen before in Connie. She was crying uncontrollably. Her mother, on the other hand, seemed somewhat removed. She retorted each accusation calmly, soon mixing Chinese and English. Connie bit her lip continuously throughout this interchange.

To try to restore some calm, I gave Connie a hug and told her I hated to see her feeling so unhappy. I said that we needed to continue exploring these problems, but I felt that Connie was too upset to do so right then. I turned to addressing more positive matters and went over Connie's progress report with both of them, highlighting her academic achievements and skills. Not that this was necessarily the best course of action, but I didn't really know what else to do. I thought the situation called for professional counseling, but this surely didn't feel like the appropriate time to suggest this. I ended the conference very frustrated. I felt I had opened Pandora's Box.

All weekend I was distracted by what had occurred. I drafted a short memo to my principal suggesting that Connie may need professional counseling and asked her for a meeting to explain. I kept thinking about Connie's threatened attempt to cut her wrists at such an early age and about her mother's emotional remoteness.

When I related the situation to the principal early Monday morning, she seemed to feel that I had overreacted. But my gut level reaction was still one of deep concern.

I went to my classroom and found Connie there early. "I'm really sorry Ms. Johnson," she said. "I didn't mean to make you feel bad." This surprised me. Again I explained how I was concerned about her feelings. She told me her mother and father had talked with her for a long time over the weekend. They both wanted her to apologize to me. "But you don't owe me an apology," I said. Still she persisted in saying she was sorry for hurting my feelings. Somehow we were missing the real problem. I told Connie I was glad she had come in to see me and encouraged her to let me know if things weren't going well. About an hour after school started, Connie's father showed up. He said hello and asked if Connie had talked to me. When I said she had, he went over to her and gave her a kiss and hug. It was the first physical contact I had seen Connie receive from either parent. She seemed content and happy.

Since that day, I became extremely aware of Connie's behavior. There were some incidents—an unacknowledged birthday present to Mai Ling, a note from a substitute that said, "It appears that there is a long-term problem between Mai Ling and Connie," and some tears. One day in March, Connie burst into tears and explained that if she didn't have her times tables memorized by the weekend, she would get spanked by her father. I talked to her mother after school that evening and explained how Connie had just begun learning multiplication and had no problem with the concept. I also encouraged her to give Connie more time to memorize the tables and not to pressure her with a deadline. I assured her Connie had an excellent memory and would have no problem with memorization. I gave her suggestions and some materials for drill and practice and strongly advised against spanking. After that weekend, Connie returned to school in a much happier frame of mind, and it appeared that the pressure was off.

One day in April, Connie asked if she could talk with me privately. She told me she couldn't stop thinking about her dog, Sparky. She still missed him and couldn't get to sleep at night because she was so sad. She had hopes of getting him back. (Connie had been told he was sent to a family in the country. Connie's mother had told me the dog had been put to sleep.) I explained to her that the dog would not return, but I also encouraged her to write down her feelings as a way to help her with the loss. The next morning there was a letter on my desk. It gave an extremely articulate description of her feelings. When I spoke with Connie, she said the writing had made her feel better. I told her that writing about painful things can be helpful and urged her to keep a journal or to continue writing letters. I received several notes before school closed, but they were all happy and positive in tone.

I had a parent conference with Connie's father in April. He was late, and I had a conference scheduled right after with another parent so we weren't able to speak for very long. I thanked him for not continuing to pressure Connie about her multiplication tables and explained she had learned them by memory very quickly. His English was not as fluent as her mother's, so communication was somewhat difficult. I saw Connie's mother several times before the end of the semester picking up her children from childcare. She always said hello, but never seemed to have time to talk. She never again approached me regarding Connie's behavior or progress.

The semester is over; Connie is moving on to fourth grade and I have seen improvement and progress, but the situation continues to haunt me. I am constantly rethinking my reactions to this child who in many ways would be considered an "ideal" student. Was the red flag alerting me to something? I think of the quote from Thoreau: "The mass of men lead lives of quiet desperation." Was this Connie? The question remains unanswered.

QUESTIONS TO CONSIDER

1. Lilly Siu, a teacher in the San Francisco Unified School District, wrote this comment about Connie's situation:

> When I first read this teacher's case I immediately thought of my own childhood. . . . Like Connie, I have a younger brother, who I often felt got "better" treatment than myself. Like her, I resented it silently, all the while keeping respect for my parents by not bringing it up. Unlike Connie, however, I had sisters to talk to, sisters who could understand my

resentment but also explain why, if not because it was fair, it was simply going to be like this. In many Asian families, particularly Chinese, it is not uncommon for parents to favor sons. It comes from the patriarchal nature of the Chinese society itself.[1]

Connie needs someone to talk to, Ms. Siu points out, and Chinese families are often too private to seek outside counseling on their own. Should the teacher have pursued outside counseling? Should she have attempted to counsel Connie herself?

2. What cultural differences do you see in the values and behavior Connie's parents and teachers consider appropriate for a young woman? Think about the spanking episodes, the insistence that Connie apologize to her teacher, and the concern about Connie's intensity regarding Mei Ling. Is it a mistake to think about Connie primarily in terms of cultural and gender issues? How else could you think about her situation?

3. Analyze how the teacher handled each of the dilemmas she encountered as she opened "Pandora's box"—bringing in the principal, asking Connie to help Annie, asking Connie to write in her journal. These are sophisticated efforts by a veteran teacher to deal with a difficult problem. Which of these efforts were helpful and why?

4. Alice A. Kawazoe, Staff Development and Curriculum Director of the Oakland Unified School District, views Connie's situation as serious:

> Connie's outburst in front of her teacher and her mother may have been disconcerting for the teacher, but was probably appalling for the mother. Connie spills out her anger and resentment about the giving away of her dog without being told, not being permitted to put pictures on the walls or talk on the telephone, the preferential treatment her brother receives, and the stealing of her letters. All this backlog of resentment boils up and out. Now she doesn't have a best friend; she is in trouble at school; her teacher is upset; her mother is frustrated; she does not feel loved. Connie has become an emotional volcano.[2]

What is the teacher's responsibility in this situation? The school district's? Could Connie's distress be a form of serious psychological disturbance, rather than ordinary cultural conflicts? Does the source of the emotional problems matter?

ACTIVITIES

1. If there is a Chinese community or resource center in your area, visit it and ask for information on the difficulties faced by first- and second-generation Chinese Americans who have come to this country. Ask specifically about gender and family relationships.

---

[1]Lilly Siu. (1993). Commentary on case 12. In *Diversity in the Classroom: A Casebook for Teachers and Teacher Educators*, ed. J. Shulman and A. Mesa-Bains. Research for Better Schools and Lawrence Erlbaum Associates.

[2]Alice Kawazoe. (1993). Commentary on case 12. In *Diversity in the Classroom.*

2. Interview a multicultural specialist on Chinese students in American schools or interview Chinese parents concerning Chinese values and traditions with regard to gender and family issues and how these harmonize with or clash with American values and traditions. Discuss how these tensions might be displayed in Chinese students and what teachers in regular or bilingual classrooms might do.

3. Read the popular literature about Chinese first- and second-generation experiences in the United States, such as Kingston (1975) and Tan (1991). Compare these accounts with your own and your family's experiences.

READINGS

Goleman, D. (1994). Childhood depression may herald adult ills. *New York Times* (January 11): B (7, 10).

Kingston, M. H. (1975). *The woman warrior: Memories of a girlhood among ghosts.* New York: Vintage International.

Tan, A. (1991). *The joyluck club.* New York: Vintage Press.

Tsai, S.-S. H. (1986). *The Chinese experience in America.* Bloomington: Indiana University Press.

Wong, J. S. (1945). *Fifth Chinese daughter.* New York: Harper & Row.

Zhang, H. (1992). "Spare a woman a beating for three days, they will stand on the roof and tear the house apart": Images of women in Chinese proverbs. In *Locating power: Proceedings of the second Berkeley women and language conference* 2: 601–609. Hall, K., M. Bucholtz, and B. Moonwoman, eds. Berkeley, Calif.: Berkeley Women and Language Group.

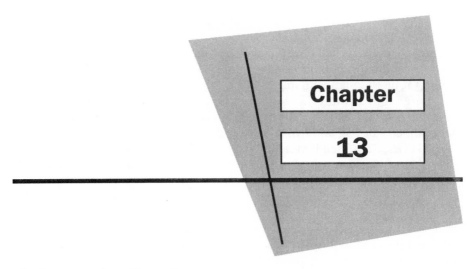

Chapter 13

Going to the Oracle:
Susan Consults the "Big Feminist"

Rachel Kleinfeld

Susan was pouring herself some orange juice when her father walked into the kitchen. "I've been thinking about your college decision," he said, as he got out the cereal. "With your talents and interest in international relations, you should really consider the foreign service. I took the exam myself, you know."

Susan smiled to herself. On the one hand, her father was finally validating her dream, suggesting that she'd be good at what she had always hoped to do. On the other hand, her dad was the one who always yelled at her mother for traveling. He couldn't even stand it when her mom came home from work a half-hour late. And here he was, suggesting that she spend her whole life moving from place to place!

Her mother apparently had the same thought. "Michael, you shouldn't encourage that type of career. It's unrealistic. You know very well you don't believe what you are saying yourself. Susan wants a career, but she'll never find a husband willing to travel around the world for her job."

She turned to Susan, "I wanted to be a teacher partially because teachers are needed everywhere; I could follow my husband wherever he needed to go. If you were in the foreign service, it would be very difficult to have a family and take care of your children. You're going to have to put two careers together when you get married, and a foreign service career will be hard to work out.

Susan looked up, surprised. Her mother was the epitome of the "superwoman" with a wonderful career, happy kids, and a good marriage. She had always struck Susan as believing in the equality of women. And here she was, telling her own daughter to give up her dreams for some man! "Why should women always have to have 'mobile' careers?" Susan thought. "Why couldn't it be the man who moved?"

Susan got up angrily, but she tried to contain it. Maybe men are different now, she hoped. After all, Mom did grow up before women's lib. She grabbed her bag and drove to school.

In class, Susan felt better. She'd attended the same school since kindergarten. Now she was a high-school junior, and everyone there knew her. Her teachers were always telling her things like "With your ability, you can do whatever you want" and "Susan's the one who sees something that needs to be done and does it well; she can always be counted on." Her classmates respected her—even the boys listened to her advice on everything from relationships to school work. At school Susan never had to fight to be equal. She knew that she was one of the brightest.

That afternoon Susan called Rob, her boyfriend. She angrily related the conversation that she had had with her parents that morning. Rob immediately told her that he agreed with her mother.

"What do you mean?" Susan yelled. "I thought we were past all that. Why is it that at school I can do whatever I want, but then, when I'm married, some man who probably isn't as intelligent as I am can make me give up my dream? Why shouldn't *he* have the mobile job?"

Rob was sympathetic. "You've got a point, but society's just not that way. Men still expect to be the primary breadwinners, and women are still not equal. No man is going to sacrifice his job for a woman. You're never going to be happy if you expect to always get your way, especially when your way goes directly against the real world."

The next day Susan could hardly wait for English class, where she would have time to write in her journal. Ms. Walker, her English teacher, made a big deal about the importance of keeping these journals. She responded to each student's writing once a week and had built up rapport with each student. As a result, her students took their journals very seriously, knowing that whatever they wrote would be kept confidential. Susan knew that her teacher was a big feminist—far more radical than Susan herself. She hoped that Ms. Walker would validate her views about women's careers. Here is her journal entry:

> I'm so furious I could scream! Everybody tells me I'm so talented—blah, blah, blah—and I keep getting these college catalogs with women doing all sorts of amazing things; and then my own mother tells me to pick a job on the basis of some man's being able to live with my choice! Then my own boyfriend tells me it's intimidating for a girl to hold a better job than her husband!
>
> Why don't teachers just tell us straight out, "You can be ten times smarter than any boy in the class, work harder, and go to a better college; but if you want a family, you might as well be content with C's and a high-school diploma. You're going to have to adapt your whole life around your husband's anyway, and the more intelligent you are, the harder that will be." Basically, women who have less initiative and fewer brains are going to be happier,

because they won't have to give up as much! So why do teachers praise me for leadership and intelligence? They're so hypocritical!

Susan threw her journal onto the pile on her teacher's desk. She slumped into her chair and wondered how Ms. Walker would respond.

QUESTIONS TO CONSIDER

1. Unlike most girls her age, Susan is very self-confident. She is known and respected for her intelligence, and she believes, as do her teachers, that she can become anything she wants to be. The advice Susan gets changes at the time she is beginning to make college and career decisions. Suddenly she is told she should not pursue certain careers if she wants to have a family. Is this advice right? Are teachers being hypocritical by encouraging bright young women to pursue whatever career they desire as though the costs and benefits are equal to those encountered by young men?

2. To some feminists, traditional gender roles are unlikely to change as long as there is an underlying assumption of male privilege. Despite their rhetoric supporting gender equity, men will not easily give up implicit privileges that keep them in positions of influence and power. What support for this perspective do you see in this case? Do you see other ways of interpreting the attitudes of Susan's mother, father, and boyfriend?

3. Susan comes from a Jewish family which offers daughters, as well as sons, substantial educational support but which also places great value on strong child-centered families. How might Susan's cultural background affect who she has become and the form of her present dilemma?

4. Susan is entering college next fall and is making serious educational and career choices. If you were Ms. Walker, what advice would you give Susan? What would you write back to Susan in her journal?

Epilogue

This is the actual letter (shortened) that Ms. Walker wrote in Susan's journal. What do you think of her response?

Dear Susan,

Ouch! I'd be angry too, if after all the encouragement you have gotten over the years, the bottom line ends up being that you need to adjust your career so you can "stand by your man." *Give me a break!* Of course, I've been lucky. My husband has always been willing to adjust to my career goals. For example, when I worked on my master's degree, he was willing to support us, when, in fact, teaching is not his passion. He enjoys working with learning disabled students, but Asian history and philosophy are what turn him on. Teaching *is my* passion, and we have often talked about how, when we can afford it, he will stay home and be a househusband and I will continue to teach.

[Ms. Walker describes an idyllic period in her marriage where her husband stayed home studying Asian history and doing the household chores while she focused on her teaching.]

The issue of children complicates things. We don't have children; we chose not to. And now I will say something which will probably tick you off—one of the reasons I chose not to have children is that I knew I couldn't teach and have kids at the same time. I am passionately devoted to my teaching; it comes first. I can't do everything, and I know *myself* well enough to know I couldn't have two careers—teacher and mother—and do as well at both as I could do at one. Clearly, though, Susan—some women can. Look at your mother.

You need to be fully aware of the rampant sexism in our culture. We give a lot of lip service to women having it all, but a lot of people still think a man who "follows" his wife around is "obviously" lazy and unmotivated, or, even worse, henpecked! A househusband is often seen as a loser—a leech who lives off his wife's earnings. Sometimes I think we've come really far in this country regarding equality; other times I think we've barely moved.

If you follow your dharma, Susan, you will make everything work out. In the end, you have to make these decisions yourself.

Love, Mrs. Walker

ACTIVITIES

1. Interview preadolescent girls and late-adolescent girls about their career goals and lifestyle plans. What would they like to do? What would their ideal life look like? Are their goals and dreams realistic? What obstacles do they face, and are they aware of these difficulties? Interview boys of the same ages. How do their responses differ from those of the girls?

2. In small groups, discuss the work and family responsibilities of members of your own families. Does anyone in the group have parents with atypical gender roles or responsibilities? Describe them.

3. Interview Jewish parents and parents of other cultural backgrounds about their expectations for their sons and their daughters. Look at the support the families give for education, for example—investing in computers, special academic camps, and lessons of various kinds. What expectations arise about who will pay for college? For graduate school? What differences do you see? To what extent are these differences cultural and economic?

4. Invite to class men and women who have both careers and families. What career choices and compromises for family reasons have the men and women made? How do they divide such household responsibilities as child care, cooking, cleaning, financial investments, driving, and yard maintenance? Which patterns of role division appear to be more successful?

READINGS

American Association of University Women (1991). *Shortchanging girls, shortchanging America*. Washington, D.C.: AAUW.

Gilligan, C., A. G. Rogers, and D. L. Tolman (eds.). (1991). *Women, girls, and psychotherapy: Reframing resistance.* New York: Harrington Park Press.

Goldschneider, F. K., and L. J. Waite. (1991). *New families, no families? The transformation of the American home.* Berkeley: University of California Press.

Greenberg, D. (1975). *How to be a Jewish mother.* Price, Stern, & Sloan.

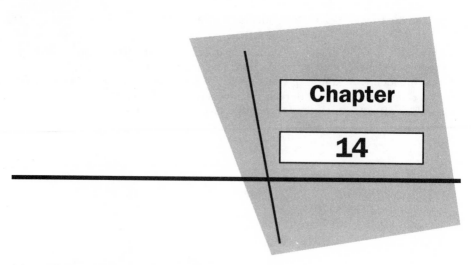

You'll Be Washing Dishes

Suzanne Yerian
Brenda Weikel

The Confrontation

Alma, the African-American English teacher from the room next door, walked into Kathleen's classroom. "Hi Kathleen. Hi Roberto. Just thought I'd see how your day went, Kathleen. What are you two doing?"

Kathleen Watson and Roberto Diaz looked up from their writing. School had just let out for students at Central High, a school located in the middle of one of the poorest and most crime-ridden sections of the city. Roberto, a bright twelfth-grade Mexican-American student from a first-generation immigrant family, had asked Kathleen to help him after school with an application he was eager to complete for Stanford University. Roberto was writing the personal essay that would accompany the application, while Kathleen typed his letter of recommendation.

"We're going over the application Roberto's submitting to Stanford," Kathleen relied.

Alma looked at Roberto, "You're applying to Stanford? Why are you applying there?"

Roberto looked pleased. "Well, I decided to become a lawyer after college. Ms. Watson thinks I have good-enough grades; so if I can get in, I think Stanford will be the best place for me to go so I can eventually get into a really good law school."

Alma frowned and sat down. "Well, if I were you, I wouldn't set foot in that place. You're going to be one of a few minority faces in a predominantly white, rich kids' school. During vacations you're going to be scrubbing greasy dishes in some restaurant kitchen because you can't eat at the dorm, and you won't have enough money to get home. Meanwhile, the rich kids—your "friends"—are going to be skiing in Europe. They're going to say things to you that are thoughtless and cruel just because they don't know any better. Your real friends are going to be the minority maids and janitors who clean the white kids' rooms and get treated like dirt for thanks. Sure, you'll get a good education, but in the end they'll never accept you as one of them. And after the whole experience, you'll have become too 'white' to fit back into your own community. Do you think it's worth it?" She paused and looked at Roberto, who had slumped into his chair. "What about your family? Aren't you going to miss them?"

Kathleen had a sinking feeling. She knew that Alma had strong feelings about being one of the few African-American female students at a predominantly white college twenty or so years ago. She also knew that Alma had become somewhat of a radical black feminist who encouraged African-American students, particularly females, to view the world through her particular lens. But how could Alma's experience as a black female have anything to do with Roberto?

"Wait a minute, Alma," Kathleen said. "You don't know what Roberto's experience will be. Even if he does have to work, Stanford is one of the best schools in the country. If he gets in, he'll have a chance at getting some scholarships and maybe a future ticket into the best law schools. This would be any senior's dream! He's too good not to apply to the best schools."

"Well, I've been there, Kathleen. You're white—you haven't. I know what it's like to be one of the few colored faces on campus. It's lonely, depressing, and degrading." Alma stood up, and walked to the door. "Listen to me, Roberto. You'll feel much more comfortable starting off in a community college where there will be more people of your own kind. Stay with your own people; keep your identity and your voice strong. How much help are you going to be to your community if you, one of the best and brightest, lose touch with your language and culture? You'll lose touch, and eventually you'll never come back." Alma got up and walked to the door. "I think you'll be happier living with your family and going to a local college, Roberto. At least think about it. Don't dive in over your head just because you have the grades." She turned and waved, "Let me know what you decide."

Kathleen was furious. Roberto was obviously distressed by the conversation. Here was a minority kid who had an excellent chance of succeeding, and Alma had to poison his mind with her separatist views. "Don't listen to her, Roberto," she said. "You may not find many Mexican Americans at Stanford, but you are the intellectual peer of anyone there. Get the right academic credentials and you can do anything you want after that—OK? Let's mail this application and see what happens."

"Yeah . . . I guess." Roberto looked confused. "My family wants me to stay close. I don't know what to do." He slumped further into his chair.

Kathleen didn't know what to say. How could Alma have done such a stupid thing?

Roberto

Kathleen Watson, a second-year English teacher at Central High, had met Roberto when he joined her after-school Quiz Bowl team during his junior year. The team met each week to practice answering academic questions in preparation for competitions with other schools throughout the region. Kathleen thought Roberto was one of the best team members. He was able to recall a lot of information, and he could do it quickly. Although Roberto was quiet—even shy—he had many accomplishments: president of his class; a member of the school's math, science, and engineering clubs; a member of the student council; active in the Key Club; and taking accelerated classes in all core subjects. As the year progressed, Roberto would frequently stop by Kathleen's class after school to ask questions about his work, to help Kathleen with a school project, or to chat. Kathleen felt she knew him well.

During the fall semester of his senior year, Roberto asked Kathleen to help him with his college applications. He had been debating whether he wanted to go into medicine or law, as he had excellent grades and high interest in both areas. Kathleen encouraged Roberto to apply to the best universities in the country, even though initially he had never considered applying to anything more than the local community and state colleges. She remembered how excited he was when he finally told her he had decided to become a lawyer and try for the best schools.

"I'm going to apply to Stanford after all, Ms. Watson. I might as well go for it, just like you said—the future Mexican-American Thurgood Marshall!"

Kathleen was pleased. Central High was 75 percent Hispanic and 10 percent black. It was located in a poor and dangerous area of the city. Few students ever got out. It looked as though Roberto would be one who did.

Roberto's Background

Roberto had been born in Los Angeles shortly after his parents emigrated to the United States from Mexico. His parents had done relatively well since then. His father had a stable job as a bus driver and earned enough money to support his family in a lower-middle-class Mexican-American neighborhood. Roberto's mother stayed home and took care of Roberto and his six younger brothers and sisters. Although Kathleen knew that Roberto's family was supportive and proud of all his accomplishments, they never came to any school functions or events. Few of the Mexican-American parents did, Kathleen discovered.

"Many of the parents or members of their family are illegal," Alma had said. "They think they would be asking for trouble by showing up. Also," she said, "many of them don't speak English and can't communicate with us very easily."

Roberto would be the first one in his family to go to college. Kathleen knew that that represented a big step for them. Whereas Roberto had been able to keep his family and school life separate when he was in high school, now he might have to live in a predominantly white college world. How would that change him? Kathleen heard a male teacher at Central tell his Mexican-American kids that if they would only "stop being so Mexican" they would do better. Would Roberto have to change in order to survive at an elite college? In Quiz Bowl team competitions, Kathleen noticed that Roberto continually deferred to the two younger white students who were less academically competent but more aggressive and self-assured than he. She sometimes wondered how well Roberto would do on a mostly white campus.

Alma

Alma was a single African-American woman who had spent eighteen years teaching English, most of them at Central High. She was an excellent teacher, but many other faculty members felt that her overt favoritism of the few African-American students at the school, particularly the girls, discriminated against both the white and the Mexican-American male students. From her many conversations with Alma, Kathleen knew that Alma considered herself to be a radical black feminist. She believed that her own experience and those of other black women could be used as the knowledge base with which to change the world.

Alma had told Kathleen that she had been raised in an extended family in the rural south. As a girl, she loved to read and to listen to her female relatives talk and tell stories. Her constant reading and the praise she received from her teachers for her academic work set her apart from most of the other children—a difference that was made worse when she won a scholarship to a large state university hundreds of miles away from her home town. Alma was eager to go, although her parents preferred that she attend an African-American college nearby. Alma's mother had cried. "You aren't going to want to talk to us any more."

For Alma—who had never been on a train, used an elevator, or had a checking account—college life was a shock. "It was the first time I had ever had to confront subtle liberal racism, sexism, and class privilege," Alma said. "My white friends and I never talked about our class differences, although we talked about race and gender. They had more money than I did, and probably never thought that my refusal to go to movies or clothes shopping or out to eat was because I was poor and had to save whatever I could from my after-school job to send home. Some of them were given more in allowance money for good times than the paycheck my parents brought home to support five kids. I hated the easy attitude these kids had toward life." Alma continued, "I didn't know any African-American professors at that time, and knew very few female professors. No one seemed to be able to help me, much less understand the problems I had. I always felt as though I didn't belong. I constantly compared myself with my friends and felt as though I didn't deserve to be there. I didn't feel good enough. In fact, my daughter had a similar experience when she went to a good school back east just a few years ago. The backlash from affirmative-action programs made it worse for her. That's the kind of experience African Americans face. It takes a lot of strength."

Alma's Aftermath

Kathleen recalled Alma's words as Alma walked out the door, and as Roberto sank farther into his seat. "I can't believe this," Kathleen thought. "A minority teacher has just done a fine job of discouraging an excellent student from applying to Stanford because he's a minority student! This doesn't make sense. Why wasn't I more forceful while Alma was here, so that Roberto could see how illogical she was in her reasoning?"

Kathleen put her hand on Roberto's shoulder. "You have a very good chance of getting accepted Roberto. Apart from a few changes that I have marked for you to look over, your essay looks very good. I'll mail the recommendation tomorrow."

Roberto nodded.

"You aren't going to let Alma's opinions stop you from applying are you? Your experiences would be different from hers—you're male, you're not black, you're from an urban area, and your family expects you to make something of yourself. You would not face the same kind of problems that Alma faced."

"Well, I'll think about it. Thanks for your help, Ms. Watson." Roberto waved goodbye and left the room.

"This is discouraging," Kathleen thought. "I'm not sure what Roberto will do. He was so excited about applying to Stanford and becoming a lawyer. Is Alma right? Should Roberto be prepared to expect the same kind of alienating college experiences that she had as an African-American female? Is the benefit of a minority individual's going to an elite institution not worth the psychic and emotional costs? What can I do to help Roberto, other than tell him that a college like Stanford might be lonely for all students, but that if he's accepted, he should try it out? It's an opportunity most students would die for. But then, what do I know about being a minority member of our society anyway? How does college experience at a predominantly white school change a minority student's perspective toward his community, and the community's perspective toward him? What would happen to his relationship with his family?"

Kathleen knew that the experiences which Alma described to Roberto closely paralleled the experiences at elite colleges reported by such African-American authors as bell hooks in *Talking Back* and Lorene Cary in *Black Ice*—books that Alma had recommended to Kathleen and that were read by students in Alma's literature courses. Both these authors had felt alienated on campus by the race, gender, and class aspects of college life, and they also regretted the distance that inevitably grew between themselves and their families over time. Kathleen could see why Alma was attracted to these books; they validated her own experiences as a bright young African-American woman struggling to find her own voice. But was it fair for Alma to use her personal race- and gender-based perspective to discourage minority students from attending schools that had relatively low minority enrollments, even if those students were as qualified as any white student to be there?

Whatever Alma had done, and for whatever reasons, Kathleen thought that it didn't seem right for Roberto. Alma's radical views would influence students and perhaps prevent minority students from taking advantage of opportunities they deserved as much as anyone. But how would she counsel Roberto? What if Alma were right?

Epilogue

A week later at a Quiz Bowl team meeting, Kathleen asked Roberto what he had done about his application. Roberto avoided her gaze. "Oh, I didn't apply to Stanford after all, Ms. Watson. I decided to go to another school closer to home. I think I'll get a good education there, too." He paused and then looked right at her: "But I'm still going to be a lawyer."

Addendum to "You'll Be Washing Dishes"

The ethnic composition of Stanford's student population for the years 1982, 1988, and 1993 is as follows:

	1982	1988	1993
African Americans	8%	8%	8%
Asian Americans	6%	14%	22%
Hispanic Americans	7%	10%	11%
Native Americans	(no data)	—	1%
Other	(no data)	4%	4%
Caucasians	(no data)	64%	54%

Sources:
Cass, J., and M. Birnbaum. (1991). *Comparative Guide to American Colleges.* New York: Harper Perennial.
College Admissions Data Handbook 1993/1994 (1993). New Orleans: Orchard House.
McClintock, J. (1982). *100 Top Colleges: How to Choose and Get In.* New York: Wiley.

QUESTIONS TO CONSIDER

1. Does Alma, as a minority individual, have the right to speak from her own experience for other minority individuals like Roberto? What does this case suggest

about who should be placed in mentoring roles with minority (or majority) students? In what ways are teachers' perspectives influenced by gender? By culture? By class?

2. Does a gifted minority student like Roberto owe anything to his ethnic or cultural community? Should teachers or others place responsibilities for one's ethnic or cultural group on students of color while they treat majority students as individuals who are free to pursue their own goals?

3. What assumptions does Kathleen make about Roberto, his family and community relationships, and his desire to apply to college? What assumptions does she make about Stanford? Did Kathleen handle the situation in the right way? What would you have done differently?

4. Alma sent her own daughter to an elite college. How do you think she would have responded if Roberto were female? If Kathleen suspects that Alma is biased in favor of females, how should Kathleen handle future advising of academically talented minority students? Should she discuss the current situation directly with Alma?

ACTIVITIES

1. Invite to class the university's director of student services or other counselors who know about the experiences of minority students on campus. Discuss what programs and resources are available for minority students and how effective they are. Include in the discussion information about the school's dropout rates for different minority groups by gender, and the reasons given for leaving school. Discuss the university's admissions standards and how gender, race, and class affect admissions, financial aid, advising, support services, and curricular matters.

2. Kathleen and Alma have different philosophical orientations toward helping students like Roberto. Set up a debate between two groups of students: Side 1 takes the position that minority students are best helped through explicit instruction in skills needed to survive in the majority culture; side 2 argues that minority students are empowered less by "making it" in the majority culture than by maintaining and promoting the language, values, and mores of their own cultural group.

READINGS

Cary, L. (1991). *Black ice*. New York: Knopf.
hooks, b. (1989). *Talking back: Thinking feminist/thinking black*. Boston: South End Press.
Lightfoot, S. L. (1989). *Balm in Gilead*. Reading, Mass.: Addison-Wesley.
Rodriguez, R. (1982). *Hunger of memory: The education of Richard Rodriguez*. New York: Bantam.

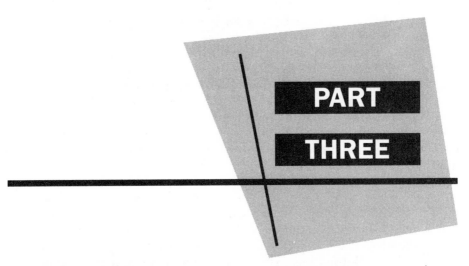

PART

THREE

Establishing Professional Standing for Female Teachers

Introduction

The cases in Part Three invite you to consider how teachers, particularly young female teachers, establish and maintain their standing as professionals. All teachers, male or female, face the task of crossing over, of changing from a student to a teacher with authority. All teachers face the problems of maintaining classroom order and handling disruptive students who challenge and test them. All teachers want to be liked, as well as to be respected.

Female teachers often face particularly acute problems of power and authority. Female socialization encourages women to be nurturant and caring, to be pleasing to others, and to use indirect strategies to accomplish their ends rather than ordering people around. Fewer women have leadership experiences—like being captain of the basketball team—that prepare them for positions of public authority. Many young women do not have the advantages of an intimidating physical size or a loud, commanding voice. Female teachers can have an especially hard time with the conflicts between being liked and being respected, being in control and being domineering. Female teachers are more likely than male teachers to be the target of sexual language on the part of adolescent male students who are feeling their own developing sexuality and physical powers.

Men and women, some suggest, have distinctive leadership styles (Rosener, 1990). Men are more apt to use "command and control leadership"—giving direct orders, enforcing clear rules, and using coercion. Women are more apt to use "interactive leadership"—sharing power, developing cooperative relationships, and nurturing individuals in ways that build their self-esteem and personal investment in the task. When problems arise in relationships, women may prefer to talk openly about them, whereas men may prefer to avoid such discussions (Tannen, 1990). In modern corporations, some argue, this "female" style of leadership offers distinct advantages (Helgesen, 1990). Although the evidence is not in, the question is intriguing: Do men and women who are successful leaders work in different, gender-patterned ways?

Leadership is a complex and subtle matter. The effectiveness of different leadership styles depends partly on the particular situation and cultural setting. African-American scholar Lisa Delpit (1988) suggests that the indirect style of exercising authority, which is characteristic of many women, does not work well in one important situation—teaching African-American students. The child-rearing styles of black families emphasize loving but firm authority, and so black students often want and expect teachers to exercise authority directly, not through veiled suggestions that are really orders in disguise. When teachers make themselves vulnerable by openly discussing their personal feelings and problems with the class, they may present themselves as weaklings.

The first two cases in Part Three—"Diane: Gender, Culture, and a Crisis in Classroom Control" and "Patsy: The Hunt for the Golden Egg"—ask you to consider the issues of gender-based classroom management styles with students of color. Both Diane and Patsy are young student teachers who prefer cooperative styles of classroom management. Both are facing serious challenges to their authority that threaten their success as student teachers. They are the targets of sexual insults. The students play on these teachers' cultural stereotypes, racial insecurities, and fears of physical violence.

Each cultural context shapes different kinds of problems. Three African-American boys hurl insults at Diane when she disciplines them on the day after a national crisis in race relations. The case asks you to think not only about effective styles of classroom management but also about racial tensions and their sexual overtones.

Patsy is doing her student teaching in a traditional Native-American community where men have always dominated women, and women still live restricted lives. The community is undergoing the pressures of social change, and gender roles are fraught with tension. A science and physical education teacher, Patsy has always enjoyed challenging the stereotypes, especially stereotypes about women. She sees herself as a role model for the young women in the community. Patsy does succeed in getting the junior-high-school girls interested in her activity-based science curriculum; but the high-school students goad her by playing offensive music, refusing to follow her directives, and rejecting any science that doesn't come straight from the textbook. The teacher aides, custodian, and others in the community turn against her, trying to run her out.

"The Day the Heat Went On" also asks you to consider the problems of sexual insults and cultural norms that are hostile to women, but in an entirely different educational setting. Ellen Collins is a young teacher eager to prove her competence at the Fleming Graduate School of Business and Public Management. As one of the few women at the school, she takes care to dress and conduct herself with professionalism. On a suffocatingly hot day, however, she removes her blazer during class and hears a loud wolf whistle. This challenges her identity as an expert on the subject at hand and turns the simple removal of a jacket into a striptease. Ellen must figure out not only how to keep control of the classroom but also how to deal with the institutional culture at this school. The problem is complicated when she realizes that the whistle came from a student who meant no offense.

As males develop physically and become aware of the power of size, voice, and strength, they may subconsciously grant respect and authority to male teachers whose masculine characteristics they are beginning to share. But they also may "play" with teachers, particularly women, whom they can intimidate. In "The Alliance," Ms. Brown, the only female mathematics teacher in the school, sees herself as having a nurturing classroom style different from the style of male colleagues. Trent, an athletic adolescent male, demands a bathroom pass during the last ten minutes of class. When Ms. Brown refuses, Trent walks out of the class, goes down to the office to talk with the male administrators about school activities, and gets his mother to complain to them that Ms. Brown wouldn't let him leave class when he had diarrhea. Rather than supporting Ms. Brown, the principal tries to negotiate a compromise among her, Trent, and his angry mother. The small issue of the bathroom pass opens up a world of large issues— gender differences in disciplinary styles, alliances between male administrators and male students, the role of principals, and the possibility of teachers' building their own alliances to turn around a disintegrating school.

The cases in Part Three ask basic questions about the nature of power and authority. Gender issues shape these problems, but they are universal.

REFERENCES

Delpit, L. (1988). The silenced dialogue: Power and pedagogy in educating other people's children. *Harvard Educational Review* 58 (3): 280–297.

Freed, A. F. (1992). We understand perfectly: A critique of Tannen's view of cross-sex communication. In *Locating power: Proceedings of the second Berkeley women and language conference* 1: 144–152. Hall, K., M. Bucholtz, and B. Moonwoman, eds. Berkeley, Calif.: Berkeley Women and Language Group.

Helgesen, S. (1990). *The female advantage: Women's ways of leadership.* New York: Doubleday.

Rosener, J. B. (1990). Ways women lead. *Harvard Business Review* 68 (6): 119–125.

Tannen, D. (1990). *You just don't understand: Men and women in conversation.* New York: Ballantine Books.

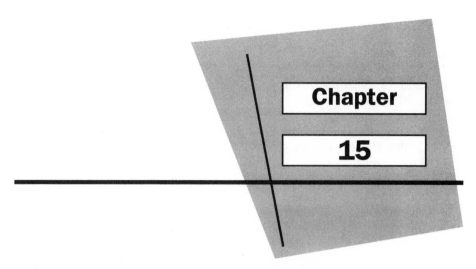

Chapter

15

Diane: Gender, Culture, and a Crisis of Classroom Control

Joan Skolnick*

The school day was over. I went back to the classroom. And I sat there. I was shaking. I felt sick. I felt these boys think that I am the biggest racist in town. Then the self-examination began. I thought back over everything . . . how I handled it. Maybe I wasn't fair to Charles. Maybe I did pick on him. Maybe I wasn't emotionally tough enough. Maybe the boys saw me as weak. I went over it and over it. Then I started writing everything down: the course of the day's events and what Charles and Demaury had done; the way they came in from lunch; the sexual name calling. And I wrote it all down so that it would be clear when I tried to explain it to my master teacher.

The Group: Demaury, Julian, and Charles

In the beginning, Demaury was the only African-American child in the fifth-grade class where I was doing my student teaching. Of the other children, about a third were Caucasian, a third Asian, and a third Latino. In

*This case is based on transcribed interviews with the student teacher, a Caucasian woman in her late twenties. Names and other identifying information have been changed. The narrative reflects her perspective only. The language of the actual transcript has been retained as much as possible to illuminate her concerns and the logic of her thinking.

Special thanks to Dr. Flora Krasnovsky (San Jose State University and the University of California, San Francisco) for reviewing the case from her perspective as an African-American psychologist and educator.

December, Julian, a street-wise kid from New York, moved to this northern California suburb and joined the class. He had gotten into a lot of trouble with school authorities in the past and had been suspended. He's Puerto Rican and black. He looked more Latino, but I think he identified with Demaury and with Charles, another black child who came a month later. I heard him saying to Demaury and Charles, "We're black." They were really into the identity of being black.

When Charles arrived, he brought a file that was really not very good in terms of attendance, test scores, and disciplinary actions that had been taken to control his behavior from third grade on. Like Julian, Charles was street-wise—that was obvious from the way he dressed. He was into criss-cross and all the rap. He was really knowledgeable. But none of the three boys was very involved in what was going on in class.

In the fall I had assigned Demaury to be my little auxiliary person to help with a drama group I had set up. Perhaps Demaury thought of me as more of a pal because of this. He was in a position of authority alongside me. I called myself the producer—I had the final word. But I let Demaury have a lot of control over the group because I thought that it was going to help him as well as the group. The drama group responded to him, and I thought it was working out really well. I wanted to give the kids ownership of their group more than perhaps I should have. Maybe Demaury thought that I was weak or passive, that he had control. So, as soon as my master teacher left the room, he really took advantage.

Demaury, Charles, and Julian hung out on the playground; they hung out at lunch. They made habits of coming in late after recess, perhaps ten or fifteen minutes late. It gave them strength to act as a group. They were like a coalition of school junior police. They knew that they had power with the other students. They knew that they had power manipulating my master teacher, and I definitely didn't try to rock the boat. I think, in fact, that they kind of took over.

Maybe I overcompensated by giving the boys a lot of respect and the benefit of the doubt, just as my master teacher did. Perhaps it was the racial thing. Maybe I was afraid they'd say, "Hey! Don't pick on us!" Maybe deep down inside it was a subliminal thing. I wasn't conscious of it.

I think also that my master teacher, Mrs. Chan, was intimidated a little bit by Demaury, because she let him come and go as he pleased a lot of the time. And she treated Charles with kid gloves.

Early on, Mrs. Chan called Charles's parents about his absenteeism. Charles got really far behind, and we were never able to keep him up to date on what was going on. I think he chose to ignore the work because it was so overwhelming, and he had a bit of trouble with his reading and writing skills. And he had trouble communicating. His grandmother said that he was a real shy kid.

Charles's grandmother was very important in the relationship between Mrs. Chan and Charles. Once the grandmother called to say that this was the first time Charles had felt respected and felt like he belonged in a classroom. From that moment on, Mrs. Chan was very loyal to him. When he was disruptive in class, she would call him aside and give him a lot of positive reinforcement.

I think that approach was working for her. But it stopped working the minute she was out of the room, or when Charles was in the library with the librarian, or in the cafeteria with the cafeteria people, or on the playground . . . or in class with me.

Mrs. Chan was very much into going to church, and I think that she and Charles's grandmother had a religious connection. I saw a touching note the grandmother had written in broken English: "You've given my Charles help. God is with you, and God is our savior. I love you." I could feel how much it meant to her that Charles was given a chance to be a functioning, happy, successful person in school.

But Charles had no connection with me and didn't feel that way about me, and so he acted out. He was like a Jekyll and Hyde. When Mrs. Chan was in the room, he was much more subservient and quiet; when I was in the room, he was like a wild man. I tried to talk with him the way she did, saying things like "I really need you to come in"—because that's where she was coming from.

I never had any contact with Demaury's mother. From what Mrs. Chan told me, Demaury was given a lot of responsibility. He was told that he was the male of the household (there was just his sister and his mother and him) and that he was in charge of "male-related activities," whatever those are. He was considered king of the castle.

When kids misbehaved in class, Mrs. Chan wrote their names on the board. If they got two check marks next to their name, they were given a citation. Two citations got them suspended. Mrs. Chan also used all kinds of after-school detentions. But it seemed as though she never even needed the check marks, because the kids responded to her. Whereas with me, the boys kept pushing, and I kept giving them chances until I was forced to give them a check mark.

But I didn't discriminate when I was teaching a lesson. I asked all the disruptive kids to focus: Nick, Michael, Chris, and the other boys who were Caucasian; or Willie, who was Latino; or Cam and Avery, who were Asian; or Charles and Demaury.

Beginning the Takeover

During that spring I did my two-week student-teaching takeover without the master teacher in the classroom. The kids really took advantage of me in a lot of ways. I wasn't an established authority figure. I wasn't comfortable with discipline at the time.

The first day of my takeover the class was being uncooperative to the maximum. I couldn't get them to quiet down. I guess I was overly emotional. I told them that the class meant a lot to me: "I have been with you all year. I've got a lot of great things planned. But I want you to *want* to be here, to *want* to learn. Because that's what this class is all about. Let's work together!" I felt myself getting weepy. I guess they saw all this as weakness.

Later I told my master teacher about this. Mrs. Chan said: "Well, that was your big mistake. You blew it. You really have to work to get them back, because if they saw you in that weakened state, they are going to think they can get to you."

From then on I tried to be more emotionally tough. Mrs. Chan later claimed that my early show of vulnerability was one of the reasons the boys tried to take advantage of me so much. I think that she saw the whole thing as resulting from my weakness.

Escalating Disaster

The day the disaster occurred was the day after the jury acquitted the Los Angeles police officers in the beating of Rodney King.

Demaury, Charles, and Julian came in from recess fifteen minutes late that afternoon. The buildup to this incident was typical disruptive behavior in the classroom, which I responded to using Mrs. Chan's method of discipline—writing names on the board, putting check marks after them, and then issuing a citation.

Charles came in first, with his shirt around his waist. He threw a basketball on table three and stopped to check his earring in the mirror. While the whole class laughed, he, Demaury, and Julian wandered around with wet paper towels on their heads. Charles poked Arlene. She screamed.

I said, "This behavior is inappropriate. You know the expectation is that you should enter the room quietly. You boys need to sit down. I will deal with your being late after this lesson is through, but for now. . . ." They cut me off. They wouldn't listen to this calm approach that I always try to have. I'm not a screamer.

I hit the bell again. "Okay boys, that's it!" I put their names on the board. "That's your warning." Demaury and Julian started to sit down.

"Charles, if you don't put your shirt on right now and get out your spelling book, I am going to have to give you a citation."

He said, "I ain't going to listen to no . . . pussy." He called me that a lot of times in from of the other kids. "You can't tell me what to do." And he called me the "p" word again.

Mrs. Chan was out in the teacher's lounge. Charles wouldn't stop. The whole classroom was disrupted. I couldn't control him. So I said, "Charles, would you like to go to the principal's office for a time out? Because it seems like you're not ready to do what the class is doing."

Demaury said, "I'll go to the office. That's better than this."

Alan joined in. "Yeah I'll go to the office too." Soon they were all piping up.

It was becoming this big, escalated disaster. So I frantically wrote out the office slip. I ordered Charles to go to the office and called to tell them he was on his way. Finally, he went.

QUESTIONS TO CONSIDER

1. How might you articulate Diane's philosophy of leadership in the classroom? How does she negotiate her relationship with the children? How does Mrs. Chan?

2. In this narrative the classroom management problems for Diane and Mrs. Chan involve only boys. Why do you think that's so?

3. Was it "weakness" to share leadership with Demaury in the drama group? Is this a flawed strategy? If so, is it inappropriate for all children?

4. How might the interaction with the boys have been different if the student teacher had been a man? An African American? What assumptions do you make about those differences?

   How might Diane's reactions have been different if the children had been Caucasian? Female?

5. What do you notice about Diane's language and explanations in her interaction with the boys after lunch? Are they speaking the same language?

ACTIVITIES

1. Observe male and female teachers with reputations for both excellent classroom management and classrooms of high academic quality. How do these teachers exercise authority and manage their classroom? Do you see gender-based patterns or differences? Be sure to construct clear definitions of key terms ("shared leadership," "tone of voice," "direct versus indirect commands"); then identify indicators of these behaviors, note their context, and consider exceptions to them.

   Develop a list of behaviors that you think characterize "male" and "female" styles of leadership. Do these excellent male and female teachers exercise authority in gender-based ways, or do they have the same basic leadership style?

   Do the same activity with male and female teachers who have difficulty with classroom management. What do you see as the bases of their problems? Are the problems of the male and female teachers fundamentally the same, or do they have gender-based problems?

2. According to Lisa Delpit, an African-American educator, many white teachers prefer to exercise authority in indirect and veiled ways that are incompatible with black cultural styles. Diane, for example, uses this language in disciplining Charles: "Would you like to go to the principal's office for a time out?"

   African-American parents are more apt to discipline children with loving but direct and firm displays of authority. "Black children expect an authority figure to act with authority. When the teacher instead acts as a 'chum,' the message sent is that this adult has no authority and the children react accordingly . . ." (Delpit, 1987:289).

Observe male and female teachers of different cultural backgrounds whose students are predominantly black. Do they exercise authority in the style Delpit argues is more culturally compatible? As in the first activity, be sure to define your terms, develop indicators of the behavior, note their context, and examine exceptions.

3. Interview female teachers in different types of schools about their experiences with physical violence and intimidation. What school policies assist them in dealing with these situations? What school and community resources are available to them? What precautions do these teachers take? What recommendations do they have for new teachers?

READINGS

Delpit, L. (1988). The silenced dialogue: Power and pedagogy in educating other people's children. *Harvard Educational Review* 58 (3): 280–297.

Kantor, R. M. (1977). *Men and women of the corporation.* New York: Basic Books.

Paley, V. G. (1979). *White teacher.* Cambridge, Mass.: Harvard University Press.

Thorne, B. (1993). *Gender play: Girls and boys in school.* New Brunswick, N.J.: Rutgers University Press.

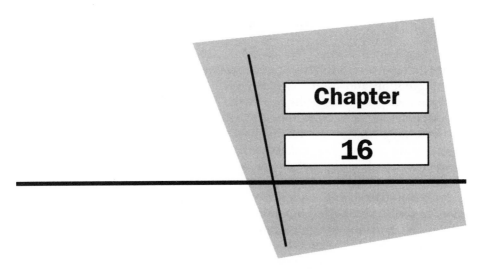

Chapter

16

Patsy: The Hunt for the Golden Egg

Gender Equity Project Teachers

The Game

"I have bum ankles!" yelled a senior-high-school girl.

Soon a chorus of kids began to call, "I have a bum leg, ankle, knee. . . ."

"I have a bowel movement!" yelled a boy.

The situation developed so fast that the student teacher, Patsy, didn't know how to curb it. She gave them her "knock it off" look, walked to the center of the soccer field, and said: "Time to begin. Set up your teams, and let's *go!*"

Ever since she arrived in Shumayuk, an Inupiat village off the Bering Sea coast, Patsy had been trying to come up with good athletic activities. The high school had a tiny gym and little equipment. The high-school students had already completed units on fitness, aerobics, Native Youth Olympics, Eskimo baseball, badminton, basketball, and cross-country skiing. Patsy decided to try snow-and-ice soccer outdoors. Spring had finally come, and she could hardly bear to be inside.

The high-school students complained that they had never played soccer in the snow and ice, that they didn't want to go outside, and that they didn't have the right shoes. But on Monday everyone had a good time.

"We are playing soccer today for gym, and we will begin *now*," Patsy said. She placed the ball in the center spot and yelled, *"Go!"*

One boy, unopposed, took the ball and quickly scored. That got them started. Play continued until Lorraine, the goalie, tried to kick the ball, missed, and landed on her back. She was laughing at first, but she didn't get up. Patsy waited a minute and then slowly walked over and watched her.

"Don't stare at me!" Lorraine said, smiling and laughing. Patsy was aware that Inupiat didn't like to be stared at, but she also knew that this girl loved attention and often played the "dumb helpless girl" routine. Patsy could not tell if she was really injured or not.

When Patsy asked Lorraine if she needed help getting up or wanted to go to the clinic, the girl lit into her, telling her that this game was stupid, that the conditions were too bad to be doing anything outside, and that she didn't want to play. Theatrically, she arose, and—milking the scene for all it was worth—hobbled like an old lady toward the school building.

Patsy ordered the students to resume play, and she took Lorraine's place as goalie. As she defended the goal, the opposing team kicked the ball as hard as they could directly at her. One of the boys on her own team would not play defense.

A kick for Patsy's goal missed, and the ball took off down the hill. Since Patsy had ducked, she didn't see where the ball went.

"Go get the ball!" Byron ordered Patsy.

"There are no out-of-bounds in this game," Patsy said. "The ball is still in play."

"The goalie is supposed to get the ball," said one of the boys.

Patsy responded, "Not true, the goalie *can* go get the ball but doesn't have to. There are no out-of-bounds. The ball is still in play."

No one moved. Patsy was fed up. She decided she would go look for the ball, and when she returned with it, they would go inside. She would have them do pushups. Then she'd take them outside to resume play. The problem was, she couldn't find the ball.

"Where is it?" she asked.

"Around that building," replied one of the students.

Patsy looked around the building, a foul-smelling outhouse, but found no ball. The kids had deliberately misled her. She told them to follow her back into the classroom and ordered them to do fifty pushups. Shirley refused, and Patsy kicked her out of class.

After pushups, the class went back outside. Patsy saw the ball far down the alley and told one of the students to get it. As Patsy walked toward him to take the ball, he acted as though he were going to throw it at her. Patsy said such a display was inappropriate and unnecessary.

"Man, what is your problem?" he demanded.

"I am not the one with the problem. You want to be treated like an adult—act like one."

"All the other team members have been running a lot," said a quiet boy. "Why can't you go get the ball?"

Were they just trying to egg her on, Patsy wondered, or didn't they really understand why she was so disappointed in their behavior? She began to explain her reasoning, when Byron exploded with complaints: She was making them play soccer outside, when they were getting hurt and wet. He had sprained his ankle. Other guys were getting hurt. Lorraine got really injured, and Patsy didn't care and wasn't fair.

"Byron, you just do not understand," Patsy said. "I am the teacher in this class, not you, and we will do the activities that I decide on. The behavior of the class will be to *my* satisfaction, not yours, or there will be consequences to pay. If you do not want to abide by my decision, you can take an F for the day. That is your prerogative. My prerogative is the activities that we will do, when we will do them, and how we will do them."

"No, *you're* the one who just doesn't understand," Byron yelled. "You just won't understand. *We don't want you here. You are not wanted here.* We won't do what you say, because *we don't want you here!*"

Patsy marched the students into the school building, told them to stay in the gym, and went straight to Darren Sawyer, her cooperating teacher. He told her that she had done the right thing, and they both went back to the gym. There Darren announced that the school would offer two gym classes for the rest of the year. One would be inside with him—gym out of a book. The other would be activities with Patsy. Each student could choose, but his class would entail homework every night and reading and reports every day. He reminded the students that Patsy's gym class had the backing of the school.

"The only injury you will sustain in my class," Darren concluded with heavy sarcasm, "is writer's cramp. We're doing this because *you* don't run the school. The principal, the teachers, and the school board run this school. *You* don't."

He turned and walked out with Patsy right behind him.

A Female Student Teacher in a Male World

Patsy had been ecstatic when she found out she would get to do her student teaching in Shumayuk, her first-choice school. After many years of trying to prepare herself for teaching and living in an Alaska village, she finally felt ready to tackle it. She looked at village teaching as a commitment to a community and a people. Her professors felt she exhibited a high degree of sensitivity and an eagerness to learn from Alaska Native people.

Patsy chose Shumayuk in large part because of Tim and Laura McNeil, teachers who had lived in this community for many years. Patsy wanted to find out what it took to be a long-term, committed teacher and what difference it would make. The system of transient teachers, she believed, created an educational climate that was not good for the students, the village, or the teachers. For this reason, Patsy did not choose to work with a well-known science teacher or to find a village in a fantastic setting. She chose to work with teachers who were committed to a community.

Shumayuk was exactly what she hoped for—a small village in a community that banned alcohol, an Inupiat culture she held in high respect. The village even had a church of her denomination. She was excited to find out that the current pastor was Native. She would teach science classes from grades 6 to 12 and might even be assistant coach of the cross-country ski team. A fantastic adventure was beginning!

When Patsy asked to become the first student teacher Shumayuk ever had, the administrators warned her that no community housing was available. Patsy ended up sleeping in a cubicle in the school. She used the home economics facilities as her kitchen, a high-school classroom as her dining area, the elementary office as her living space, and the elementary school's only bathroom as her toilet and shower.

Patsy knew that privacy would be nonexistent. The first week she arrived, the toilets were backed up, smearing the bathroom with human waste. The smell was overwhelming. Toilets backing up, she soon learned, were routine. But the cubicle wasn't so bad. Patsy had lived in a tent for five months at a time. She could handle it once more. After all, everyone in Shumayuk was crowded into small houses.

Gender Issues and Science Teaching

Patsy was not only the first student teacher in Shumayuk but also the first female high-school teacher in several years. The last female high-school teacher, people told her, had been run over by the students and had left not only Shumayuk but also teaching.

The first hint of the community's attitudes toward women came when she observed Darren Sawyer's junior-high-school social studies class. He had married a Native woman, and so he had a personal as well as a professional perspective on the local culture.

"Now let me get this straight," Darren was asking incredulously. "You are saying that girls are not as smart as boys? There is something genetic so that girls can never be as smart as boys?"

"That's right!" answered a chorus of students, mostly eighth-grade girls. Most of the boys weren't saying anything.

"Girls are just dumb," one female student said.

"Well, you have already told me that girls can't be good athletes. . . ."

"Yeah, that's right," one girl said. "Girls are stupid, and girls are weak."

No one was smiling. Darren continued: "So, if girls can't think and girls can't do well in athletics, what can you do?"

"Nothing!" another eighth-grade girl exclaimed, straight-faced. She appeared to be serious!

"Gee, I'm glad I'm not a girl growing up in Shumayuk. I wouldn't want to think I am good for nothing. What does that say about how you feel about yourself?"

As Darren gathered up his books, he said, "You have a lot of work to do here, Patsy."

Patsy thought the girls had been joking, but Darren later told her they had not been. Women have no place as authority figures within the culture, he explained. The last female teacher at the high school, he said, had given up trying to discipline them. He exhorted Patsy to remain firm and not to negotiate. She should be authoritarian, he advised her. He gave several examples where male high-school students literally ran their homes and ordered around their mothers and grandmothers.

Patsy felt she was ready for the challenge. She had experience in the field of science. She was full of innovative teaching ideas. As a female in science, she had faced bias and discrimination before. Besides, she did not fit the mold of the typical female anyway. Not only was she teaching high school and teaching science and math, but she was taller than most men in the village. She was single and without children, when all the village women of her age had children whether or not they were married.

Patsy enjoyed being different. She went to church, which no other local teacher did. One day she was delighted to surprise men cutting fire-wood when she was skiing 10 miles from town. She was amazed that people were afraid to venture far from town without vehicles or guns, especially women. Patsy was not afraid and thought it amusing that people were in awe of this feat. She was hoping that she would be a good role model for her female students.

Patsy also approached instruction differently than the other high-school teachers. Science class before Patsy's arrival had been a matter of reading from the book and copying the answers to the questions at the end of the chapter. Patsy taught the students how to read carefully. She tried to get them to think about the process of doing science rather than just doing experiments in a cookbook fashion. She tried to incorporate into her lessons examples of scientific principles from village life. Her junior-high science class centered on activities, labs, and educational games.

After the expected period of initial testing, the junior-high students settled down and accepted Patsy as their teacher. Even though she had been warned that some junior-high students had severe emotional and behav-ioral problems, these students seemed to catch on to Patsy's style of teach-ing. They realized that they would have a lot more fun doing science Patsy's way than just reading the textbook. Two junior-high-school girls went from barely passing grades to getting A's and B's, and another girl's grades rose from F's to C's and D's.

Patsy also helped out with science mini-lessons for the kindergarten class and assisted in field trips and activities. The kindergarten class and Patsy started writing letters and notes back and forth, and Patsy was their "guest speaker" on a few occasions. When Patsy got them to sit still for a 20-minute lesson, she knew she was getting them intrigued with science.

With the high-school students, however, the situation was out-and-out warfare. The initial testing seemed to intensify rather than recede. The students did not treat any other high-school teacher the way they treated Patsy. Every day she had to send students outside the room or to the princi-pal's office and flunk them for the day.

Even though science was all around them, the students could not make connections between science in the classroom and science in the world outside the classroom. They were not interested in learning how to think when they had already learned how to read a textbook and regurgitate it for an exam. They vehemently resisted anything new or different, even though they were bored and uninterested in their classes. Whatever Patsy tried went wrong—like the time she took the students outside to examine the snow vehicles, and one girl sprained several fingers by getting her hand stuck in a vehicle's track.

Of the twelve high-school students in the school, Patsy had constant problems with five of them. One student, whose father was the head of the local school board, quit school after a confrontation with Patsy. At least the principal had backed Patsy. While the student came back after a week, she sought out fights with Patsy.

Patsy did not feel comfortable with the authoritarian methods of discipline the other teachers used. She tried to speak with students individually to explain her actions and reactions. She entertained questions. She tried to be reasonable and appeal to their desire to be treated as adults. But when it became apparent that the students viewed her methods of discipline as a personal weakness, she tried other methods. After talking with the male high-school teachers and observing the ways they disciplined students, Patsy tried their methods—sarcasm, anger, yelling, flunking students who were misbehaving, sending them to the principal's office. None of these methods seemed to work any better than hers, and Patsy did not feel comfortable using them.

The Tape of 2 Live Crew

As Patsy prepared her lunch one afternoon, music started blaring from the gym. The boom box had been placed on the shelf next to the home economics room where she was eating. Irritated by the volume of the music and her lack of privacy, at first Patsy paid no attention to the words of the rap song. She was soon shocked to hear the sexually explicit lyrics of 2 Live Crew. She stepped into the gym and turned off the tape recorder.

"Hey! What are you doing? We're allowed to play music after lunch," the boys yelled.

Patsy explained that it was not the music itself, it was that music in particular which was unacceptable on the basis of the lyrics. The language of the tape was inappropriate for school and would not be tolerated. By the time Patsy had walked back into the home economics room, not only had the offensive tape been put back on, but the volume had been increased. Patsy turned and walked back into the gym, where only Byron remained, shooting baskets. She snapped off the tape recorder, took the tape, and started to leave.

"Hey, you have to right to take that tape. That's not even my tape!" Byron protested.

"No, Byron, you have no right to play that tape here. And it's your problem that it is not your tape." Patsy walked out, slipping the tape into one of the pockets of her jumper.

Byron followed, furious, yelling at her to give back the tape. Patsy thought he would give up, but he kept walking after her.

"Byron, knock it off! You are not getting anywhere—you are only making things worse for yourself! Just button your lip!" said Patsy, turning toward him.

Byron faced Patsy, hands tightly clenched into fists with arms bent. He was trembling in anger and yelling over and over that Patsy had no right to take that tape and should give it to him.

Patsy ducked around him, intending to go to the principal. To her amazement, Byron continued to follow her, screaming as he went. Lorraine joined him, saying it was her tape and she wanted it back. To Patsy's immense relief, the students left, and she located the principal. He told Patsy to keep the tape. After he talked to the students, he said, he would return it to them.

Patsy asked, "You're going to give it back to them?"

Tim said, "Yes, I will."

Patsy locked the tape in her locker. She did not want to have the tape on her person and certainly did not want to return the tape to the students. Nothing was being done for her benefit, she thought. The students would speak with the principal, but no one had apologized to her or served any punishment. She was in a daze.

At the end of the school day, Tim asked Patsy for the tape. Byron and Lorraine were trailing behind him, laughing and joking. Patsy had no choice but to walk over to her locker, retrieve the tape, and hand it to the principal. The principal handed it to the students. Patsy felt that she was the one who had been punished and abused.

The rest of the week that same tape blared in the gym every day at lunch. The best way to handle it, Patsy decided, was to skip lunch and escape to her cubicle. To her, the tape represented the students' victory over her authority.

Detentions

The one disciplinary method that Patsy found successful was detentions. Students had to stay 45 minutes after school, and Patsy claimed detentions as time for the students to help her with her work—setting up bulletin boards or tying strings for an educational game. Students could not socialize or do homework during a detention.

One day Patsy sent Lorraine to the principal's office during science class. After class Patsy went to the office to ask Lorraine what had set her off. Lorraine told Patsy to "Fuck off!" Patsy was shocked that a student would say that to a teacher, and in the principal's office. Patsy gave her another detention and told her to go to lunch. As Patsy started to leave, she turned around to say something, and Patsy and Lorraine bumped into each other. Lorraine pushed Patsy. Putting both hands on Lorraine's shoulders, Patsy told her to calm down and leave when she was calm.

Lorraine's mother, Alice, was a regular substitute in the school and happened to be there that day. Patsy told her what had just taken place.

"I wouldn't let her get away with saying that at home," Alice said.

"I don't intend on letting her get away with it in my class either," Patsy replied.

Later that day Alice and Lorraine approached Patsy about serving the first detention that day rather than the next. Lorraine had made special plans to get away for the weekend and didn't want to serve a detention on Friday afternoon. Why couldn't Patsy change her plans so that Lorraine wouldn't have to ruin her Friday afternoon? Patsy was irritated and reminded them that a detention was a consequence of Lorraine's actions. Patsy was not going to change her plans for the convenience of a student who was being punished.

Friday afternoon, Lorraine began her detention and brought with her several friends. Patsy separated the other students from Lorraine and set her to work on a bulletin board. Larry, the custodian and Lorraine's uncle, came in. He started harassing Patsy, telling her that she couldn't handle her classroom or teaching, that she needed a break from work, and that she was suffering from spring fever and blaming the students for her own problems. Lorraine jumped right in and agreed with her uncle. Patsy had stopped her work when the custodian came in to talk but quickly decided the best response was no response at all. Patsy went back to her work, and the custodian went back to cleaning.

Larry and his wife, Wendy, had spoken with Patsy a few weeks before about detention slips Patsy had made up and sent home. Patsy's idea had been to send home a detention slip that the student and a parent or guardian had to sign before the detention. Patsy had thought it would open up communication between herself and the parents, and the parents would know more of what was going on and how their children were being disciplined.

Larry and Wendy questioned whether Patsy could make up such a form as the detention slip and start instituting detentions without first checking with the local school board. The tone of the conversation was pleasant. Larry and Wendy said they thought the detention slips were a good tool to keep parents informed but did not think a student teacher had the authority to start enforcing such a policy. Patsy had discussed detentions with the principal before implementing them, and Tim had said it was her choice. Patsy had never thought about approaching the school board with a matter this minor.

Patsy discussed the meeting with Larry and Wendy with the principal and asked again about the detention slips. The principal said they did not need school board approval to institute detentions; if she felt detentions were valuable, she could use them.

Patsy was also concerned about the friction that had already developed between her and Wendy, who was a teaching aide in the primary grades. Patsy respected Wendy, as did the other teachers. But Patsy noticed that if she ever disciplined Wendy's daughter, Shirley, Wendy was particularly unfriendly. Patsy was surprised, because she knew that Wendy had almost completed her teaching credential and should appreciate the importance of discipline in teaching. Patsy had tried to encourage Wendy to finish her credential and had thought they would get along well.

The principal explained that Wendy was jealous of Patsy. Wendy might have been the first student teacher at Shumayuk, not Patsy, except that her husband had not allowed her to finish her education. Wendy was no longer taking classes. Every time Patsy tried to encourage Wendy to finish school, said the principal, she was pouring salt into Wendy's wounds.

The Lockout

Tim had told Patsy to lock the door to her cubicle right from the start, but Patsy had not seen any need to. Her few valuable items were in a locker in the hallway, and she did not feel threatened. But after the problems with Byron and Lorraine, Patsy decided to lock her door. She felt she was losing her privacy. One morning, three different people walked in on Patsy when she was in the bathroom taking a shower or in her cubicle dressing.

In April, Patsy's university supervisor was observing her, and Patsy went down to the kitchen to see if she could get her supervisor some juice. She left her bookbag and books on the cot with the room key in full view on the small desk. When she returned a few minutes later, the door was shut and locked. Patsy thought that was odd—surely she would have remembered locking the door, since it usually stuck and it took a couple of tries to lock it.

Patsy remembered that once before she had gotten locked out and had gone to Larry, the custodian, for a spare key. Patsy approached him for the spare key, apologizing for somehow getting locked out. But Larry said he had no spare key to that door.

The principal could not find a spare key either. They tried to pry open the window from the outside, but that didn't work. Rather than break the window to get inside, Tim decided he would have the custodian saw off the door handle to the room.

"Poor thing, now we have to saw off the lock, and you won't be able to lock your room anymore," Larry said.

Patsy was shocked to realize that Larry had been working just outside her room when she left, and his tone of voice was an admission that he had locked her out of her room. When she told Tim what had happened, Tim said he wasn't surprised and to try not to let it get to her. Her university supervisor suggested she pleasantly ask Larry why he did it. Tim said that would do no good—he would just deny it, and then Patsy would have the additional problem of having made an accusation. Patsy knew the custodian was baiting her, and she was glad to see that her university supervisor could witness her situation firsthand.

As soon as the doorknob was sawed off, Larry sat down on the cot and said, "Well, looks like you can't lock your door anymore, doesn't it? That's too bad—now what will you do? Looks like you'll just have to trust us now, doesn't it?"

Patsy left the room.

Later that morning Tim instructed Larry to remove the doorknob from the junior-high classroom and put it on the door to Patsy's cubicle. Tim kept the extra key himself.

Talking to an Elder

Did the entire village hate her and want her to leave? Had she tried to make too many changes in the classroom? The junior-high students did not seem to have problems with her and her teaching. So why did the high-school students?

Patsy decided to ask one of the village elders for his opinion. While fearful of making cultural mistakes, Patsy decided to ask him frankly if she was doing things that were insulting or culturally inappropriate that she didn't realize. Patsy knew the man from church, and several of his children were on the ski team that Patsy was helping to coach.

To her surprise, the elder told Patsy that the village as a whole thought she was doing a fine job, and that he personally would like to see her return to Shumayuk as a full-time teacher. He cited examples in which some of his children had commented on what they had learned in her classes. His children liked her as a teacher and coach. The students she was having problems with, he said, were known to be troublemakers. Many parents, he added, did not teach their children to respect teachers or education, but it was not her personally.

Patsy and the elder spoke for some time. In the olden days, he said, the harshness of the physical conditions disciplined people. Childhood was an indulgent time, and children were considered precious because many died before adulthood. As a child grew up, the elements would discipline them soon enough, and life would be harsh. There was little need for discipline in those days.

His explanation regarding the detention slips was also revealing. To some parents, he said, if a child needs discipline at school, that is the teacher's responsibility, not the parents'. Sending home a detention slip was like pointing a finger at the parents.

The Easter Egg Hunt

On the Saturday night before Easter, Claire, one of the women Patsy met at church who had a husband on the school board, stopped by Patsy's room and asked for her help in hiding eggs for the village's Easter egg hunt. Patsy was happy to help, thinking this would be a positive community activity to join and assist, and great fun for the young children. Perhaps her participation in a pleasant community activity would help her relationship with the village and ease tensions.

Claire especially asked Patsy for help in hiding the "golden egg," wrapped in shiny gold foil and containing a note for $50. About twenty of the two hundred eggs they would be hiding had notes for money rewards. Last year, Claire told Patsy, the golden egg hadn't been hidden well, and people found it much too quickly.

Patsy was not pleased when she realized that she would have to get up at 3:30 A.M. to hide the eggs, but she decided to go ahead.

As Patsy, Claire, and Naomi, a friend of Claire's, worked to hide the eggs around every home with children, she was surprised to find a house with adults still up, gathered on the porch. She asked the young men if they wanted to help hide the eggs, but they refused. Following Claire's instructions, she hid the golden egg in a remote spot, near some spruce trees by the airstrip.

The next morning Patsy was awakened at 6 A.M. by children begging for hints about where she had hidden the golden egg. She was dismayed to find that the majority of the eggs had been retrieved not by the children of the village but by the adults. The young men who had been up at 3:30 in the morning watching her hide the eggs had gathered them up, including the ones with money notes.

Patsy was disgusted to think that the adults would take these eggs from the children, especially on Easter. The children kept coming to her all day long, begging for clues to the golden egg. Some had been searching in vain since 6 A.M. Claire said she had children participating in the hunt and so she did not want to know where the golden egg was hidden and did not want to talk to Patsy about giving hints. Naomi had left town to go fishing for the day and wanted nothing to do with the Easter egg hunt. The other teachers seemed to think the situation was hilarious. That's the reason, they said, that they didn't get involved in village affairs.

If the golden egg weren't found by 8 P.M., the village council said, Patsy should retrieve it. When the time came, Patsy started walking from the school building to the airstrip to get the egg. Along the way children joined her. When they asked her who would get the money, she told them to ask Claire, as the decision was not hers to make.

Accompanied by her entourage, Patsy walked onto the airstrip. She was surprised to see about twenty people, mixed between adults and children, combing the airstrip road again and again. No one was looking off the road. Patsy went directly to where she remembered hiding the egg, praying it was where she thought it was. To her relief she could see the egg from the road. She quickly picked up the egg, and the children started shouting that the egg hunt was over. People came over asking where the egg had been hidden. Patsy started to explain, when a cloud of smoke swept into the airstrip. It was Claire on her four-wheeler, rushing toward Patsy as fast as she could and yelling, "Don't pull the egg! Don't pull the egg! The IRA Council decided you shouldn't take it until 9 P.M.!"

Patsy just stood there, hand outstretched toward Claire, with the golden egg in her palm. The crowd yelled their disapproval. Now, not only had she hidden the golden egg so that people couldn't find it, but she also disregarded the IRA Council's directions in retrieving it. Who did she think she was, anyway? The crowd was clamoring for the golden egg to be rehidden so that someone could find it before 9 P.M.

Patsy made it back to her cubicle before the tears came. The egg hunt seemed like a perfect setup to her. Instead of improving her relations with the village and doing something positive, she had succeeded in alienating more people and found herself much more likely to be condemned. How could this happen? she thought. Why can I try so hard just to fail so miserably? How could I have foreseen this? What could I have done to have prevented this whole thing?

Epilogue

Patsy decided to talk with the principal, Tim McNeil.

"I can give you four reasons why you are having these troubles with the high school," Tim explained. "First, you are female. Second, you are new. Third, you are temporary. And, fourth, you are young. Don't take it personally."

She had heard this advice before. Although the other teachers were nice to her, they did not seem to grasp how she felt.

When Patsy talked with Darren Sawyer, her cooperating teacher, that weekend, he finally caught on to how desperate Patsy was feeling. When he told her not to let it get to her or make her think about leaving teaching, Patsy exclaimed "*Think* about leaving teaching!" She said she had wanted to leave Shumayuk weeks ago and would have packed her bags in an instant. The gravity of the situation dawned on him.

After talking for hours with Patsy, Darren decided to speak with every one of the high-school students on an individual basis. He would look over their grades and emphasize to them that Patsy was, indeed, a real teacher, that her grades counted, and that they should begin to treat her as a teacher.

The students' immediate response stunned Patsy. Their behavior was exemplary, and most were trying academically. Evidently, most of the students were shocked to discover that after getting four weeks of F's, these grades counted. Patsy wondered if the concept of student teacher had never been explained to them. She began to understand their view that school with Patsy was just "play school."

All along Patsy had been telling them that she had the same authority as their regular teachers, but she had no authority to tell them she had authority. Patsy was thankful that Darren had spoken with them. But why did it have to get to this point before anything was done?

QUESTIONS TO CONSIDER

1. Describe Patsy's attitudes toward the role of women and what she sees herself accomplishing as a role model and teacher of science in this traditional Native American community. Then describe the community's attitudes toward women, the social changes the community is undergoing, and the tensions these changes create. Refer to specific incidents, such as Wendy's difficulties in completing her education because of her husband's opposition.

   Teachers in culturally different environments face hard choices when their own deeply held values clash with the established values of the community. Should Patsy define herself or let Darren Sawyer define her as an agent of social change?

   Is changing community behavior and attitudes toward women a matter for Patsy, the school faculty as a whole, or the school board? Or should the matter be left to the community? Consider the influence of Title IX legislation outlawing gender discrimination in educational programs.

2. Patsy is caught in a dilemma typical of women entering male-dominated fields such as business—whether to adopt a traditionally female style of group leadership by sharing power or to assume a "command and control" style of management more characteristic of males (Rosener, 1990). How does Patsy handle this dilemma at different points in this case? What happens when she first uses the egalitarian style of leadership she prefers? What happens when she tries to adopt the management methods of her male colleagues?

   If you were advising another female science teacher who would be teaching in this community, what leadership style and ways of relating to students would you advise? What would you recommend she do to prevent what happened to Patsy from happening to her?

3. Describe the views of the school administrators toward women and the support they gave Patsy. What did the administrators do that helped her, and why did these actions help? What did the administrators fail to do?

4. Darren Sawyer attributes Patsy's problems to being new, female, young, and temporary. What are the personal and institutional sources of a teacher's authority?

   Do you agree with Darren Sawyer's explanation for Patsy's problems, or do you see something else in Patsy's style of exercising authority that might lead adolescents to goad and defy her?

   How else might Patsy have handled such conflicts as the students' rebellion in the ice-soccer game or the offensive music?

5. Teachers entering culturally different communities are often told to become involved in community affairs and not isolate themselves with other teachers. The experienced teachers are amused by the way Patsy is "set up" in the Easter egg hunt.

What does Patsy's case suggest about the advantages of teachers' participating in the activities of culturally different communities? What does it suggest about the dangers and risks? How did Patsy become unwittingly involved in long-standing political and social conflicts in this community?

ACTIVITIES

1. Construct short scenarios that present issues of authority which you have read about or observed in schools. Some of these scenarios might be taken from the case of Patsy, such as the music incident or the doorknob incident. Ask other students or experienced teachers how they think the teachers should deal with each situation. Do males and females have different perspectives or advise different courses of action?

2. Interview new male and female teachers, and ask them how they established authority during student teaching? During their first and second years of teaching? As student teachers were they able to establish authority on their own? Did an established teacher have to intervene on their behalf? What school policies helped or hindered them? Do you find differences in how the male teachers and the female teachers established authority?

READINGS

Cohen, S. S. (1989). Beyond macho: The power of womanly management. *Working Woman* 14 (2): 77–81.

Kleinfeld, J. S. (1975). Effective teachers of Indian and Eskimo students. *School Review* 83 (2): 301–344.

Martin, E. (1984). Power and authority in the classroom: Sexist stereotypes in teaching evaluations. *Signs* 9 (3): 482–492.

Rosener, J. B. (1990). Ways women lead. *Harvard Business Review* 68 (6): 119–125.

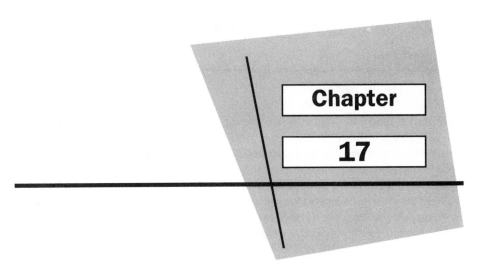

Chapter

17

The Day the Heat Went On

Abby Hansen
From *Harvard Business School Case Series**

PART A

When a malfunctioning heating system sent the classroom temperature up near 90°, Ellen Collins, a first-year assistant professor of Finance at Fleming Graduate School of Business and Public Management in Toronto, encountered an unexpected interruption. Although she always made it a rule to wear a jacket while teaching, the heat had become so stifling that she unobtrusively shed her blazer and draped it over a chair before turning back to the chalkboard. No sooner was Ellen's back turned than, from the rear of the large amphitheater-shaped classroom where sixty students sat, there came a long, loud wolf-whistle.

The Instructor

Before accepting her tenure track post with the Finance teaching staff at Fleming, Ellen, a recent Ph.D. in Economics from the University of Chicago, had already done two years of postdoctoral research in International Banking at the school. She was married, thirty years old, 5'4" tall, and slim, with collar-length brown hair, blue eyes, and a soft speaking voice. "Many of my male colleagues try to be tough," Ellen told the researcher, "and a few are really rough. But I don't admire that style and it wouldn't work for me anyway. I'm not tall; I can't physically dominate a large room; and nobody has ever called my voice 'booming.' I would never 'wipe the floor' with students, as they call it here—grill them so they look stupid in public—but there are teachers who do it regularly."

The School

Fleming Graduate School of Business and Public Management in Toronto enjoyed an admirable reputation for producing successful leaders who assumed influential positions all over the world. Advancement in this faculty was highly prized, as was its well-known master's degree, awarded after a two-year program to 430 students each year—about 25% of them women. The faculty ratio was similar.

At Fleming, the 500 first-year students were divided into units of 80 to 100 students called "learning groups" (LGs). Each LG met daily at 8:30 A.M. in a particular classroom permanently assigned to its use, and took three hour-and-a-half-long case discussion classes in a row with just one break for lunch. The first-year curriculum included nine different courses, most of them taught by the case method. Class participation usually counted heavily in course grades. Teachers "floated" from classroom to classroom to lead discussions with the LGs. Spending so much time together, and facing the pressure of the heavy workload, the LGs usually developed strong internal bonds. Most instructors described the LGs as self-protective.

The Situation

In her first year at Fleming, Ellen taught Finance to two LGs—III and VI. LG III had another woman teacher, but aside from Ellen, LG VI had only male instructors. These, according to her, constituted a mixed bag of personality types whose net effect was to create tension in the members of the group. Ellen mentioned various teachers whom LG VI thought "distant but cooperative"; some they thought "too strict" or "too lax"; one they thought "brilliant"; and one they thought "a tyrant." The "tyrant," Charlie Brennan, was their instructor in Organizational Psychology (OP). A notable practitioner of the tough style of teaching, Charlie started class on the dot of the hour, held students' presentations to a prescribed number of minutes, and had once made a lasting impression on the women of LG VI by calling a special meeting for them during which he said that because the professional world of bureaucracy had high standards for female decorum, he, too, would tolerate "no messy purses, no ungainly leg-crossing, no sloppy attire" in his class. According to Ellen, several women in the group described this meeting to her and mentioned how insulted Charlie's message had made them feel.

To make matters worse for Ellen, she usually taught LG VI immediately after Charlie's OP class with them. On these occasions Ellen found the group "so wound up that I had to do something to get them to relax before they could get their minds on the Finance class." To this end, Ellen made it a ritual to give them a few opening minutes for nervous joking. When one fellow began to use these openings for mildly flirtatious humor directed at Ellen, she tried to deflect it with good-humored shrugs. Once he opened the prediscussion joke session by saying, "Now, Ellen, smile if you have a secret crush on me!" Ellen was taken aback, but when she heard the LG laughing she good-naturedly smiled, too. "Aha! I knew it!", the student crowed, but he was laughing and Ellen read the incident as harmless and proceeded with the Finance discussion. Nonetheless, she considered his sexual undertones inappropriate and was very relieved when the jokes did not escalate any further in the direction of bad taste.

Although Ellen's relations with LG VI were generally satisfactory, she recalled having noticed right away that "the women in the group seemed demoralized. All the student association officers in this LG were male, and the women behaved particularly quietly in class, more so than in my other group, LG III. When one of the women spoke, the males tended to look bored or fidgety, as if Finance was so complex a subject that no female could possibly have anything worthwhile to say about it. I think Charlie Brennan was responsible for this intimidating atmosphere."

Ellen mentioned a further obstacle to her success with LG VI: a peculiarity of the scheduling at Fleming decreed that Finance should start in the spring semester—much later than most other courses—so that the students could accumulate technical background in economics and accounting and learn how to study by the case method before tackling its complexities. For Ellen, however, the late start also meant that she "inherited a section that had already set its social norms in the complete absence of women instructors." Nonetheless, Ellen hoped that LG VI would accept her simply as someone who could lead them through discussions of the Finance cases.

When she agreed to teach at Fleming, Ellen knew that its institutional culture could be very rough on women. Although women were significantly represented in the union faculty, only five women were tenured out of a senior faculty of 100 members. No one found Charlie Brennan's condescending attitude toward his female students particularly unusual. The master's-degree students at the school had a reputation for playing pranks, and those they sprang on women teachers often had sexual overtones. For example, when one woman teacher discovered that some fellows in her LG had hired a belly dancer to interrupt her class, she managed to intercept the woman and bar her from the classroom. But this lack of taste was quite common in all sorts of joking at Fleming.

Ellen mentioned to the researcher that, after her course with LG VI was over and she spoke less formally to some of the women of the group, they mentioned having been deeply offended by many things in their first year at Fleming—not only Charlie Brennan's speech, but the general level of obscenity in the LG's humor and the tacit assumption of so many male students that women couldn't possibly say anything useful about public administration. Ellen also mentioned that LG VI had included "three extraordinarily bright women—but oddly enough these three seemed to be having just as hard a time, for different reasons, as the less-gifted, more intimidated ones." Ellen described these three as "outstanding and outspoken," but she noticed that when any one of them began to speak, the rest of the group, male and female alike, put on expressions of bored tolerance, and "sarcastic chuckles" could be heard in the room as if to say "there goes old Sue, being so damned brilliant again—ho hum." Ellen felt "sorry to see these three—all of whom later won high honors, by the way—being almost systematically ostracized by their peers. All in all, I think their experience here was pretty negative, despite the honors. That just underlines the fact that women—all women—have a very tough time at Fleming."

Given this strained atmosphere and her late entry into the academic program of LG VI, Ellen worked hard to prepare herself to make a good impression on the group. "It sounds trivial," she smiled, "but women must worry about wardrobe in these public situations. If you look too frilly, you come across as an *airhead;* but if you look too severe, you're a *schoolmarm.* There's another aspect to dress here, too. Most of the male teachers begin class by removing their jackets and rolling up their shirtsleeves. Women can't do that because shedding an article of clothing in front of sixty students in an amphitheater might seem perilously close to some sort of striptease. I can't imagine any image less likely to bolster authority!"

The day the heat went on was a day in early April of her first year teaching at Fleming, during the third week of the Finance course. Ellen had worn a typically conservative outfit: dark skirt, high-necked white blouse, woolen tweed blazer. Unfortunately, by afternoon, the weather had turned unexpectedly warm. At 1:00 P.M. when she entered their classroom, Ellen noticed her LG VI students were all casually dressed; several were in running shorts. It was instantly apparent to Ellen that somehow the heat in their classroom had been turned on by mistake. Ellen got about fifteen minutes into the discussion before beginning to feel extremely uncomfortable. She was putting a student's key points on the board when "the temperature felt as if it had gotten up near 90°. The students were all slumping. I was trying to listen to the speaker, but I, too, was beginning to succumb to the incredibly cloying atmosphere. That room was always stuffy. Now it was dizzyingly hot." As the student continued, Ellen stepped back from the board, shrugged out of her blazer as unobtrusively as possible, and turned to drape it over the chair that stood behind the instructor's desk near the blackboard. Then she turned to walk back to the board. As soon as her back was turned, the wolf-whistle rang out from the top row, where, Ellen knew, "a bunch of drinking buddies sat together." For a split second, anger crashed over Ellen. What nerve! How childish! What an insult! She clutched the chalk tightly and wondered what response to make.

PART A: QUESTIONS TO CONSIDER

1. How would you respond to the wolf whistle if you were in Ellen's position? Consider the various options she has.

2. What did Ellen have to lose if she handled the matter poorly? What would be the implications for the women in the class?

3. Should Ellen respond differently depending on her views of the motivations of the man who whistled at her? Consider the possible interpretations of the wolf whistle—sexual appreciation? Insult? Challenge to authority? A compliment?

4. How has Ellen chosen to manage her classroom dress and appearance? How are her options affected by her gender? Would you advise her to continue wearing a jacket to class?

5. How has the atmosphere in the class that students attended before Ellen's class affected their behavior in her class? In what ways can she manage the class to create a different atmosphere?

6. Although this incident takes place in a professional school, similar problems of managing appearance and authority occur for female teachers in elementary and high-school settings. These problems are especially acute for student teachers and young teachers whose age may be close to the ages of their students.

    How would you advise a young female teacher to dress in different types of school settings?

    What if a young man in a high-school class let out a wolf whistle? Would you advise a teacher like Ellen to act the same way as in this professional-school situation? Why, or why not?

PART B*

Ellen Collins Recalls the Incident

I knew these characters sitting in the top row, and I didn't consider any of them basically hostile, although my instantaneous reaction to the whistle was pure fury. I felt like lashing out, but I immediately rejected the possibility of responding with angry words because it seemed important, somehow, to show that I hadn't been rattled. The idea of calling on a woman student in the hope that she would complain on my behalf occurred to me. That might bolster the women as a group and offer more effective correction than I, as the insulted party, could make.

But I knew that the women in LG VI were demoralized. They were a fairly young group—their average age was 25 (about two years below the average male age)—and they had far less than the typical four years of business or government experience the males had. I had noticed that they acted self-effacing. There was a lot riding on me as their only female teacher. If I called on one of them to defend me, not only would I put her on the spot but she might simply swallow the insult and thereby help create an even worse impression of passivity.

I realized that both I and the women students in that room had much to lose by a wrong response. I don't mean that I deliberated for hours before responding to the whistle. But some form of all these thoughts did rocket through my mind as I stood there. What I did was instinctive. I did not look in the direction of the whistle. Instead I waited for a pause from the speaker, wheeled around to face the part of the room farthest away from where the whistle had originated, and called on a male student. I chose a reliable fellow who I knew would have something pertinent to say, and asked him a direct, simple question relating to something I had just put on the board. While he answered, I collected my thoughts. The class went on with no further jarring incidents.

Ellen Reflects on Long-Term Consequences

Oddly enough, I think there might be some level on which this incident—and my not getting rattled by it—did me some good. I ended up the year with far better teaching evaluations than LG VI gave Charlie Brennan, and he's considered one of the real "old pros" around here. By the way, I think I know who whistled, and I don't think he really meant any harm by it. It was an attempt at humor, quite spontaneous, and flat-footed rather than malicious. The student I'm thinking of happens to be an average guy—average intelligence, average looks—but he has a frankness and naivete that are refreshing at Fleming. He's the sort who would offer daring comments in discussion without calculating every syllable for effect in the interests of his precious course grade. In retrospect, I'm still not certain of what that whistle meant. Perhaps it was a sort of compliment—a recognition that I'd finally joined the club by doing what the men did and teaching without a jacket. I also think this incident could have landed me in real hot water if I'd acted flustered or showed the instantaneous fury that I really did feel. As LG VI's only woman teacher, I was a symbol for all women at Fleming at that moment, and one false step could have crippled my relationship with this group and my credibility as a leader. To me, though, this relatively minor incident is just one of many signs that women live under microscopes at places like Fleming. And—for the record—I still wear a jacket when I teach.

PART B: QUESTIONS TO CONSIDER

1. What do you think of Ellen's response? What are the limitations in the ways she handled the situation?

2. Should Ellen have said anything in public about this incident? Should she have spoken privately to the person she suspected?

3. This institutional culture tests and teases women, both as students and faculty. If you were a faculty member at this graduate school, what steps might you take to change this culture? What could you do as a student at this school?

ACTIVITIES

1. Interview female teachers about sexual comments, insults, and compliments that they have received from their students in and out of the classroom. Ask for details about the context. Exactly what happened? What was the setting and tone of the situation? Who were the students? How did the teachers respond to these situations, and what was their reasoning? What kind of responses were more successful?

2. Interview women who have positions of authority in male-dominated fields—high-school principals, school superintendents, managers of business corporations, partners in major law firms. Ask them to describe the pressures of being a woman in their situation. Do they dress of act in specific ways in response to these pressures? Do they see themselves as acting like their male colleagues or in ways that reflect their gender?

   Interview men in the same fields about the problems they see facing women. What styles of dress or action would they recommend for a woman they would like to see succeed? Do they think the women should act as they do or in ways that reflect their gender?

READINGS

Geis, F. L. (1985). Sex of authority role models and achievement by men and women: Leadership performance and recognition. *Journal of Personality and Social Psychology* 49 (3): 636–653.

Martin, E. (1984). Power and authority in the classroom: Sexist stereotypes in teaching evaluations. *Signs* 9 (3): 482–492.

Tischler, N. G., T. L. Morrison, L. R. Greene, and M. S. Steward. (1986). Work and defensive processes in small groups: Effects of leader gender and authority position. *Psychiatry* 49 (3): 241–252.

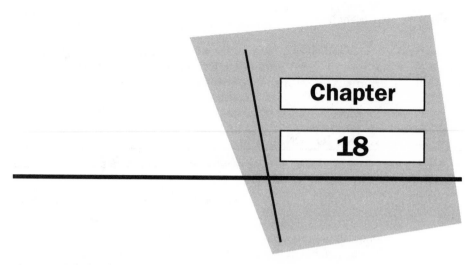

Chapter

18

The Alliance

Gender Equity Project Teachers

The Bathroom Pass

"Mrs. Brown, I have to go to the bathroom. I've had to go real bad since the beginning of class."

I looked at Trent and then at the clock. It was 12:48. "Trent, there are only 12 minutes left. Class will be over at one o'clock, and then you can use the restroom." I shifted my attention to Anne, who had her hand in the air.

For several days I had been expecting Trent to ask permission to use the restroom in order to test me on an issue he had discussed with me a couple of days earlier. Trent had asked me what I thought of a student who asked to use the restroom during class and a teacher who refused to let him go. "A counselor told me it was a form of child abuse if a teacher wouldn't let a kid use the bathroom."

I explained to Trent that the 15-minute breaks between class provided the time to take care of student's personal needs. Trent didn't accept my reasoning. "If you have to go, you have to go, and you should be allowed to go."

Now, I couldn't tell if Trent really had to use the restroom, or if he was testing me. I suspected he was testing me in front of the other students. Trent was very social. He liked to get out of class whenever he could and meet his friends in the hall. My classroom policy had always been no passes except in an emergency. I strongly believe in letting students know how much I value the academic time in class, and how much they should value it, too.

Trent gave me a long look, walked back to his seat, picked up his books and leather jacket, and headed for the door. "Write me up," he said, and walked out.

Immediately after the bell rang, I went to the office with Trent's detention form. The office keeps track of how many detentions the student has and the forms that notify parents of what has happened. I was surprised to see Trent in the office lobby talking with Mr. Hammet, the principal, and Mr. Gregory, the vice-principal in charge of discipline.

"Mr. Hammet, we need to put a time on the school calendar for our Timber Carnival," Trent was saying. "We want to have it during Spirit Week."

After a few moments of confusion, I realized that Trent was not talking about leaving my class early and not being permitted to use the restroom. I was seeing a completely different Trent. In contrast to his behavior with me, he was very respectful of the two administrators. Was he buttering them up before I told them what had happened in my class? Trent was one of the jock stars of the school and active in the school's social events. He had to deal with the administrators all the time.

My plan to tell the administrators what had happened was delayed when a teacher rushed into the office yelling about a fight that had broken out in the lunchroom. Mr. Hammet and Mr. Gregory left immediately, and I realized I would have to wait to settle this matter until after school. Trent and I looked at each other. "I have to go to shop class," he said, and walked away.

After School

When school was dismissed, I went to the office and told Mr. Gregory what had happened. Believing I had school policy to back me up, I mentioned the numerous requests I had from Trent's class to leave the room for one reason or another. "I sprained my finger." "I need a pass to go to the nurse." "I need to call my mom so she can pick me up after school." "I need a drink of water." "I have to get a tissue to blow my nose." At one point, student requests were getting to be such a problem for so many teachers at the school that Mr. Hammet told the faculty at a staff meeting to "Just tell them no!"

When I reminded Mr. Gregory of this policy, he quickly corrected me. The school, he said, didn't have a blanket policy on passes. Every teacher ran his or her class differently. At the staff meeting, Mr. Hammet was merely stating what he thought each teacher should do individually. I was surprised. I thought the faculty had discussed this issue and the importance of time on task often enough that we had, unofficially perhaps, agreed to enforce a no-pass policy. Not only did we not have a school-pass policy, Mr. Gregory said, but at Trent's mother's request, Trent was not to serve after-school detention. Instead, he would serve a day of in-house suspension when he had accumulated three detentions. I felt as though my feet had been knocked out from under me. If teachers were in charge of their own classroom discipline, then why wasn't my pass policy being supported?

The next day Mr. Gregory told me that Trent's mother had called. She was angry that her son had not been permitted to leave class to go to the bathroom. She said he had diarrhea, and she wanted to schedule a parent conference immediately with the teacher who wouldn't let her son leave under those conditions. I could tell Mr. Gregory was upset with me for letting the situation escalate to this point. "Couldn't you have given Trent lunch detention instead of sending him to the office?" he asked. I told Mr. Gregory that I didn't monitor detentions during my lunch break. I felt discipline was the office's responsibility. "You're going to have to discipline your own students," he said. "Office-generated detentions might not be an option for teachers anymore."

Later, Mr. Hammet called me into his office wanting to know what had happened with the student in my class who had diarrhea. After I explained the situation, he said, "There won't be a meeting with Trent's mother after all. In the future you're going to have to be more clear, Mrs. Brown, about when and how students may leave your room. I would personally warn students that exceptions to a no-pass policy would be made, but only rarely." When I left the office, I wondered if an agreement had been made on the phone with the parent and if it no longer mattered what policy or learning environment I wanted to establish in my own room.

The next day Trent and I met with Mr. Gregory in his office. Trent explained that after he had left my room, he had gone to the bathroom, put his books in his locker, and had gone to the office. Mr. Gregory looked at Trent and said, "The detention will be dropped this time, but understand: It is not child abuse for Mrs. Brown or any other teacher to ask you to wait." I was stunned. I felt as if I had been disciplined, not Trent.

Background

I have been teaching for nearly ten years, the last six at Timberville High. I've taught different levels of algebra, computer programming, trigonometry, and analytic geometry. The math department has six teachers. I am the only woman. We all work well together and accept each other's differences in teaching and in personality. The other math teachers are more strict in the discipline policies than I am. I sometimes wonder if my more nurturing teaching style or my gender makes students challenge me more. The male teachers don't have to make as big an issue of the rules as I do, and when they have a problem with a student, they are more strict and inflexible about the consequences.

The Class

Twelve of the eleven boys and twelve girls in my class are repeating the course from the year before. Only eleven freshmen are taking the class for the first time. Three of the students who are repeating come from the resource room. Three other students failed Algebra I the year before and have been dropped back to elementary algebra. Two of these students, Jeff and Don, are extremely bright. Jeff recently commented that the only reason he attended school was to find out where the parties were on weekends. Even though both students are failing, I feel they are misplaced in my class. They already know the content and don't take the tests seriously. I feel they would be more challenged in a higher-level class, but they both need to pass this class before they can move on.

Three other students are brothers and sister. Katie, whom I had in the same course last year, sits in the front of the room and has been a model student. She says she wants to pass this time so she doesn't have to be in the same class again with her brothers next year. Her older brother, Dan, often comes to class late with a pass from the office or has an unexcused tardy. He behaves as though he has just rushed back from someplace or is impatiently waiting to get somewhere else, with little concern for the math in between. Dan is also participating in the STARS drug intervention program and is usually absent once a week for his group's meeting. Katie's younger brother, Sam, has a learning disability and occasionally asks to work in the resource room because the class is too noisy.

Three other boys are athletes on the football and basketball teams. Bill's personality appeals to many of the girls in the class. Bill and his female "fans" work on note-passing skills more than they work on their math skills. Mark, a sophomore, is starved for attention and frequently interrupts my instruction by sighing, leaning back in his chair, or slamming his book down on the desk and then apologizing. He tends to do what's necessary to get the class focused on him instead of the lesson. He seems to know which buttons to push without suffering too many negative consequences. Phillip, a senior, has math anxiety. It took the administration weeks to track him down and get him to attend class. He would still be skipping out if he didn't need the class to graduate.

It's difficult to predict from day to day how this class will respond to me, to each other, and to the lesson. It depends on who is absent, who arrives late, and who has been pulled out for counseling, the office, or other programs. Some days the class is like riding an out-of-control roller coaster.

The School

Timberville High School, home of the Lumberjacks, has nearly seven hundred students who are bussed in from as close as 2 miles and as far away as 40 miles. Many of our students have a reputation as being rough, undisciplined, and disinterested in academics, compared with students at the other two high schools in town.

The administrators consist of one principal and three vice-principals, responsible for discipline, attendance, and extracurricular activities, respectively. In the six years I have been at Timberville, I have noticed a change in how discipline is handled by the administration. In the past, discipline policy had firm consequences attached to misbehaviors. If a student did not show up for detention, the student spent the next day at in-school suspension. A further violation of rules resulted in a three-day out-of-school suspension.

During those years, students were not allowed to be in the building unsupervised half an hour after the last bell. Students were only allowed to be in the building if they were participating in sports or club activities and had an adult sponsor.

The present policy appears to be much more relaxed. More students stay after school just to hang out. The administrators don't question kids about why they are in the building, and so students can roam the halls freely, do their homework, or talk with friends. The school's vandalism problems have skyrocketed.

Also, the school district has adopted a new policy toward students who have had drug or alcohol offenses. There is a greater effort to keep the kids in school attending drug intervention programs, rather than having them suspended and out wandering the streets, as in the past.

But the students who don't fight the system seem to be the ones who end up getting punished with detentions. The chronic offenders appear to get more breaks by getting concurrent detention time, complaining the loudest, or having their parents complain. When parents complain, the administrators now seem to reevaluate the situation and compromise. Some teachers have pointed out the inconsistencies in the discipline policy. Several female teachers have commented that male administrators don't support them when students are written up for discipline matters. As one female teacher said, "When I give a detention, I expect the administration to back me up. I don't expect my professional judgment to be questioned."

End of the Issue?

Three days after the meeting with Trent and Mr. Gregory, this case seemed to be over—or was it? Trent didn't receive any discipline for leaving my room without permission. I had made a judgment call about his leaving the class based on the conversation about abuse and the manner in which he had approached me about the pass in class. I still think he was testing my authority. I expected the administrators to back up the detention I had given Trent, whether it was a school policy or my own. If this had happened to another student whose mother had not been involved, the detention would have gone through. I wondered if the administration's actions would have been the same if Kent "Viking" Harrison, a strong male disciplinarian from the P.E. department, had written Trent up instead of me. I guess I'll never know.

QUESTIONS TO CONSIDER

1. Describe what Ms. Brown and Trent's mother each expect from the school principal. What dilemma does the principal face, and how does he see his role?

   If Trent's mother is unsatisfied with the way this situation is resolved, she
   could escalate the problem by calling or writing the school board and requesting
   action against the teacher or administrators or writing a letter to the local newspaper. Ms. Brown, as well as the principal, faces risks in this situation. Considering
   these possibilities, as well as the importance of supporting teachers and maintaining school discipline, what would you have done if you were the principal?

2. Think about this situation from Trent's viewpoint. How do you think he sees Ms.
   Brown? What is he learning about gender roles and about building alliances and
   gaining power?

   What would you advise Ms. Brown to say or do the next time Trent claims he
   needs a bathroom pass in the last few minutes of class? Do you see ways for her
   to gain authority and power?

3. How did the problem of the bathroom pass develop in the first place? Think about
   the way Ms. Brown defines her teaching role; her differences in disciplinary style,
   as well as gender, from other teachers in the mathematics department; the
   physical characteristics of the participants in the case; the nature of school
   policies; the informal organization and social relationships at the school; and the
   changes in the school over time. The issue of bathroom passes contains a world
   of difficulties.

   In the long run, what would you suggest Ms. Brown do to head off future
   problems of this type? Consider both what she could do in her own classroom and
   also what alliances she herself could build in the school.

ACTIVITIES

1. Interview the administrator in charge of discipline at a secondary school. Ask
   such questions as these: Is there a schoolwide hall-pass policy? Are passes the
   decision of individual teachers? Who was involved in creating this policy? How is
   it implemented? What administrative support do teachers receive in classroom
   management dilemmas? Under what circumstances would teachers not receive
   full administrative backing? How are conflicts between teachers and parents
   handled? Do some teachers have a more difficult time managing disruptive students? What are the common characteristics of these teachers, if any? What does
   the administration do to assist these teachers?

2. Follow a referral. If a student is given a referral during a class that you observe,
   follow the paper trail from the classroom through the office. Write a short summary that describes the situation and states the reason for the referral, including
   both the student's and the teacher's point of view. Note the kind of information
   requested on the referral form, the person who will be notified, any action that is
   taken as a result of the referral, and the justifications for that action. Examine a
   day's or week's worth of referrals to the office. Do male and female teachers

seem to have different reasons for referring students? Is the administrative response to similar problems equivalent for male and female teachers?

READINGS

Freed, A. F. (1992). We understand perfectly: A critique of Tannen's view of cross-sex communication. In *Locating power: Proceedings of the second Berkeley women and language conference* 1: 144–152. Hall, K., M. Bucholtz, and B. Moonwoman, eds. Berkeley, Calif.: Berkeley Women and Language Group.

Lakoff, R. T. (1992). The silencing of women: In *Locating power: Proceedings of the second Berkeley women and language conference* 2: 344–355. Hall, K., M. Bucholtz, and B. Moonwoman, eds. Berkeley, Calif.: Berkeley Women and Language Group.

Lortie, D. C. (1975). *Schoolteacher: A sociological study.* Chicago: The University of Chicago Press.

Martin, E. (1984). Power and authority in the classroom: Sexist stereotypes in teaching evaluations. *Signs* 9 (3): 482–492.

Tannen, D. (1990). *You just don't understand: Men and women in conversation.* New York: Ballantine Books.

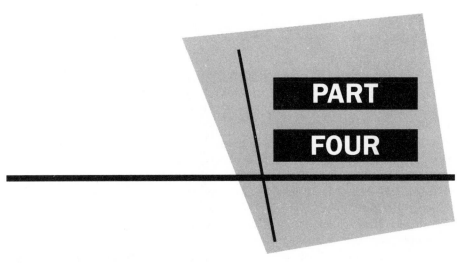

Sexual Harassment in the Schools

Introduction

Catcalls, compliments, hugs and kisses, bra snapping, soulful looks, snide leers, a boy pressing a girl up against her locker—walk through a high-school hallway, and you will see it all. Many of us are so used to this behavior, especially among teen-agers, that we hardly notice it at all. The world of adolescents is changing. As a result of cases brought before state and federal courts and of complaints brought to the Office of Civil Rights in the Department of Education, standards for what is acceptable behavior and what is sexual harassment are undergoing radical change.

Protection from Sexual Harassment

Title IX of the Education Amendments of 1972 prohibits schools from discriminating based on gender. This legislation has been interpreted as well to protect students from a "sexually hostile environment" in classrooms, buses, and playgrounds. A central problem for schools is that social standards are shifting, and we lack consensus on the meaning of a "sexually hostile environment." As Eaton (1993) summarizes the problem:

> Another important question is the definition of a "sexually hostile environment." The Office for Civil Rights defines it as one characterized "by acts of a sexual nature that are sufficiently severe or pervasive to impair the educational benefits" offered by the school and says that the existence of such an

environment "is determined from the viewpoint of a reasonable person in the victim's situation."

Some court decisions, however, seem to be in conflict with the OCR definition. The U.S. Court of Appeals for the Second Circuit, in a case involving Yale University, ruled that the harassment had to be so severe as to deny *all* educational benefits—for example, by forcing a student to drop out of school.

For teachers, this evolving area of law raises fundamental questions that go beyond what constitutes sexual harassment. The question is not simply what schools or teachers can be held liable for. The central issue is what schools should be teaching about respect for the dignity and freedom of other people and the privacy of their bodies. School regulations and discipline policies communicate critical messages to students about what behavior is acceptable and what is not.

Many students, both male and female, find sexual comments and contact so upsetting that they cannot learn. Being the talk of the school, having your name and sexual habits emblazoned on the restroom walls, being pinched or mooned—such behaviors have academic consequences. In a national survey of sexual harassment conducted by the American Association of University Women (1993), many students with such experiences said they didn't want to come to school and found it hard to concentrate in class. Boys were also victims of sexual harassment. Girls, far more than boys, however, reported that such harassment interfered with their school work.

Most of us will agree that schools should prevent sexual harassment and should teach students respectful ways of treating other people. The problem is that we decidedly do not agree on a definition of sexual harrassment. What is harassment, and what is harmless flirting? What is clumsy flirting? Many adolescent girls—aware of their developing bodies and proud of their unfolding beauty—dress to be noticed. Should we then discipline boys for noticing them?

The subjective nature of sexual harassment is also a matter of concern. Suppose a young man brushes up against a girl in a sexual way. If she likes the attention, do we then call it flirting? If she dislikes it, do we then call it sexual harassment? Many are troubled by a definition of bad conduct that carries disciplinary consequences and depends on the subjective feelings of the young woman, rather than on the objective behavior of the young man.

Can and should schools monitor the sexual behavior and language of students? Many worry that sexual harassment is yet one more problem—rooted in the home, the media, and the larger society—that has been thrust on the schools. Must schools monitor every use of the "F" word in the hallways? If schools are to be held responsible for sexual harassment on the bus, then are the schools also responsible for sexual harassment at the bus stop? What about on the walk to the bus stop? Schools have limited professional resources (time, funds, and energy); if the schools expend their resources on this problem, less will be left to deal with other problems.

These are the kinds of issues the cases in Part Four ask you to consider. By talking about concrete cases, we can move toward shared agreements about what sexual harassment is and for what the schools should take responsibility. The first case, "The Boys on the Bus: Bad Language or Sexual Harassment?" presents the famous story of Cheltzie Hentz, which made headlines around the world. When six- and nine-year-old boys called seven-year-old Cheltzie a "bitch" and told her and other little girls that they had "stinky vaginas," Cheltzie's mother charged the Eden Prairie School District with failing to stop sexual harassment. The Office of Civil Rights investigated not only the teasing of Cheltzie but also the kind of sexual behavior among older children that many people take for granted.

The next case, "Lisa's Complaint," centers on how schools should handle complaints about sexual harassment. When the boys in Lisa's English class make sucking and moaning sounds behind her desk and push her up against her locker, the assistant principal urges Lisa to write a formal complaint. Lisa writes the memo but then refuses permission for the school to deliver it to the boys. According to the school's official policy on sexual harassment, the school can do nothing without Lisa's permission. Is something wrong with such a policy?

Protection from False Charges of Sexual Harassment

Most sexual harassment occurs between students and other students, not between students and teachers. When it comes to sexual relationships between teachers and students, we have no disagreement: Teachers should not have sexual contact with their students and should not make sexual advances to students. If they do, they may well face criminal charges and loss of their teaching licenses. School administrators who neglect to protect students from sexual misconduct on the part of teachers also face the specter of huge damage suits, a result of the path-breaking 1992 Supreme Court decision *Franklin v. Gwinnett County Public Schools.*

The problem is that teachers, as well as students, also face the specter of false charges of sexual harassment. People's sensitivities have intensified because of the attention the issue has received in the workplace, the schools, and in public life. In the current atmosphere, teachers worry that innocent behavior—hugging a child who is upset—might be interpreted as sexual behavior. Teachers fear that angry, vengeful students might level false accusations against them. Students sometimes develop a crush on a particular teacher. These romantic feelings—always difficult for teachers to handle with sensitivity—could be twisted as well into undeserved charges of sexual harassment.

Teachers' lives and careers have been destroyed through such accusations. In one famous case, Roderick Crochiere, a music teacher in Connecticut, was fired for improperly touching one of his music students on the knee (Conkling, 1991). When newspaper headlines accused him of "fondling" the student, the publicity drove him to a mental breakdown. The full story did not come out until years later. What had been labeled "fondling," it turned out, was actually "falling." Crochiere, legally blind in his right eye, was leaning over to read the music on his student's music stand. To keep his balance, he accidentally placed his hand on her thigh. He apologized for touching her where his hand should not have been. The young girl reported what happened to her mother, and the school authorities did not properly investigate.

The last two cases in this section, "When Good Intentions Aren't Enough" and "Who Is the Victim?" present real-world cases in which teachers were accused of sexual harassment. These are cautionary tales, to help you think through the minefields in this sensitive area. One case, however, has an ending that may surprise you.

REFERENCES

American Association of University Women (1993). *Hostile hallways: The AAUW survey of sexual harassment in America's schools.* American Association of University Women, P.O. Box 251, Annapolis Junction, MD 20701-0251.

Conkling, W. (1991). Presumed Guilty. *Teacher Magazine* 2 (8, May–June): 33–38.

Eaton, S. (1993). Sexual harassment at an early age: New cases are changing the rules for schools. *Harvard Education Letter* IX (4, July–August): 1–5.

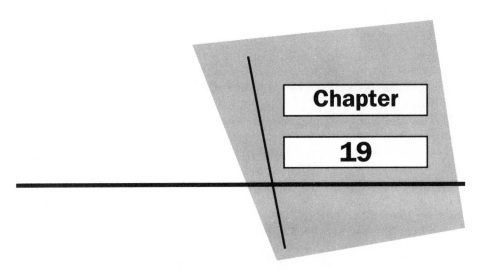

Chapter

19

The Boys on the Bus:
Bad Language or Sexual Harassment?

Judith S. Kleinfeld*

"Many days I would pick Cheltzie up . . . and she was crying. The first thing she'd talk about was, 'Mom, I've got to tell you what's happening on the school bus.' "

Cheltzie's mother, Sue Mutziger, was talking to a reporter. Many children get teased on the school bus, but Cheltzie's case had turned into national and international news. At seven years of age, Cheltzie was the youngest child ever to bring a charge of sexual harassment, according to the U.S. Office of Civil Rights. One of the boys accused of harassing her was only six years old; two of the others were nine.

In early March Ms. Mutziger first called the school district about the boys' behavior. Her daughter was upset, she said, because the boys on the bus were using foul language. The coordinator of the school district's transportation department rode the bus the day after this telephone call to check out the situation. He did not hear any profanity, he said, but he did observe a lot of disruption. The coordinator warned the children that they would be disciplined for swearing, and he called Ms. Mutziger to discuss what he had seen.

When the coordinator called Cheltzie's school principal, the principal

---

*This case was written from materials secured under the Freedom of Information Act from the Office of Civil Rights, Region V, including the OCR statement of findings, the settlement agreement, interviews with major participants in the case, and newspaper articles from the files. The following articles were especially useful: Rhonda Hillbery, "Taunts on the School Bus Spark Girl's Sexual Harassment Complaint," *Los Angeles Times*, December 1, 1992, A5; Nan Stein, "School Harassment—An Update," *Education Week*, November 4, 1992; and Jon Tevlin, "Don't Even Think of Harassing Little Cheltzie," *Minnesota Monthly*, January, 1993, 44–64.

said that she had already heard about the problem. The principal counseled the six-year-old boy. She suspended one of the nine-year-olds for a day, and the other received a 1-hour detention for his behavior, which was written up on the bus slips.

But Cheltzie's problems did not end. About a week later Ms. Mutziger wrote to the transportation coordinator to say that Cheltzie had been the target of sexually abusive language (including "shit bitches," "small penises," "scum-fucking pigs," "go and suck your dad's dick"). According to Cheltzie's day-care provider, Cheltzie and another girl were chased off the bus by a first-grade boy calling them sexual names. The two girls were in tears, screaming and hysterical.

Cheltzie's mother wrote lengthy letters to the school district and spoke before the school board about the problems on the bus. In the school superintendent's view, the district was dealing with the issue. The two nine-year-old boys, he pointed out, were special education students. Their rights and legal procedures for dealing with them had to be taken into account. Furthermore, the superintentent emphasized that he wanted to "problem-solve and not punish."

A few weeks later the two special education students were transferred to the special education bus for the rest of the year. The principal had already counseled the six-year-old boy, whom Cheltzie named as her chief attacker. The boy received no punishment other than the earlier detention. This was not enough punishment, Ms. Mutziger said. The school district was doing far too little. A couple of times, for example, school officials got on the bus and talked to the children about foul language. She demanded more training about sexual harassment for both students and staff. She demanded that adult monitors or videocameras be placed on every school bus.

The superindendent responded that videocameras would cost $500,000, but the money was not his primary concern. "We don't want to treat this thing like Big Brother with a camera on every bus," he said. "We want the students to develop self-discipline. This is a societal problem," he argued. "The schools can't be responsible for the language children use with each other any time during the school day and on the bus."

Superintendent McCoy was proud that Eden Prairie had taken the lead in developing a sexual-harassment policy some years earlier. When he became superintendent, he set the goal of having females in 50 percent of administrative positions. "Do the job right, and you get promoted even if you're a woman," was his theory.

Typically, the school district considered sexual touching to be a violation of its sexual-harassment policy. But sexual slurs, especially among young children, was considered a case of "bad language," not "sexual harassment." Children of six or seven don't even know what the words mean, said school officials. But now that Cheltzie's story had become national news, they said, children would claim sexual harassment in their fights. "They'd say that someone had touched their 'private parts,' " said the principal of

Cheltzie's school. "But when you asked them to show you where, they'd point to their shoulder."

Next fall, the school district told Ms. Mutziger, they would make sure to deal with Cheltzie's problems. The district selected a veteran bus driver for her daughter's route, and Cheltzie sat directly behind the driver. Cheltzie's problems on the bus ended, but the problems of the school district were just beginning. That fall Ms. Mutziger filed a sexual-harassment complaint against the district with the U.S. Office of Civil Rights, Department of Education.

The school district, Mutziger charged, violated Title IX of the Education Amendments of 1972. The district had not dealt with sexual harassment against her daughter and other female elementary- and middle-school students. Given the hostile climate, she argued, female students were denied equal educational services because of their sex. Sexual harassment of students, she said, went far beyond Cheltzie's problems. She had gotten many calls of support from other parents whose daughters were the target of sexual harassment on the bus, in the hallways, and on the playground. In the middle schools, parents told her, young girls are continually called "sluts, bitches, and whores." When the parents complained to the school counselors or principal, they said, their complaints were ignored. Putting a veteran bus driver on the route and moving her daughter's seat behind the driver may have solved Cheltzie's problem, but it certainly hadn't solved the problems of other little girls.

Many held the same view. We are used to a society in which boys make sexual jokes, snap girls' bras, and grope at their bodies, argued Nan Stein of the Center for Research on Women at Wellesley College. Just because it happens every day, just because witnesses and bystanders see it, just because it happens in public, doesn't mean it isn't sexual harassment. The situation is a "national disgrace." Whatever we tolerated in the past, we should set new standards.

Others considered the Cheltzie case ridiculous—a prime example of using the law to deal with issues that should be dealt with in schools and neighborhoods. Sexual-harassment charges because a six-year-old boy was using naughty language? Why hadn't Sue Mutziger called the boy's mother before filing the case with the Office of Civil Rights? Critics charged that Sue Mutziger was a publicity hound who exploited her daughter like a stage mother. She had hired an attorney who specialized in book and movie deals, not in the legalities of sexual harassment. Mutziger and her attorney had called a press conference partly to announce the creation of a clearinghouse for information about sexual harassment among students "Stop the BUS! (Behavior Unruly Sexual)."

"Anita Hill brought to the attention of America the problem of sexual harassment. Cheltzie brought it home," said the attorney in a prepared statement at their press conference. Cheltzie and her mother had been featured on talk shows like *Good Morning America* and *Sally Jessy Raphael.*

National publications like *Newsweek* and *People* magazine interviewed them. Was this good for Cheltzie?

If any child abuse was going on here, one social commentator bristled, the abuser was Cheltzie's neurotic mother. Sue Mutziger was after big bucks, said the cynics. The U.S. Supreme Court had just handed down a decision in the cases of Christine Franklin that enabled victims of sexual harassment to sue and collect financial damages from school districts. In another case in the news, a Minnesota court had awarded a young woman $15,000 because of mental anguish she had endured when school administrators had not acted fast enough to remove sexual vulgarities about her from the restroom walls. Financial penalties were also awaiting a school district that hadn't done enough to quash a list circulating through the high school that described twenty-five girls and their sexual attractions.

A single parent working on a master's degree in counseling, Cheltzie's mother dismissed all such accusations about her hidden motives. She was limiting the public exposure her daughter got. Anyway, it was good experience for Cheltzie, who wanted to be a model. In Mutziger's view, anyone who raises the uncomfortable issue of sexual harassment will face such demeaning accusations. But the issue was her daughter's emotional health. What little boys learn about how they can treat little girls teaches men how they can treat women.

Social critic Camille Paglia, commenting on television about a similar case, was more concerned about what the little girls were learning about standing up for themselves. This is just another case, she argued, of trying to protect middle-class white girls from every hurtful experience in life. We do them no favor.

Suppose Cheltzie hears the same language in a neighborhood park? asked a teacher. Will her mother sue the park system? What if Cheltzie hears the same language in the grocery store? Will her mother sue the store owner?

In the middle of all this controversy and media attention, the Office of Civil Rights conducted its investigation of the events. Was seven-year-old Cheltzie Mutziger sexually harassed by six- and nine-year-old boys? Had the school district failed to take effective action to protect Cheltzie and to prevent a sexually hostile environment toward girls in its schools?

QUESTIONS TO CONSIDER

1. Would you call what happened to Cheltzie on the bus "sexual harassment"? What about the sexual slurs, grabbing, or bra snapping that happens to intermediate-school girls? What makes something sexual harassment? Does the age of the children matter?

    Suppose a boy grabs for another boy's crotch—another incident reported in the Eden Prairie School District. Should this behavior be written up on the forms required to report sexual harassment?

2. Why did it make so much difference to the Office of Civil Rights and to Ms. Mutziger to label what happened on the bus as "sexual harassment" rather than "bad language"? What do the two different labels imply in terms of symbolism and remedies?

3. According to common definitions, whether an action is considered to be sexual harassment depends on the female's reaction, on whether she sees the attention as wanted or unwanted. Some criticize this standard as being too subjective—the male's behavior is an offense or not, depending on how the female sees it, rather than on the objective behavior itself. Others argue that it is obvious whether or not the female wants the attention.

   Consider the following situation. You are a teacher walking down the hall, and you see a high-school male drop his notebook. An attractive girl bends down and picks it up for him. "I give you a 10," he says. The girl looks pleased.

   You have just witnessed an "ass check." Should you say or do anything? What if the girl looked angry and upset? Should you then say or do anything?

4. Was the school district right to allow more tolerance for the misconduct of special education students, who may have less control over their behavior? Or should these students be held to the same standards as others when it comes to sexual language and behavior?

5. Do you agree or disagree with Superintendent McCoy's view that putting video-cameras on every bus would create a Big Brother atmosphere and undermine the goal of teaching students self-discipline?

6. What do you think Cheltzie was learning from the way her mother handled the bus situation? How would you have handled the problem if you had been Cheltzie's parent?

7. As the media played up Cheltzie's story, the anger and hostility surrounding her increased. Other children at school teased her. If you were Cheltzie's elementary schoolteacher, what would you say to the class? Would you do anything to protect Cheltzie?

8. Schoolchildren are often teased severely in ways that create a hostile school environment that interferes with their learning. To call a girl "fatty," for example, may upset her far more than calling her a "slut." Should the schools prevent this type of teasing as well?

Epilogue

[Keep in mind that sexual harassment is an area of the law that is in a state of flux and evolving. The Office of Civil Rights, Region V, in Chicago, decided this case on the basis of many considerations—relevant federal legislation, the policies of the school district, the particular facts of the case.

This decision should not be regarded as "the law" on the matter of whether sexual slurs by primary-grade students constitutes sexual harassment. Rather, this is the decision that the Office of Civil Rights made in one region, given this particular set of circumstances.]

The Office of Civil Rights (OCR) decided that Cheltzie had been sexually harassed:

> Sexual harassment is defined as verbal or physical conduct of a sexual nature, imposed on the basis of sex, by an employee or student, which is unwelcome, hostile, or intimidating. . . .
>   The existence of a sexually hostile environment is determined from the viewpoint of a reasonable person in the victim's situation.

Even if the boys and girls in the primary grades did not know the meanings of the words, the OCR ruled, sexual harassment had occurred. "In this case, there is no question that even the youngest girls understood that the language and conduct being used were expressions of hostility toward them on the basis of their sex and, as a clear result, were offended and upset."

The OCR did not accept the school district's contention that special education students should be treated differently. "The rights of students with disabilities," the report stated, "may not operate as a defense of behavior which singles out students, because of their sex, for adverse consequences."

Not only had sexual harrassment occurred, said the OCR, but the school district failed to correct it. The coordinator's initial investigation

> did not satisfy the criteria for a complete and thorough investigation: questioning of students was done on the bus and without the privacy necessary to enable students to talk freely without worrying about "tattling," no records were kept of the discussions with students, the complainant's daughter was not questioned, the identity of all of the students identified as possible perpetrators was not established, and the nature and scope of the problem itself was understood only as swearing or bad language rather than harassment directed at female children.

The OCR also found that other students in the intermediate grades in the school district had been sexually harassed. A sexually hostile environment had arisen on bus routes and a playground and in school hallways.

The school district did not accept the OCR's decision, disagreeing both on matters of fact and on whether or not the district was in violation of Title IX. Nonetheless, the district entered into a voluntary settlement agreement to end the matter. According to the settlement agreement, the school district would take further steps to define specifically what misconduct constituted sexual harassment, to determine in each individual case whether sexual harassment occurred, to document each occurrence, and to develop disciplinary sanctions. Parents, students, and school staff would be informed about the sexual-harassment policy. Staff who failed to respond appropriately would be reprimanded or disciplined.

ACTIVITIES

1. Discuss in small groups your personal experiences regarding sexual language and sexual touchings as a child. What was the adult response? How did you feel about it? What did you do to avoid it? Were there any instances in which you enjoyed the sexual attention? How did it differ from attention that is considered harassment?

   Write a definition of sexual harassment, in your words. Does your definition apply to young children?

2. Ride a school bus and observe students, or observe them on the playground or in the hallways. Note sexual language and sexual touchings. How do the students and the adults respond? Which behaviors would you classify as sexual harassment, and why?

3. Talk to a school principal about how sexual-harassment issues are handled. What is done about bad language, and how does the principal distinguish that from sexual harassment? How would the principal handle slurs written on the wall, sexual gestures or language in the hallway, and sexually hostile behavior by special education students?

   Does the school or school district have a formal policy about sexual harassment? If so, obtain a copy, and ask the principal to describe how the policy is carried out.

READINGS

Eaton, S. (1993). Sexual harassment at an early age: New cases are changing the rules for schools. *Harvard Education Letter* IX (4, July–August): 1–5.

Stein, N. (1992). School harassment—an update. *Education Week* (November 4).

Strauss, S. (1988). Sexual harassment in the school: Legal implications for principals. *NASSP Bulletin* (March), 93–97.

Will, G. (1993). Liberals going on playground patrol. *Seattle Post-Intelligencer* (September 24), A13.

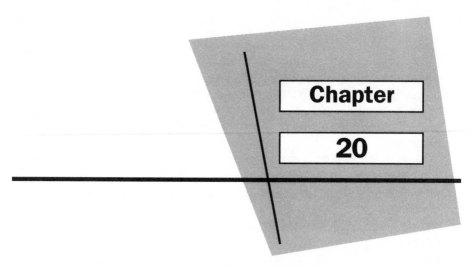

Lisa's Complaint

Edward Miller*

Lisa Jackson, 14, kept her eyes glued to the poem that Mr. Wickman had just asked the ninth-grade English class to read, but she couldn't shut out the kissing and sucking sounds coming from behind her. She remembered her friend Joanne's advice: "The creeps just want to see you react. Don't give them the satisfaction."

The sounds changed to heavy breathing and low moaning. Lisa's face flushed. Finally she turned her head and whispered, "Stop it, Bobby."

Bobby Marshall, who sat directly behind Lisa, chuckled and looked at his friend Richard in the next row. He and Richard were teammates on the freshman football squad.

Bobby leaned forward and made a lewd comment about Lisa's breasts. He spoke just loudly enough for Richard to hear. The boys giggled and sputtered.

Lisa looked up at Mr. Wickman with a pleading expression just as he asked the class, "Who's finished reading the poem?" Peering out from behind his desk at the front of the room, he saw Lisa's upturned face and said, "Lisa? Good. Will you tell us what you think the poet means here by the word *sleep*?"

Lisa looked down again quickly, ashamed and confused, and said nothing. Mr. Wickman made a mark in his daily grade book. Behind Lisa, Bobby said, "I'll see you in my wet dreams, baby."

•

*Reprinted with permission from *The Harvard Education Letter*, Vol. 9, No. 4, July/August 1993, p. 5. Copyright © 1993 by the President and Fellows of Harvard College. All rights reserved.

Ann Danton, the guidance counselor, said to Assistant Principal Caroline Morgan, "I think you ought to talk to Lisa Jackson. After the assembly on the new sexual harassment policy, she gave me the impression that she might be a victim. I've been worried about her anyway. She's failing English and math. She's always struggled with language arts, but I feel she could be doing better. Something's troubling her."

Caroline retrieved Lisa's file. Her grades were mostly C's and D's, but there was no disciplinary record. Her teachers described her as "immature" and "lacking social skills."

Soon Lisa was sitting nervously in the young assistant principal's office. Caroline closed the door. "Lisa, you were at the assembly when I explained the definition of sexual harassment, weren't you?" Lisa nodded. "Is somebody doing that to you?"

Lisa looked as if she were about to cry. "Yes," she said at last, "but I shouldn't have said anything to Ms. Danton. I don't want to get anyone in trouble."

Caroline moved her chair closer and put her arm around the girl. She again explained the school's policy on harassment, emphasizing that the first step in making a complaint did not involve punishment. "You're not getting anybody in trouble," she said. "You're the one who's got the trouble, and it's important to do something about it."

After much prodding and encouragement, Lisa poured out the whole story. Bobby, Richard, and three other boys had been making sexual comments for several weeks. Bobby had also pushed Lisa up against her locker and squeezed her breast and buttocks. The latest thing was the noises in class.

Caroline was a little surprised when she heard the boys' names. They were not what she would call "troubled" kids; they were "regular" guys, well liked by students and staff.

Caroline and Lisa pulled their chairs up to the computer and called up the sexual harassment memo format that the principal's harassment task force had developed. Though Lisa struggled to find the right words, with Caroline's help she wrote a memo to Bobby and the other boys, following the format called for in the harassment policy. She described in specific, graphic detail what they had said and done, how it had made her feel, and what she wanted them to do about it.

"When you said 'I'll see you in my wet dreams' in English class on Monday," she wrote, "I felt embarrassed and dirty. When you made sucking sounds and talked about my 'tits' I felt angry and ashamed. And when you pushed me and touched me in the hallway last week I was afraid. I don't want you to say those things anymore and I don't want you to do those things anymore."

•

Lisa sat pensively reading the finished memo over and over. She knew that the next step was for Caroline, as assistant principal, to deliver the memo in person to each of the boys and to warn them officially. Though there would be no punishment or disciplinary hearing at this stage, if Caroline received any further complaints of sexual harassment about them, she would take formal action.

But Caroline needed Lisa's permission to deliver the memo.

"No, I can't do it," Lisa finally said. "This paper will just make things worse. I don't know what they might do to me. Please, Ms. Morgan, don't say anything to them."

Nothing Caroline could say would change Lisa's mind. And the school policy strictly prohibited delivering Lisa's memo without her written permission.

QUESTIONS TO CONSIDER

1. What, if anything, should Caroline Morgan do now? Would it be wise to talk to other school administrators or staff about the case? To Lisa's parents? What might she say to Mr. Wickman, the English teacher, or to the freshman football coach? What kinds of written records should she be keeping?

2. How realistic are Lisa's fears of retaliation?

3. What are the school's legal and ethical responsibilities toward the students involved in the case? For example, what would the legal ramifications be if Caroline Morgan takes no additional action and the following week Bobby Marshall forces Lisa Jackson into the football team's equipment room after school and rapes her?

4. What if Lisa had given Caroline permission to deliver the memo, and Bobby had denied the charges, called Lisa a liar, and demanded a hearing? Should he get it?

5. Judging only from this brief version of events, do you think there might be problems with this school's policy on sexual harassment? For example, should students be required to write a letter to the perpetrators before the school will handle the problem? Elizabeth Bradley (1993), assistant superintendent for instruction in Hamburg, New York, points out, "If Lisa had been punched, would we have told her that she needed to write a letter to her attacker before we were able to do anything?"

ACTIVITIES

1. Following is the actual text of the harassment policy of the high school at which the incidents in "Lisa's Complaint" took place. The policy appears in the student handbook. Read the policy, and identify its strengths and weaknesses. Consider what injustices to victims, perpetrators, and innocent students might be done through this policy and how these injustices could be prevented.

2. Identify chilling effects that this policy might have on freedom of speech and on the discussion of controversial issues and ideas in the classroom.

3. Rewrite the harassment policy to correct the problems you identified in activities 1 and 2.

Harassment Policy

Harassment of any kind is strictly prohibited at [name of high school]. Harassment refers to conduct, behavior, or comments that are personally offensive, degrading, or threatening to others. This policy refers to, but is not limited to, insulting or harmful comments or actions based on a person's race, gender, religion, sexual orientation, national origin, or disability. It is important that students understand and be sensitive to the fact that what might seem acceptable or even well-intentioned can easily be hurtful and demeaning to the recipient. Examples of harassment include, but are not limited to, threats, sexually suggestive remarks, unsolicited physical contact, unwelcome and insulting gestures, and the display or circulation of written materials or pictures that are degrading to any individual, or any ethnic, religious, or gender group.

Any student who feels that he or she has been the victim of any form of harassment should report this immediately to a teacher, counselor, or administrator. These reports will be treated with utmost sensitivity to the feelings and wishes of the person reporting the incident. Every effort will be made to assist the individual or group in communicating to the offender the exact nature of the incident, the feelings it created, and a clear request that the behavior stop immediately. A response to a reported case of harassment will occur only with the consent of the aggrieved party.

Procedure for Handling Cases of Harassment

When a student accuses another student of harassment, the "victim" is encouraged to write the "harasser" a letter as soon after the incident as possible, using the format below. After the letter is written—and an administrator or teacher can help the student write the letter—the principal hand-delivers the letter to the "harasser." When delivering the letter, the administrator tells the student that the letter is not a disciplinary action; rather, the letter is meant to communicate with the student and to educate the student about the impact of his/her actions. If the harassment stops, nothing further will happen. However, if it doesn't stop, serious consequences will occur.

Letter Format (printed on letterhead)

Date
To: (Name of "harasser")

- Describe exactly what happened, when it happened (how often it happened), and where it happened.
- How did this make you feel? (angry, embarrassed, helpless, uncomfortable, etc.)
- Request that this behavior stop. Explain that if it stops, nothing further will be done about it; but if it doesn't stop, it will be considered harassment and further action will be taken.

Full name and signature of student writing the letter
cc: (Administrator)

READINGS

Bradley, B. (1993). The burden of harassment. *Harvard Education Letter* IX (6, November–December).

Hentoff, N. (1992). *Free speech for me—But not for thee.* New York: HarperCollins.

Roiphe, K. (1993). *The morning after: Sex, fear, and feminism on campus.* Boston: Little, Brown.

Stein, N. D. (1993). Sexual harassment in schools. *School Administrator* 50 (1, January): 14–16, 19, 21.

Strauss, S., and P. Espeland. (1992). *Sexual harassment and teens: A program for positive change.* Minneapolis: Free Spirit Publishing.

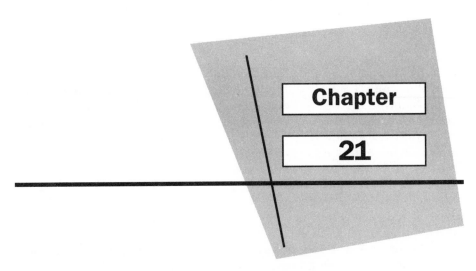

Chapter

21

When Good Intentions Aren't Enough

Samuel S. Wineburg*

Her name was Rosa, and I was her teacher. Strikingly pretty, she struggled over texts easily managed by an able fourth-grader. But Rosa was 15, and a member of my Title I remedial English group in an inner-city high school in northern California. She sat in my third-period class with a permanent scowl on her face, expressing her discomfort to Luis and Carlos, the two other native Spanish speakers in the group. To me, she said little except for curt inquiries about her grades and what she needed to do to avoid an F.

Rosa lived in a Spanish world. She spoke Spanish at home, at her job in a *taqueria,* with her friends, and, prior to her freshman year in high school, in her public school classes in southern California. Rosa considered English an intrusion, a trial to be endured. When I asked her what she planned to do for the written portion of her driving test, a test she desperately wanted to pass, she responded triumphantly by opening her purse and brandishing the official instruction manual—*en español.*

The differences between us were deep and, in moments of frustration, unbridgeable, I thought. Here I was, a gallant Jewish liberal, educated in an august New England college, out to bring the salvation of education to the under-privileged of the inner city. After my first few weeks at the school, I diagnosed the problem as one of relevance—what intelligent person in his or her right mind could get motivated by reading about the production of paper in British Columbia or the habits of beavers in Vermont? I asked my students what they were interested in, and their answers—Madonna, AC/DC, Kiss, Prince—made up my mind. I knew it! To hell with basal readers;

*Reprinted with permission of the *Phi Delta Kappan* (Volume 68, Number 7, pages 544–545, 1987).

bring on *Rolling Stone, Tiger Beat,* and, in a pitch of daring, the issue of *Time* with the "Private Life of Michael Jackson" emblazoned on the cover.

Relevance, I quickly learned, was but a mote in the larger configuration of problems that I was to encounter. The deeply held assumptions that I brought into the classroom were only slowly surfacing in my consciousness.

Foremost among these were beliefs about the importance of written texts and the central place they should occupy in even the most mundane of existences. Reading was the lifeblood of my own existence, an act so sacred that I failed to recognize even the possibility of apostasy. Sure, my students said that they hated reading and that books were boring, but I interpreted these sentiments as defense mechanisms, developed over years of failure and disappointment.

As the year wore on, however, I listened to and reflected on my students' comments. I sensed that books and texts—indeed, the whole act of reading—were instrumental to them. They represented something to do to *get* something else, like a driver's license or a passport. Sneaking a book underneath the covers with a miniature flashlight and savoring the stillness of a house in slumber was a world foreign to my students.

Most of all to Rosa. Nothing I did seemed to reach her. When I tried speaking Spanish, she muttered derisively, *tortuga,* turtle.

Undaunted, I keep trying. I brought in articles about Madonna, her idol, and I encouraged her as she stumbled over the simplest sentences. Sometimes she would try, usually with a brush in her hand to let me know that reading would not get in the way of her grooming, but I didn't care. I was pleased by any sign of progress.

When Luis and Carlos snickered as Rosa tripped over "easy" words, I fumed and let them know that I would have none of it. In my reading group, attempts to learn would not become the butt of cheap jokes. Rosa sided with her ridiculers and turned against me, crumpling up articles and tossing them on the floor. With her characteristic scowl, she announced that my attempt to engineer a learning experience was really "pretty stupid."

I could understand Rosa's frustration (or so I thought). But what really perplexed me was the way she acted when we bumped into each other in the hallways or in line in the lunchroom. On such occasions, she was all smiles. She never missed the opportunity to whisper to her friends, "El es mi maestro en inglés." I wondered to myself about the ways I had structured my reading groups, and despite the assurance of my supervisor (an able woman whom I respected highly), I concluded that my "educational environment" was sterile. There was nothing personal about it.

I have always valued teachers who are genuinely interested in their students, who learn their names quickly, who are aware of day-to-day changes in their students' lives. One morning, Rosa came to the group with a new hairdo. Insead of straight jet-black hair flowing down onto her shoulders, she wore it up, in carefully crafted curls.

What I said was innocent enough: "I really like your hair, Rosa." I wanted to let her know that she was not just any student, but an individual, someone I could compliment not just on her reading but on other things as well. It was a nicety (actually, the curls looked artificial and I didn't *really* like them), a social grace, a well-meaning way of letting her know that I noticed.

Soon afterward, Rosa began cutting class. In the hallways, she averted her eyes and pretended not to notice me. When I issued a "pink warning slip" to her counselor, she showed up for class, but as soon as I asked her to read, she heaved her chair against the wall and dashed from the room in a huff. What had I done? Where had I failed? Beverly, my supervisor, also wanted to know.

Two weeks passed before Beverly told me that Rosa had been transferred to another reading group. Beverly said that she had a few questions to ask me. The assistant principal wanted to know whether I had ever said or done anything that might have led Rosa to thinking that I had any "noneducational" (a delicate way of saying prurient) interest in her.

Me?! A pedophile?! A white Jewish liberal in the tradition of Kozol and Kohl? Come off it! Beverly's questions became more pointed. Was it not true that I had mentioned to Rosa that I liked her hair, that I had said that I liked her blouse? Well, yes, but it was a ploy, part of an effort to personalize the classroom, to make a more humane place. Was I aware, Beverly asked, of what it means for an older man to remark to a 15-year-old Roman Catholic *chicana* from a traditional home that he "likes her hair?" But I was only trying to. . . . No, I didn't know. Given my background, how could I have known?

This story is true. Although I was unable to help Rosa, I did get a glimpse of the complexity of cultures in conflict. We bring to the classroom a freight of cultural assumptions—assumptions so deeply embedded that it can take an incident as unexpected as this to shock us into an awareness of our differences. "Innocent" and "well-meaning" are truly in the eyes of the beholder.

QUESTIONS TO CONSIDER

1. How does the teacher diagnose the problem with Rosa? What does he see as the basic problems, and what strategies does he decide to try?

2. What assumptions does this teacher make regarding how to create good relationships with students, particularly women? Consider the problem of authenticity, when he says he likes her blouse and hair.

3. The teacher says, "Given my background, how could I have known?" How do you think the teacher's own cultural background affected how he responded to Rosa? Should he have known how what he was doing would be interpreted? How could he have found out?

4. Could Rosa have understood this teacher's behavior quite well, on the basis of her own years of experience with teachers, and reported him to the assistant principal as another way to resist learning to read English? With the benefit of hindsight, how would you advise a new student teacher in this classroom to approach Rosa?

ACTIVITIES

1. Write a story about an event that occurred in your life in which a well-meant action on your part was completely misinterpreted by others. Identify the assumptions you held before the event. What did you learn? Develop some generalizations that might be instructive to teachers working with students of different genders or cultures.

2. View films that portray examples of misunderstandings which arise from differences in gender, class, and cultural backgrounds. A popular example is *Educating Rita* (1984), starring Michael Caine and Julie Walters, in which conflicts between an older male professor and a young female student center on both class and gender differences.[1] An academic example is *Multicultural Britain: Crosstalk* (from the National Centre of Industrial Language Training, Commission for Racial Equality, London, England; produced by John Twitchin).

   Identify the miscommunications that arise from differences in the characters' backgrounds, and suggest how these problems could be addressed.

READINGS

Bilingual Education Office, California State Department of Education. (1986). *Beyond language: Social and cultural factors in schooling language minority students.* Los Angeles, Calif.: Evaluation, Dissemination and Assessment Center, California State University, Los Angeles.

McIntosh, P. (1990). White privilege: Unpacking the invisible knapsack. *Independent School* 49 (2): 31–36.

McKenna, T., and F. I. Ortiz (eds.). (1988). *The broken web: The educational experiences of Hispanic American women.* Berkeley: Thomas Rivera Center and Floricanto Press.

[1]We are indebted to Diane Brunner for this teaching suggestion. A discussion of this film, from a feminist perspective, may be found in Diane Brunner, "*Educating Rita* and the Struggle for Voice," Department of English, Michigan State University.

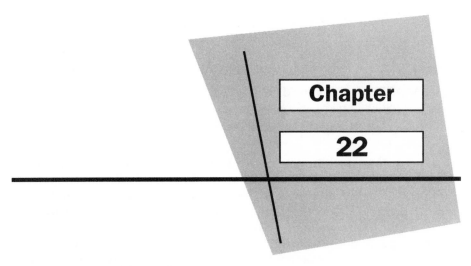

Chapter

22

Who Is the Victim?

Traci Bliss

Shannon Rice, a senior at McCally High School, was a straight-A student who had received early admission to an Ivy League college. Statuesque at 5 feet, 9 inches, Shannon was known throughout McCally as a "real flirt." Jeffrey Monroe, thirty-three years old and a tenured history teacher, was aware of her reputation when he hired her as his student aide. He said his decision was based on her fine performance when she was a junior in his advanced placement U.S. History course. Boyish and athletic, Jeffrey called himself a "family man."

In December 1991, Jeffrey received a full-faced glamour photo from Shannon with the following inscription: "To Mr. Monroe—a great, terrific, nice-looking, nice-bodied, looks like a good sex partner (hopefully I'll find out) kinda guy. luv ya." A month before receiving the picture, Jeffrey had been talking with Shannon and several of her friends about the contents of a letter. Suddenly, Shannon blurted out, "He ate her out, and she gave him a blow job." Without batting an eye, Jeffrey wrote *fellatio* on a piece of paper and handed it to Shannon, saying, "Look that up in the library."

Jeffrey Monroe discussed these incidents with his principal on March 13, 1992, when Shannon Rice brought the following charges against him: terroristic threatening, harassment, harassing communications, and sexual abuse in the third degree. Two days later, Monroe was suspended from McCally without pay for "conduct unbecoming a teacher." In compliance with state statutes, Dr. Herman Boyd, Monroe's superintendent, submitted a report to the Education Professional Standards Commission. The report included a third incident between Monroe and Rice which occurred on Valentine's Day. Mr. Monroe had given a handful of store-bought candy hearts to Ms. Rice during a break in the class period. She returned the hearts with her handwritten inscriptions, including the following:

> Then, stick your dick in.
> Stick it everywhere.
> Do you want to fuck me?
> I luv your big dick.

According to Dr. Boyd's report, Monroe's suspension was based on his "inaction" relative to Ms. Rice's conduct. Boyd cited the student code of conduct, which "establishes that teachers have responsibility to maintain a positive professional attitude and behavior toward all students." Boyd went on to write, "Your keeping of the picture and the candy hearts depicts failure to maintain a professional attitude and behavior toward her." Jeffrey's explanation was that he did not believe Shannon was trying to seduce him but rather was just being flirtatious, and for that reason he never told her that the conduct was improper.

Exactly six weeks after his suspension from teaching, Jeffrey was tried in a state district court on charges of harassment and sexual abuse in the third degree. The other two charges against him—terroristic threatening and harassing communications—were dropped. The state statutes applicable to Jeffrey Monroe's case provide the following definitions of the two charges for which he was tried:*

A. Harassment. — (1) A person is guilty of harassment when with intent to harass, annoy or alarm another person he:
   (a) Strikes, shoves, kicks or otherwise subjects him to physical contact or attempts or threatens to do the same; or
   (b) In a public place, makes an offensively coarse utterance, gesture or display, or addresses abusive language to any person present; or
   (c) Follows a person in or about a public place or places; or
   (d) Engages in a course of conduct or repeatedly commits acts which alarm or seriously annoy such other person and which serve no legitimate purpose.
   (2) Harassment is a violation.
B. Sexual Abuse in the Third Degree. — (1) A person is guilty of sexual abuse in the third degree when:
   (a) He subjects another person to sexual contact without the latter's consent.

Shannon did not appear at the trial, but in a deposition she stated that the teacher had sent gifts from lingerie stores, called her at home and talked sexually, showed her pornographic materials and letters, made numerous sexual suggestions, and touched her breast and warned her not to tell anyone about it.

The jury found Jeffrey Monroe not guilty of sexual abuse but con-

---

*The state supreme court later ruled that the state statute on harassment containd unconstitutional interference with freedom of speech.

victed him of harassment—a misdemeanor for which he was fined $250. He remained suspended from his position at McCally for the remainder of the academic year; for the 1992–93 year he was assigned to Conard, another high school in the same district.

In late May, Superintendent Boyd made a second report to the Education Professional Standards Commission to provide full facts and circumstances concerning the conviction on sexual harassment charges. Included was Jeffrey Monroe's response to the first-semester incident, when he told Shannon Rice to look up the word *fellatio*. "Monroe wanted her to understand there are other words that we have that relate the same message in a much more genteel way. In retrospect, Mr. Monroe realized it was probably a mistake."

Jeffrey Monroe then sent his own letter requesting that the commission, composed mostly of teachers, not conduct a hearing to determine whether he should have his teaching certificate revoked: "I have already served the suspension without pay, and the related criminal charges received much publicity, resulting in severe embarrassment to me and my family. I feel that I have been punished severely enough." Mr. Monroe said that he recognized that his failure to report receipt of the materials from Ms. Rice in a timely manner was an error in judgment. He also wanted the commission to be aware of his excellent teaching record.

In October 1992, the Education Professional Standards Commission held a five-hour hearing in the case of Mr. Jeffrey Monroe. Accompanied by his wife, Monroe brought character witnesses who testified on his behalf. The prosecuting attorney for the commission produced no witnesses. The findings of fact from the hearing included the following points:

= Mr. Monroe chose not to appeal the harassment conviction, even though he believed the charges were unfounded, because of the publicity that would result from the continued litigation.
= The jury's decision that Mr. Monroe was not guilty of sexual abuse supports his assertion that he did not have any improper physical contact with the student aide.
= Mr. Monroe testified that he never made any improper comments or suggestions to the student aide and did not have any physical contact with her. He admits that he made an error in judgment by not reporting to his superiors sexual comments made by the student aide.
= The principal of Conard High School testified on behalf of Mr. Monroe. He has been satisfied with his work and wants him to continue teaching at Conard.
= Jeffrey Monroe stated that as a result of the charges and conviction he has changed his teaching style to put more distance between himself and his students.

The prosecuting attorney recommended a temporary suspension of Jeffrey Monroe's license, citing the results of the criminal proceedings. The commission concluded that while Monroe did exercise poor judgment with regard to the student aide, the evidence did not support suspension of his teaching certificate. The case was dismissed on October 7, and Monroe continued teaching at Conard High School, to which he had been transferred.

QUESTIONS TO CONSIDER

1. Jeffrey Monroe was suspended for "inaction" when Shannon Rice made advances toward him. In his view, he had done nothing except ignore Shannon's behavior. Should he have taken action? If so, what should he have done, and at what point? If he had returned the picture and the candy, as the superintendent suggested, would his professional responsibilities have ended? Should he have contacted the principal? Shannon's parents?

2. Do you share Monroe's viewpoint that he did not do anything wrong? What should he have done about the "fellatio incident"? Could he have created a supportive environment for Shannon's behavior?

3. Teachers sometimes find themselves the recipient of genuine affection from students. How would you handle the following situation, which is not unusual? A young male teacher received several love letters (none with sexual language) from one of his senior students. The teacher wanted to stop the behavior but also wished to be sensitive to the student's feelings. He met in his office with her and explained that he was glad to have her as a student but that the letters were not appropriate. He returned her letters but said that he was flattered by her feelings. What do you think of this teacher's response? If he had come to you for advice, what would you have told him?

Epilogue*

Almost three years after the Education Professional Standards Commission voted to allow Jeffrey Monroe to retain his certificate, he came before the commission a second time. The allegations focused on his having had sexual intercourse with a minor female student and sexually harassing other female students. On this occasion, the commission revoked his certificate for fifty-five years based on "immoral acts with students."

QUESTIONS TO CONSIDER

1. The Education Professional Standards Commission made its first decision about Jeffrey Monroe without foresight about such future events. Considering the evidence they had at the time of the earlier incidents, do you agree with their decision?

*We received this epilogue about a year after the case was written.

2. What is the school administration's responsibility in such situations? Analyze the reasons for Monroe's transfer to another school. Consider what happened to his students when he resumed teaching. What other actions could the administration have taken?

ACTIVITIES

1. Look up the professional code of conduct for teachers in your state. The code is usually available from teachers' union representatives or from the state licensing board. Did Monroe violate this professional code of conduct? In what ways? If the code does not cover his behavior, would you revise it to do so? How?

2. Interview male and female students about whether they or their friends have ever received sexual attentions from a teacher. Ask them what, if anything, they did about it, and why. Consider their responses in light of the power differences between teachers and students.

3. Interview counselors and teachers' union representatives about their experiences with sexual accusations on the part of students and sexual encounters between students and teachers. What do they see as the central issues? How do they recommend teachers and students protect themselves?

READINGS

Sorenson, G. T. (1991). Sexual abuse in schools: Reported court cases from 1987–1990. *Educational Administration Quarterly* 27 (4, November): 460–480.

Strauss, S. (1988). Sexual harassment in schools: Legal implications for principals. *NASSP Bulletin* 72 (506, March): 93–97.

Valente, W. D. (1990). School district and official liability for teacher sexual abuse of students under 42 U.S.C. Section 1983. *West Education Law Reporter* 57 (3): 645–659.

Zirkel, T. A. (1988). Wrongs by Wright: Liability for sexual abuse. *Phi Delta Kappan* (February), 451–452.

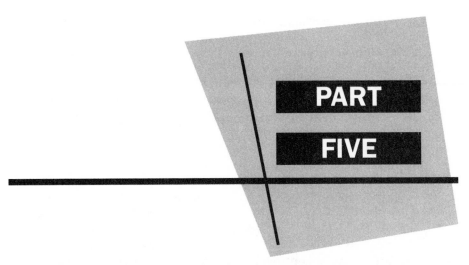

PART

FIVE

Sexual Slurs, Sexual Stereotyping, and the Marketplace of Ideas

Introduction

At the center of intense and important debates in American society is a conflict in fundamental values—the importance of freedom of speech versus guarantees of equality and respect for women. This value conflict is at the heart of bitter controversies about censorship, pornography, and speech codes in schools.

From the perspective of many feminists, our society—indeed the very language we speak—has been constructed with a bias that privileges men (Spender, 1980). The words we use exert a powerful influence on our thoughts and our attitudes. If we use words like *chairman* rather than *chairperson*, we construct the view that men, rather than women, hold roles of leadership and power. If we use the pronoun *he* and omit the pronoun *she*, we communicate the view that females are too unimportant to deserve mention.

Similarly, the images of females in literature and in the media shape what we believe girls and women are and can do. If we read constantly about models like passive Becky in Mark Twain's *Tom Sawyer*—a girl who cries and waits to die when lost in a dark cave while plucky Tom figures a way out—we will assume that females give up when trouble comes and that males have the courage and competence to solve problems. If we want to improve the status of females, we must change our language and our images—no matter how uncomfortable and daunting a task it might be.

The most damaging and degrading images, in this view, are those which portray females in sexual terms. Sexual representations place women in a subordinate position, as people whose basic function lies in giving pleasure to men. This sexual exploitation humiliates women and prevents them from full and equal participation in American life (MacKinnon, 1987). As a government institution, entrusted with socializing children, public schools should present respectful images of females that underscore their equality with males.

In opposition to this viewpoint are those who consider freedom of thought and expression as the most vital of our rights, guaranteed to all American citizens in the First Amendment to the Constitution. In this view, freedom of speech is a precious liberty easily brushed aside in the pressure to accomplish some immediate good—the elimination of offensive language, the creation of community, the desire to spare people's feelings. In every historical period, people strive to eliminate the heresy of their times, to suppress some idea they find hateful and offensive.

According to this perspective, freedom of speech is important to liberty itself, to our sense of personal freedom and dignity. Freedom of speech is vital to the political discussion in a democracy and vital to the search for truth. Only in a free marketplace of ideas can we hear different voices, some of which will be in error, some of which will be hateful, but some of which will speak new and valuable truths. As the famous historian C. Vann Woodward argues in his report on freedom of expression to the Yale Corporation, "The history of intellectual growth and discovery clearly demonstrates the need for unfettered freedom, the right to think the unthinkable, discuss the unmentionable, and challenge the unchallengable" (Hentoff, 1992, 115).

Unless schools educate children about the value of freedom of speech, say advocates of free speech, we will lose this right and protection. "Liberty lies in the hearts of men and women," Justice Learned Hand eloquently puts it (1944, 190). "When it dies there, no constitution, no law, no court can save it."

In opposition to this view, MacKinnon (1987, 208–209) argues that women had no voice in creating the Constitution, a document that protects the freedom and privilege of white men. The marketplace of ideas is a "capitalist metaphor," and freedom of speech has been used "to defend Nazis, the Klan, and pornographers."

This powerful language underscores the high stakes and intense emotions of this debate. Schools are socializing institutions and public school-teachers act as agents of the state. What schools and teachers do makes a great difference—the speech they use, the literature they teach, the values they communicate, and the spirit of their classrooms.

Part Five begins with two cases about very different educational settings in which freedom of expression comes into conflict with respectful language towards females. In the first case " 'T' Is for T-Shirt . . . and Take It to Court," Mark, an excellent student with no intention of creating trouble, wears to school a *Co-Ed Naked Band* T-shirt that his parents gave him for Christmas. In the view of the physical education teacher, the T-shirt sends a sexual message; it thus violates the dress code of the physical education department, which aims to create an emotionally healthy atmosphere for young women in the high school. Acting in the tradition of civil disobedience, Mark and his parents protest. What is at stake, they argue, is the constitutional right to freedom of speech.

The T-shirt case takes place in a public high school. In this setting, the courts have held that school officials have broad, but not total, discretion to regulate dress and language that is disruptive to the educational mission of the school. Is Mark's protest a form of protected political speech?

The second case, "Jockeying for Position: The Battle Over Classroom Speech" takes place in a quite-different educational arena, where the conflict is far more complex—Harvard Law School. This educational institution is a private university, not a public high school, and its students are adults preparing to be lawyers, not adolescents receiving a general education. Professor Ian Macneil is stunned when he gets a letter from the chair of the Harvard Women's Law Association accusing him of making sexist comments in class and writing a textbook that perpetuates images of female subordination. Professor Macneil denies that his language is sexist, and he mounts a counterattack. He accuses the women of seeking to destroy his reputation without giving him the opportunity to respond; he accuses them of "mud-slinging McCarthyism."

The next two cases raise issues concerning the images of women in literature and in students' writing. Again, the age of the students and the type of educational setting may affect your perspective about these issues. We therefore present them in two settings: a public high school and a private women's college. In "The Girls at Central—They Sure Got Nice Behinds" the teacher asks a reluctant writer, José, to write about something he knows and cares about. José writes this sentence, "This Girls in Central they sure got some nice Behnds. It is just Beutiful. . . ." Should Mr. Andrews encourage José to develop his writing and thinking, even if he locates beauty in girls' behinds?

In "March in Minneapolis" the professor, Pam Higgins, is teaching a John Updike story entitled "A&P." This literary classic portrays the sexual thoughts of a young male clerk who sees three girls in bathing suits shopping at a beach-town grocery store. Infuriated by the degrading, sexist images of women, some students ask Pam why she would ever assign such an insulting story. How should teachers deal with literature that contains what some may see as stereotyped, insulting images?

The language that you choose to use as a teacher and the language you encourage your students to use communicates your political positions about gender issues, whether you want it to or not. The literature you assign communicates a view of the world. Great art and great literature portray complicated truths and realities that some may find offensive. Students will write and speak in ways that challenge and offend. We hope these cases offer you the opportunity to think through these crucial and complicated issues.

REFERENCES

Hand, L. (1944). The spirit of liberty. In *The spirit of liberty,* ed. I. Dilliard. New York: Knopf, 1960, 189–191.

Hentoff, N. (1992). *Free speech for me—But not for thee.* New York: HarperCollins.

MacKinnon, C. (1987). *Feminism unmodified: Discourses on life and law.* Cambridge, Mass.: Harvard University Press.

Spender, D. (1980). *Man-made language.* London: Routledge & Kegan Paul.

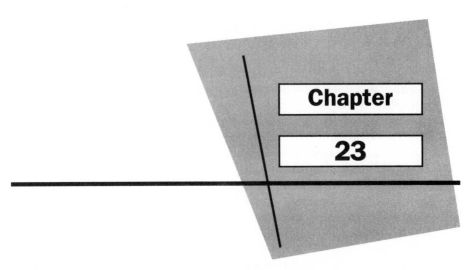

"T" Is for T-Shirt . . . and Take It to Court

Paris Finley

Surveying the packed meeting room, school board member Jack Mullins figured he was in for a long night. Mark, a high-school senior, and his parents had come with an attorney from the American Civil Liberties Union. Preventing Mark from wearing his T-shirt, they argued, was a violation of his constitutional right to freedom of speech.

The teachers at the high school were presenting a petition asking the school board to uphold the dress code, which banned lewd, vulgar, or obscene clothing. The issue had been the subject of newspaper stories and letters to the editor in this small town for weeks.

"At least no one disagreed with the basic facts," Jack Mullins reflected. Mark Evans had worn to physical education class a T-shirt emblazoned with the message *Co-Ed Naked Band. Do It to the Rhythm.* His parents had given him the shirt for Christmas because he played in the school band.

The physical education teacher, Sharon West, was an outspoken feminist at the school, and she had raised the issue with Mark. "Hold on, Mark," she had said, holding up her hand as a stop sign when he started to run his laps. "That shirt—you know the rules. Either change it, or turn it inside out."

"This shirt's OK," Mark had argued.

"If you don't change the shirt, you'll get a zero for the class," she intoned.

"All right, then give me the zero! I'll go to the office!" Mark spun around and left the gym.

Sharon West was surprised. Such behavior was unlike Mark, an excellent and usually cooperative student.

Jack Mullins figured he knew what was really going on. Mark had told the town newspaper that the incident had not been a planned provocation. But Mullins knew the family, and he knew that principles were important in their household.

Mark's father had often voiced his view that feminism and other politically correct movements had reached the point where they were threatening the constitutional right to freedom of speech—freedom to express views that others may find offensive or even hateful. Mark was casting himself in the role of the Iowa high-school student in the famous case of *Tinker v. Des Moines Independent Community School District* (1969). The student in *Tinker* had worn a black armband to school as a protest against the war in Vietnam. Iowa school officials had banned the armband. The case had gone up to the Supreme Court, and the student had won. The Court had held that students and teachers do not "shed their constitutional rights to freedom of speech or expression at the schoolhouse gate." But the Court also had upheld a school's right to regulate students' dress and deportment.

Sharon West was also one to stand on principle. She had been instrumental in helping to formulate the physical education department's dress code. She was concerned about the extent of harassing behavior toward girls in school, and she was adamant about creating an emotionally healthy tone in her classes, free from hostility and sexual harassment. The department's policy read:

> Students are prohibited from wearing any clothing or accessory which jeopardizes the health or safety of other students. Students are prohibited from wearing clothing which is lewd, vulgar, or obscene. Students are prohibited from wearing clothing which advertises drugs, alcohol, or tobacco.

The members of the department interpreted "health" to include "emotional health," and thereby enjoined shirts that were sexist or hostile to any particular group.

The principal had upheld Sharon West and the physical education department. Refusing to accept his ruling, Mark and his parents were appealing to the school board. If the board ruled against them—the ACLU attorney had made clear—they would take the issue to court.

Jack Mullins put on his public face—impassive, noncommittal—and began to listen to the testimony. Mark's parents outlined their position:

> Some think this case too silly to bring to court, but Mark is not demanding the right to wear a T-shirt with sexual innuendo. He is making a much more important point: Ideas we dislike must be permitted to ensure protection for ideals we cherish.

Most of the public testimony took the other side:

> Mark is confusing the right to speak with the unrestrained exercise of that right. Responsibility is the hidden cost of living in a free society [Local pastor].

> Isn't this really a privileged male power trip using up the time, energy, and money of the rest of the town's citizens? [Female teacher].

Sexual harassment is like a mosaic. It's made up of bits and pieces, but it isn't easy to see until it's done. The school must do its best to stop it—one piece at a time [Female teacher].

We are responsible for fostering an atmosphere in this building. The shirt interferes with our basic mission [Principal of the high school].

Several students pointed out that the dress code was unclear. Some teachers were strict, some medium, and some didn't say anything no matter what they wore. Other students, including girls, had worn *Co-Ed Naked Band* shirts to school.

Mark Evans himself held a complex position about the matter. He didn't believe that students should wear sexually suggestive shirts to school. He didn't even want to. Such T-shirts, he believed, should be *censured* but not *censored.* He was acting out of conscience, in the tradition of civil disobedience. As he told a local newspaper reporter: "I want to set an example for students that they need not accept everything authority says. I think we're raising a generation of people who will end up believing that they really have no freedom of expression if it offends somebody."

The testimony went on and on, with each position blurring into the next.

"What did it all boil down to?" Jack Mullins asked himself. "What is at stake here? And which way should I vote regarding the dress code?"

QUESTIONS TO CONSIDER

1. The issue of freedom of speech goes to the core of our society. According to the First Amendment of the United States Constitution, "Congress shall make no law . . . abridging the freedom of speech, or of the press. . . ." Even if speech offends people or hurts people's feelings, advocates insist, a free marketplace of ideas is essential to a free and democratic society. In the famous words of Oliver Wendell Holmes, "If there is any principle of the Constitution that more imperatively calls out for attachment than any other it is the principle of free thought— not free thought for those who agree with us but freedom for the thought we hate" (*U.S. v. Schwimmer,* 1928).

   To many feminists, the principle of free speech has been a paternalistic umbrella under which women have been silenced and victimized. Free speech, they claim, has been used to defend men who control and use women to sell products or indulge in sexual fantasies such as those represented in pornography. Words and images can be used in harmful and threatening ways, particularly by a dominant group. If the law is meant to protect citizens, why is it not fashioned to protect women and members of minority groups to the degree that it protects white males? Is the law a tool of control by the dominant group?

   These competing positions about a great and important question underlie the small issue of Mark Evans's T-shirt. If you were a school board member, would you support Mark's right to wear the T-shirt, or would you take Sharon West's position? Explain your stand.

2. Testing the limits of the dress code, Mark later wore to school a shirt reading: *See Dick drink. See Dick drive. See Dick die. Don't be a Dick.* As a teacher at the school, what position would you take about this shirt? Why?

   Considering the graphics and sexual innuendos that you have seen on the clothing teen-agers wear, where would you draw the line?

3. One teacher at the school adopted the policy of forbidding statements of a sexual nature in class. He noted positive course evaluations from female students describing their enhanced ability to concentrate and learn in this atmosphere. If you were a teacher at the high school, would you adopt a similar policy? Why, or why not?

Epilogue

The school board ruled against Mark Evans and adopted a dress code similar to the one proposed by the physical education department. With the support of the ACLU, the Evans family took the case to court. The judge refused to issue a temporary restraining order against the school district's dress code. As of this writing, the issue is in federal courts.

ACTIVITIES

1. Collect a sample of suggestive or sexual statements that have appeared on T-shirts, posters, and signs in your community. Where should schools draw the line about what can appear on T-shirts and posters in the school? What criteria are you using to make your decision? Would your criteria change depending on the age of the students? Why?

2. Interview the principals of high schools and elementary schools to see how they deal with suggestive or sexual messages that appear on students' clothing and on posters in school. What issues come up, and how are they handled? Does the school district have a policy about this matter? If so, how is the policy interpreted and carried out?

READINGS

Fish, S. (1993). *There's no such thing as free speech and it's a good thing, too.* New York: Oxford University Press.

Hentoff, N. (1993). *Free speech for me—But not for thee.* New York: HarperCollins.

MacKinnon, C. A. (1993). *Only words.* Cambridge, Mass.: Harvard University Press.

Roiphe, K. (1993). *The morning after: Sex, fear, and feminism on campus.* Boston: Little, Brown.

Sunstein, C. R. (1993). *Democracy and the problem of free speech.* New York: Free Press.

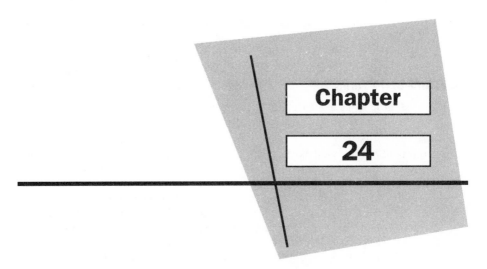

Chapter

24

Jockeying for Position:
The Battle over Classroom Speech

Ian Macneil

PART A

Ian Macneil, a professor at Northwestern University School of Law, was pleased to be invited to be a visiting professor at his alma mater, Harvard Law School, for the 1988–89 academic year. The author of a standard book on contracts, Macneil was scheduled to teach the required first-year Contracts course.

In a *Boston Globe* article on the later controversy, Robert Lowe pointed out that Macneil was a professor in the "Paper Chase" tradition:

> Macneil revived the ancient custom of taking attendance and reporting no-shows for disciplinary action, his students say. He wouldn't let his pupils duck the Socratic line of fire and his questions sometimes seemed relentless.
>
> "He humiliated people," said one student. "He can come down hard on you," said another. "But after class, he's the nicest guy."

In the middle of spring vacation Professor Macneil received the following letter from Bonnie Savage, chair of the Harvard Women's Law Association:

> Dear Professor Macneil,
>
> Repeated instances of sexism in both your contracts textbook and your classroom discussions have been brought to the attention of the Women's Law Association. Furthermore, the Women's Law Association understands that student discussions since October with you and with members of the administration have failed to effect improvement. Just this week students were as-

signed to read page 963 of your textbook, containing the following quote from Byron's "Don Juan" beneath a section entitled, "Jockeying for Position: The Battle of the Forms":

> A little still she strove, and much repented,
> And whispering, "I will ne'er consent,"—
> consented.

A quote about a sexual "jockeying" for power, depicting a woman struggling, repenting, and being dominated, has no place in a contracts textbook. Such remarks not only reveal inappropriate and sexist attitudes but also pose a more serious problem: the Byron quote exemplifies the attitude that "women mean yes when they say no." By quoting such a work inexplicably and out of context, you are promoting a dangerous misperception which has come under fierce attack, particularly in the evolution of rape law.

The following examples show that this is not an isolated incident. . . .

[The letter continues with three other examples from Professor Macneil's textbook and two examples from class discussions.[1] The letter continues:]

> When you encounter gender-specific language, you often have a flippant, disparaging remark to make about the possibility that the language might be sexist:

> "Posner was the grandfather—or should I say grand*mother*—of this idea. . . ."
> "That would be a strawman—or do we use that word any more?"
> "I admit it, I am paternalistic—or do I want to say 'maternalistic'?"
> "Sauce for the goose, sauce for the gander—I don't know, is that sexist?"

> Sexist language is not a joking matter for many of your students. By using sexist language, you encourage sexist thought and, in essence, promote hostility against women, something not foreign on this campus.

> A professor in any position at any school has no right or privilege to use the classroom in such a way as to offend, at the very least, 40% of the students. Indeed, sexism is an affront to the entire law school community. Only by respecting all members of a classroom can a professor earn the respect of even one.

Copies of this letter were sent to the Dean, Dean-Designate, Vice Dean, Appointments Committee Chairman, and the Senior Student Affairs Coordinator.

Macneil later said of this:

> The HWLA letter came like a bolt out of the blue as, among all the slings and arrows concerning the course, there had never been a hint of such concerns from anyone. I knew the class considered me a first-class bastard, but a sexist in the sense of that letter? For just a few minutes alone in my office I felt as if someone had kicked me in the stomach. Twenty-odd years of successfully negotiating academia's ever-enlarging minefields of sensitivity, and now one had blown up right in my face.

---

[1]For the sake of brevity, the other charges and Professor Macneil's responses are given in the appendix to this case.

QUESTIONS TO CONSIDER

1. Do you consider the quotation from Byron's "Don Juan" or the other examples quoted from the textbook and classroom discussion to constitute "sexist language" and "sexist attitudes"?

2. Whether or not the Byron quotation is an apt analogy for the point Professor Macneil is making, would you advise him to retain it in his textbook or to leave it out of a later edition? What is your reasoning?

3. Should Professor Macneil attempt to find out how many students in his classroom may find his classroom language and examples "sexist"? If he finds out that only a miniscule number of women in his class are offended—for example, two or three students out of a hundred or so—would you advise him to change his style of language use in the classroom? What if larger numbers are offended?

4. What, if any, threats to academic freedom do you see in the letter Bonnie Savage wrote on behalf of the Harvard Women's Law Association?

5. What do you think Ms. Savage and the Harvard Women's Law Association are trying to accomplish with this letter? Should they have scheduled a private meeting with Professor Macneil to discuss the situation? Why might they have chosen not to do so?

6. How would you advise Professor Macneil to respond? Would you suggest that his approach be conciliatory or that he defend his classroom examples and language? Should he make apologies? Should he launch a counterattack?

PART B: Professor Macneil's Response

Professor Macneil responded to this letter with a letter of his own to the HWLA, care of Ms. Bonnie Savage. He sent copies of both Ms. Savage's letter and his reply to all the students in his class and all faculty at the Harvard Law School. His letter reads:

> How to address this letter is a puzzlement. Ms. Savage's letter to me of March 23 was signed as being "for" the Harvard Women's Law Association. I can, therefore, only assume that she speaks for and is authorized to speak for the entire association. The following is, therefore, addressed to the association collectively, and not necessarily to individuals who may not have had the opportunity to know of or approve of Ms. Savage's letter.
>
> I note that you have convicted me of the sin of sexism. This conviction has been the result of proceedings of which I was in fact unaware, of which I was given no notice, and in which I have not been heard.[2] The conviction is based on statements of an unnamed informer or informers. (Hereafter informer.) Punishment has already been administered in the form of mud

---

[2]Professor Macneil is referring to the constitutional concept of "due process," meaning that people with charges against them must receive notice and an opportunity to be heard before a determination of guilt is made and punishment inflicted.

being slung on my name. No doubt you will, at a moment suiting you and with the same respect you have thus far shown for fair process—to say nothing of common courtesy—announce what, if any, further punishment is to be administered.

Your indictment/judgment of conviction raises a great many issues apart from the foregoing.

One question is your purported standing to raise the issues you have on behalf of all the women in my class. Throughout the year I have had a great many complaints about the course from students of both sexes. Of this great quantity of complaints I can recall only two which had anything to do with gender. Neither of these were general complaints but referred to specific matters (see below). A meeting on December 7 was attended by around 60% of the class, at which a wide range of complaints were voiced. Not a word was said about any alleged sexism. Another meeting will take place shortly at which any student concerned about alleged sexism will have the opportunity to make his or her complaint.

Respecting the substance of your examples of alleged sexism, I have no apologies to make. I shall treat them one by one.

Casebook

The quotation from Byron's Don Juan is in fact a perfect summary of what happens in the "battle of the forms."[3] In that struggle each party—without regard to his or her sex—strives to make contracts on his or her own terms, says that he or she is not making a contract on the other person's terms, and just as firmly goes on and makes one knowing that the other is insisting on their terms, i.e., each side consents while whispering he or she will ne'er consent. One of the key points of the casebook section and its classroom treatment, is that consent is never a purely on-off phenomenon in which people ever consent 100% to anything. Parties always consent more to some things than to others. They also may really not consent at all to something while at the same time consenting to something entirely inconsistent with their non-consent. Whatever may be the effect of that point on analyses of rape law, I can hardly refrain from teaching it. It is fundamental to understanding a key aspect of contractual relations and contract law.

[Professor Macneil responds to each of the other charges made by the Harvard Women's Law Association and concludes with a discussion of his alleged "sexist" language:]

Gender-specific language. Your letter clearly implies that it is possible to avoid ever "using sexist language." In fact it is impossible to speak English as it is

---

[3]The "battle of the forms" is a topic in all first-year contract courses. In many commercial sales, the seller and the buyer each use different standard forms for a sales agreement or a purchase order. Each side uses a form with "boilerplate" language that gives itself certain advantages— like the question of which side bears the loss in the event of an unexpected strike. Since business deals must often be made quickly in response to the market, neither side wants to waste time and money negotiating other's form but then goes right ahead with transaction— signing its own form, for example, and shipping the merchandise. The Byron quotation is an analogy to this situation: The young woman refuses, saying "no" but goes right ahead with the sexual relationship.

normally spoken without using words which zealots would insist are sexist. If I were to stop my students—male or female—every time one of them used a possibly gender-specific word to express an idea or identify a non-gender-specific person or subject the class would come to a grinding halt.

I certainly often have a light remark about gender-specific language when it is juxtaposed to a non-gender idea, as it is in the four examples you give. The joke is about the difficulties of using the poor old common everyday English language to do everything everyone wants to do with it. And my reasons for interjecting the joke is to call attention to those inadequacies. I would have thought you would applaud that where the inadequacy concerns gender.

I might add that in all four instances you mention I was (and am) genuinely puzzled about the extent to which, if at all, anyone would consider use of the word or phrase to be sexist. The joke in those cases was aimed in part at myself for wondering about it.

I doubt if I ever said "I admit" to being a paternalist. The very first day last fall I announced to the class that I took an interest in their welfare, which could only be described as paternalistic. At that time I also mentioned the lack of a good non-gender word for paternalism, and joked about my coining a word, "waternalist," using the Swahili root "wa" which means people. (It also picks up the idea of community which I was trying to stress in this institution of excessive individualism.)

We have quite different views of what humor is all about. To you humor is flippant (lacking proper respect or seriousness), disparaging. To me humor is one of God's greatest gifts in getting through life. It is what makes it possible for the human race to survive its many aches and pains, to salve the sores of human existence, to soften our hostilities and conflicts so that we can continue to work together.

I have now responded to your specifics. I shall now sum up my view of this whole affair. It reeks of McCarthyism. In McCarthyism there was One Simple Truth, and the McCarthyites were the sole interpreters of that One Simple Truth. Certainly no one was permitted to laugh about their interpretation. The Nonbelievers would either convert to that Truth or be rooted out. In the McCarthy era faceless informers in classrooms reported on Nonbelievers. The McCarthyites used words—Red, Commie-lover, Pinko—lacking precise meanings; these were highly pejorative while not quite constituting slander or libel. In the McCarthy era fair procedures existed largely to be set aside. Under McCarthyism the most common punishment was slinging mud on the victim. The mud was indelible; seldom, if ever, could it be scraped off without leaving a bad stain. And always the mud was flung first, fair procedures, if any, coming after it was too late.

You too believe there is One Simple Truth about the immensely complex nature of human relations. You too believe that you are the sole interpreters of that One Simple Truth. You too prohibit humor as blasphemy. You too will either convert or root out the Nonbelievers if you possibly can. You too rely on informers faceless to the victim. You too use a pejorative, not-quite-libelous word, Sexism. This is a word with two quite distinct dictionary meanings, but is largely defined by the eyes of the beholder. You too care nothing for fair procedures. Your weapon too is indelible mud. And you too have flung the mud first—procedures, if any, to come after it is too late. And in one respect you go even beyond the McCarthyites—they never told us we had to abandon our mother tongue in order to survive in their paradise.

I resisted the original McCarthyism; I have resisted McCarthyism in its many guises since then; and I shall continue to resist it to the best of my ability now.

Meanwhile in my class I shall continue to try my fallible best to treat every one of my students as the individual he or she is, to treat all of my students equally and courteously, to soften the bumps and bruises of a rigorous course of study with humor where I think it may help, and to concentrate on the increasingly difficult job of trying to teach law students to become professionals.

Because this matter concerns all the students in my class, I am sending copies of your letter and this reply to them. As it raises important issues for the school, I am doing the same respecting my colleagues on the faculty.

Stories appeared on the affair in the *Boston Globe* and *The Harvard Crimson*. When the HWLA failed to respond to the issues raised in Macneil's letter, he wrote the following letter to The Harvard Law School Record:

On April 3 I sent the Harvard Women's Law Association a detailed answer to each of the charges it made against me of "sexism." . . . (This caused the reply to be "extremely lengthy"—it sometimes take a lot of clean water to try to wash off mud.)

Has the HWLA responded to each—or to any—of those answers to its charges? No. Has it withdrawn the charges with, or even without, apology? No. What has it done? Its President, Bonnie Savage, has in effect simply reiterated to the press all the charges as originally made. And she has tried to deny the original smear while leaving it entirely intact: "We never called him a sexist." Speak of Nineteen Eighty-Four! If accusing someone of "repeated instances of sexism" does not constitute calling someone a sexist, what does?

All this is shoddy, unlawyerlike, reminiscent of Senator McCarthy, and entirely consistent with HWLA's prior conduct.

Savage has also revealed a complete lack of understanding of the difference between speech as an expression of ideas and speech as an attempt to intimidate. Savage is under the erroneous impression that principles of free speech confer not only the right to express views, but also the right to have the hearer agree. "Our point was to go on record with the problem and get him to change." "The language of his response contains words which aren't meant to say 'I don't understand, educate me,' . . ."

It is true, of course, that "insisting" that listeners agree is a social commonplace. But it becomes both offensive and dangerous to academic freedom whenever the insistence is intended to and does create fear. This can occur whenever the speaker has power. Students can, and often have through the ages, made life miserable for teachers with whom they disagree. The HWLA has such power and intended to exercise it. It is, to put it politely, disingenuous for its representative to deny this.

Savage has also been quoted as saying "Our decision was not to go public [in making the charges]." Consider the facts. A large student political action organization adopts at a "general meeting" of its membership a letter making serious charges against a faculty member and sends copies to five of the highest officials in the Law School. All of these necessarily must discuss such a serious matter with a good many other people. Can Savage deny with a straight face that such charges will become almost instantly public through the efficient rumor system of the school, and, indeed, of the law school world generally?

Anyone the least familiar with the situation now obtaining on many American campuses, including this one, would recognize the HWLA's intention to instill fear and to intimidate rather than to convince. But if there were any doubt of that, Savage has laid it to rest. Savage, in explaining the HWLA action, has twice been quoted as saying "We thought he might be considered for tenure." This statement removes any doubt as to why a copy of the original HWLA letter was sent to the Chairman of the Faculty Appointments Committee. Clearly anyone holding *any* of the views erroneously attributed to me by HWLA is not fit in the eyes of Savage to serve on the Harvard Law School faculty. The HWLA letter was intended to prevent such an appointment, not simply to express views on the subject of sexism. That neither HLS nor I ever had any intention of my visit becoming a permanent appointment reduces not one whit the danger this effort poses to academic freedom. The HWLA attack stands, and is surely intended to stand, as a lesson to all teachers here, present and prospective. As the French generals said of the executions after the 1916 mutinies: "Par example pour les autres."

Savage seems quite offended that I sent copies of the HWLA charge and my response to members of my contracts class. This in spite of the fact that the HWLA letter clearly purported to speak on behalf of all the women in my class, and clearly raised issues of which all the class was entitled to be informed.

Savage also seems to think that for some reason it was inappropriate to send copies to the faculty (after I sent the original to her). "Maybe he doth protest too much." You are damned right, Ms. Savage, I protest. But you are wrong that it is even possible to protest too much when principles of academic freedom are attacked this way. Given the shoddiness of the HWLA procedures and the flimsiness of the HWLA charges, undoubtedly Savage would have preferred those charges and my response to be made public only through the distortions of the rumor mill. It hardly served her interests to have them clearly set out so those most directly concerned could read them in the original. But it served the interests of truth.

My course in contracts engendered numerous complaints. Those surfacing publicly concern my efforts—vain ones respecting many students—to insist that students act like professionals in the classroom respecting participation, preparation, attendance, and promptness. . . . Less publicized complaints concern the content, focus, and pedagogy of the course. It is not my intention to justify here either the course or the pedagogy. But readers of the Record should be aware that the HWLA's trumped-up charges of sexism were simply surrogates for other highly controversial issues. Savage was quoted in the *Boston Globe:* "The students who came to us wanted some outlet for their frustration. . . ." You bet!

The final volley came in a note in the HWLA Newsletter, entitled "WLA Makes No Apologies":

Recently, WLA has been, ironically, the focus of much attention resulting from a letter we sent to Ian Macneil, Robert Clark, James Vorenberg, Todd Rakoff (Appointments Committee Chair), David Smith (Vice Dean), and Gwendolyn Bookman (Senior Student Affairs Coordinator). The letter voiced the concerns of various women who were disturbed by Macneil's sexist behavior in his Contracts class.

It is the Administration's responsibility to ensure that women are not encountering overt or sub rosa discrimination in the classroom. WLA responded to these women's concerns by bringing them to the attention of the appropriate individuals: the Professor and the Administration.

Macneil vehemently denied the allegations, admitting that our quotations are accurate but denying that our interpretation of them is correct.

Professor Macneil's response was distressing in many ways. Apart from being paternalistic ("Had you and your informer paid more attention to the course and less seeking to be offended you might have recognized the pedagogical point of the Don Juan quotation, and not thought its inclusion "inexplicable.") he it [sic] is trying to silence women's voices. He calls the women in his class who came forth "informers" and "McCarthyites." More importantly, he absolutely refuses to consider that from *their* perspective, his behavior was offensive. They were the ones who felt disturbed by his textbook and his classroom language to the point where their study of the material was interrupted. A teacher who sought to be fair and effective would want to address the criticism, not by defensive denial, but by listening, trying to understand, and attempting to make the classroom comfortable for all. There is no excuse for a hidden curriculum which makes women unable to concentrate on the official curriculum.

Finally, it is ironic that so much attention has fallen on the WLA. The focus should be on this Professor's behavior and the Administration's response. Why hasn't the Administration defended our attempt to eliminate sexism? Why hasn't the Administration censured Macneil for trying to silence our legitimate criticism? Or, why hasn't the Administration reassured students that they should continue to come forward with similar concerns?

WLA will not be silenced by Macneil's histrionics. The women in his class found his behavior offensive to them as women. That is what should be remembered and addressed.

Epilogue: Professor Macneil's Later Reflections

It never occurred to me not to do exactly what I did, which was to fight back as best as I could by answering the charges specifically. It took no courage, there was simply nothing else to do. (I can't say the same for walking into the classroom thereafter.) In many ways I was fortunate: I was a one-year visitor who neither expected to be asked nor wanted to stay at Harvard; I had a well-established permanent position at Northwestern; and I was looking forward to retirement from teaching within a few years. Whether I would have thought there was nothing else to do if I had been a young untenured member of the Harvard faculty, I cannot say. My one career fear was that the HWLA attack would jeopardize my relations with women students at Northwestern the following year. I am happy to report that it did not. Teaching the Northwestern 1989–90 contracts class—about 45 per cent women—was the high point of my teaching career in terms of relationships with a class.

I did not believe for a minute that any student in the class, male or female, was "disturbed by [my] textbook and [my] classroom language to the point where their study of the material was interrupted." I do believe that two or three individuals in the class had their antennae out for anything to relieve the anxieties created by a demanding Socratic classroom. The HWLA charges reveal how far they were willing to go to find something. My belief was reinforced by the anonymous course evaluations submitted at the end of the course a few weeks later—excoriating about most everything, but silent on the subject of sexism.

If I were rewriting my casebook, I would delete the Don Juan quote, not because it is not in point or because it is sexist—it is neither. The quote and its point can, however, be misconstrued by someone unable to see it clearly because of fear of rape. As I am deeply sympathetic to women's fears of rape I do not think the pedagogical value of the quotation is worth that cost.

Given the serious issues of academic freedom raised by both the substance of many of HWLA's charges and by its procedures, Harvard's institutional response to the events described—or rather lack of it—particularly interested me. There were many quiet, supportive visits to my office from faculty colleagues, as well as similar comments on casual meeting in the hall, at lunch, etc. A number of staff members—mostly female—let me know they considered the charges utter nonsense, and praised my response. Since there is something of a generation gap on these issues, it may be noted that most of these staff members were younger women. The Vice Dean called a couple of times offering school administration help in any way possible. (I rejected this for two reasons. First, I needed no help, and it was not for me—a visitor—to tell the Law School to help itself. Second, the kind of help which would in fact have been proferred would almost certainly have been an effort to smooth the waters, rather than to face the issues.) One faculty member used the HWLA letter and my response in his constitutional law class as a vehicle for exploring free speech issues.

What, however, was prominently absent was any collective felt sense of threat to academic freedom leading to any institutional expression of concern. The closest to any official public reaction—indeed, so far as I am aware, any public reaction of any faculty member—were independent statements from the Chairman of the Faculty Recruitment Committee and the Dean, made to the reporters. The former was quoted:

> I am very sorry to find that this kind of thing takes place between students and professors at this school.

The Dean was equally neutral:

> You have a professor who is strong-minded and has a way of teaching class and a typical group of strong-minded Harvard Law School students. Its not surprising there are some sparks. I'm optimistic they will work out these issues.

The failure of anyone at Harvard Law School to recognize publicly the dangers to academic freedom of the kind of politicized classroom HWLA sought to impose on faculty and students alike or the methods it uses was disappointing, but certainly came as no surprise to me.

QUESTIONS TO CONSIDER

1. The article "WLA Makes No Apology" argues that a teacher who wanted to be "fair and effective" would respond by "listening, trying to understand, and attempting to make the classroom comfortable for all." Do you agree? What are the issues here?

2. In an article in the *Boston Globe*, Bonnie Savage is quoted as saying: "We didn't like the content of his speech. In a way he's saying we didn't have the right to write that letter. Free speech comes on both sides."

   Is Professor Macneil indeed trying "to silence" his feminist critics? Is he unwilling to grant to them the rights of free speech he claims for himself?

3. Would you consider Professor Macneil's response to the HWLA "paternalistic" or the opposite of "paternalistic"? Should he have adopted a stance more conducive to creating community, or is this situation simply one where someone is going to win and someone is going to lose?

4. Should the Harvard Law School administration have intervened in this controversy? In what ways? On whose side?

5. What were the costs and benefits of the controversy for Harvard Law School? For Professor Macneil? For Bonnie Savage and the HWLA? For creating an atmosphere at Harvard Law School that is respectful of women's perspectives? For preparing competent attorneys effective in the profession of law?

ACTIVITIES

1. Imagine that the HWLA had brought its charges of sexism to Professor Macneil first. What would have happened? How would he have responded? Could they have reached a compromise? Role-play this scene.

2. List the cost and benefits to the various actors in this case: Bonnie Savage and the HWLA, Professor Macneil, the Harvard Law School as an institution, the administrators, the men in the class, and the women who support Professor Macneil. What actions might each of these characters or groups take to improve their outcomes? Can you identify courses of action that would have improved the outcomes for all the parties?

READINGS

Bernstein, R. (1990). The rising hegemony of the politically correct. *New York Times* (October 28): E1.

Hentoff, N. (1992). *Free speech for me—But not for thee*. New York: HarperCollins.

MacKinnon, C. A. (1993). *Only words*. Cambridge, Mass.: Harvard University Press.

Appendix: Jockeying for Position

This appendix details the other charges made by the Harvard Women's Law Association and Professor Macneil's responses.

Excerpt from Harvard Women's Law Association's Letter: Additional Charges

From Your Textbook:

- Your comparison of exchange relations to "any mutually successful making of love" (p. 20, n. 7), which uses inappropriate sexual imagery and reduces the sexual relation to a commercial exchange
- Your statement, "Habit, custom and education develop a sense of obligation—call it socially constructive or paranoid as you will—to preserve one's credit rating not altogether different from that Victorian maidens felt respecting their virginity" (p. 59), giving credence to the idea that a woman's sexual life is a reflection of her worth, when in fact you allude to an artificial standard that society imposed on women of the Victorian Era
- Your single and isolated use of the female pronoun to refer to a secretary (p. 890), thus perpetuating a stereotype

From Class Discussions:

- When debating a point with a female student, you remarked: "I don't want to beat you into submission or anything," a comment evoking a male power structure to silence a woman's voice
- When discussing a case in which a 12-year-old boy was required to give up the specific vices of alcohol, smoking and gambling, you joked that at least not *all* vices were being denied the poor boy: "He was left *girls*, you know," thereby implying that women are a commodity for male use

Excerpt from Professor Macneil's Letter: Additional Responses

With respect to page 20, note 7, I suggest that you read the whole note:

> The sharp notion that my goals equal your costs is a discrete-transaction concept.[1] In relational patterns my goals may equal your goals and my costs your costs; while exchange takes place, it is in such circumstances muted psychologically in that it is not thought of by participants as a discrete exchange. Consider, for example, any mutually successful making of love.

Evidently your informer totally misunderstood not only this footnote, but the whole nature of relational patterns, which we had then been studying for three days. You either have done the same thing or have simply not troubled to investigate what the note in question is about. This is made manifest by your statement about reducing "the sexual relation to a commercial exchange." The note conveys precisely the opposite message.

---

[1] A "discrete-transaction" is a single transaction, not necessarily repeated—like buying a pair of shoes. In buying shoes, the buyer's goal—to get the shoes—requires payment of the seller's cost—the price of the shoes. Professor Macneil is pointing out that in other types of relationships, both parties may share the same goals and costs. When making love is successful, in his view, the experience is mutual with both sharing the same joys and experiencing the same disappointments.

Your comment on this footnote also raises serious questions about academic freedom. My own personal attitude towards "making of love" happens to be extremely old-fashioned and as far away as it is humanly possible to get from reducing "the sexual relation to commercial exchange." But there are a great many people who have vastly differing views about sexual relations. Indeed there are those who think that commercialism has infiltrated all human relations, sexual or otherwise. There are those who applaud this and those who abhor it. They are entitled to express these thoughts without fear. It will be a sorry day for intellectual liberty when a teacher in this Law School cannot safely express the views which you and your informer attributed to my footnote.

The reference to Victorian maidens also must be read in context:

> In any society—communal, centrally planned, capitalist, or something else—habit, custom, learning and education, and legal reinforcement of behavior conforming to the norms they establish, in great measure supply the stability necessary for specialization and exchange. For example, in middle America one learns to protect one's status as a good credit risk well beyond what self-interest may dictate. [Habit, custom and education develop a sense of obligation—call it socially constructive or paranoid as you will—to preserve one's credit rating not altogether different from that Victorian maidens felt respecting their virginity.] [Brackets added.]

You have stated that the bracketed words give "credence to the idea that a woman's sexual life is a reflection of her worth, when in fact you allude to an artificial standard that society imposed on women of the Victorian era."

This comment baffles me. I cannot understand how anyone could conceivably read that paragraph and find anything in it relating to the intrinsic worth of anyone—either of "one" or of "Victorian maidens"—the two subjects in the sentence. The only possible "worth" I can see to which you might be referring is economic worth, since the analog is to credit ratings. Perhaps you equate someone's economic worth to their intrinsic worth as a person; I do not.

Once again your comment gives rise to problems of academic freedom. You are entitled to your apparent view that the conduct of a person's sexual life is not a reflection of his or her intrinsic worth. I am entitled to mine that it is. You are also entitled to your view that what I described was "an artificial standard that society imposed on women of the Victorian era." I am entitled to my view that it was an integral part of a society in which both sexes had power and which had its goods and its bads for both sexes, just as this one has its goods and its bads for both sexes. In short, I do not believe that a teacher is obliged to or should accept a particular view of history simply because some of his or her students hold that view keenly.

Your next example of my alleged "sexism" is the use of a single and isolated female pronoun to refer to a secretary "thus perpetuating a stereotype." This was the subject of one of the two complaints I mentioned earlier. Last week two students came to my office and asserted that this "she" in the casebook (published in 1978) violated my own (not objected to) principle for male-female usage adopted in my 1988–89 supplement. It probably does violate that principle adopted more recently than the date of the eleven year old casebook. At any rate, I had long since made a notation on my own copy of the casebook to rearrange the thought in any future revision to avoid any reference to the sex of the secretary. I showed this to the two complaining students, and they seemed quite satisfied.

Once again questions of academic freedom are raised by your insistence that such usage must be expunged. The fact is that there are quite a few jobs in this country which tend to be heavily or even entirely filled by persons of the same sex. One example, both in 1978 and now, is secretarial work. Using words and constructions which pretend that those occupations have become sexually balanced smacks too much of Orwell's *Nineteen Eighty Four* to suit me, even though I often do so. Moreover, it may very well be that recognizing the very real fact of sexual imbalance by sex-identifying pronouns will hasten rather than slow movements towards balance in those occupations. If these views cannot be expressed through ordinary usage, because others such as you disagree with them, we are indeed well along to losing our liberties.

Class Discussion

I turn now to your indictments/convictions relating to class discussions.

"I don't want to beat you into submission or anything." I make remarks along these lines quite often to students of both sexes. The occasion for doing so is when the student is saying or seems about to say he or she agrees with me, but I sense that may not be the case, but rather surrender to a louder voice. When one teaches vigorously and demandingly there is a serious risk of pushing students into this position. Far from evoking "a male power structure to silence a woman's voice," these statements are an acknowledgment, probably a clumsy one, that I may have already exercised too much "teacher power to silence a student's voice," be that student male or female.

Hamer v. Sidway,[2] Willie, the 15 year old boy whose uncle in 1875 offered him $5000 if he refrained from "drinking, using tobacco, swearing, and playing cards and billiards for money." I said something along the lines "I hope you noticed that he was left girls." (To the best of my recollection I have never used the word "vice" in discussing this case, this year or any other year. That is your term, not mine.) This remark aroused one of the two complaints mentioned above. I thought at the time and still think that the complaint is utterly absurd, and that one can find sexism, no matter how defined, in the remark only if one is hoping to be, and very actively seeking ways to be, offended. Anyone who thinks that a joking remark about adolescent interest in adolescents of the opposite sex implies that "women are a commodity for male use" has serious problems understanding other human beings, male or female.

I have serious reasons for making the remark. Why did a mid-Victorian uncle trying to "improve" Willie, say nothing about sexual activities? Was the omission because the uncle was a "modern" respecting sexual activities? Because he held a double standard in which Willie, but not Willie's sister, could indeed do as he pleased on that score? Because he thought it unnecessary even to mention such a subject respecting what were then called "nice girls," and it did not matter respecting "not nice girls" or prostitutes? Because the subject

---

[2]This case illustrates an important concept in contracts—"consideration," or the benefit and detriment which turns a promise into a legally binding contract. The uncle's promise to pay Willie did not legally bind the uncle unless Willy suffered a detriment as a result of it, for example, giving up something he might have liked, such as smoking.

was unmentionable at a family gathering? Or was the omission simply because Willie was (according to the opinion) already doing the things specified, and had yet to offend his uncle respecting any sexual activities? Or was it something else?

Given present widespread views respecting sexual relations, adolescent as well as adult, as well as a common lack of historical knowledge, it is by no means clear to me that most students will even notice the omission unless it is called to their attention. Given the difficulties students tend to have with the doctrine of consideration, which is why the case is in the casebook, there is no time to deal with the foregoing questions in class (unless a student raises them, which no one ever has). A joking reference may cause some students to reflect on them later. Had your informer done so perhaps he, she, or they, would have seen that there may be some important feminist issues underlying that omission.

Had you and your informer paid more attention to the course and less seeking to be offended you might have recognized the pedagogical point of the Don Juan quotation, and not thought its inclusion "inexplicable." If you will find an equally concise, apt, and literate quotation elsewhere which makes this point without sex-identification, I shall be delighted to use it in any future revision of the casebook.

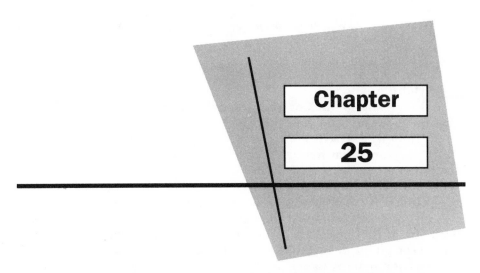

Chapter 25

The Girls at Central—They Sure Got Nice Behinds

John Martin

PART A

Mr. Andrews sat behind his desk, watching the ninth-graders squirm in their seats. They were awkward and restless, mostly African-American and Latino, mostly just kids. He contemplated the scene in front of him, trying to settle the doubts and anxieties playing tag inside his head. In today's lesson plans, he wanted them to write in their "journals." Not journals really, just a folder with a name on it that held a few pieces of lined writing paper with not much of anything written on them.

He wanted them to write, to be writers. He thought of himself as a writer and wanted them to join him. The product of a large public high school himself, he then went to a privileged, private university where he discussed educational theory and methodology, including teaching writing as a process. He wanted desperately to merge his ideals with the academic and personal realities of the students sitting in front of him.

He had an idea. The students in his class have complained often about the irrelevancy of the work they were given. Irrelevancy is his word. What they say is: "I don't like this"; "It's boring"; "This sucks"; and "I don't ever need to know about this stuff." He wanted to make a writing assignment mean something to them—for their sake, and for his.

The bell rang. Mr. Andrews passed out paper, and the students cringed.
"What's this for?"
"We gotta test?"
"I ain't gonna do it."
"Just hold on a minute, and I'll explain what you have to do."

"I'm not doin' nothin'."

"Yes, you are."

"Huh?"

"I want you to think of what you did this last weekend, OK? Tell me what you did, who you did it with—"

"Uh-huh. You *really* wanna know?"

"Come on. What you did, the people you were hanging out with, and that sort of thing. Tell me all about your weekend."

Most of the students looked down at the paper and did nothing. Adults would say that their faces showed a little too much "attitude."

Mr. Andrews prompted them impatiently. "Put your name and date down first. If you can't think of anything to write, don't worry about it. Just write, 'I can't think of anything' over and over. Something will come to you."

"What if nothing happened?"

"What if all I did was sleep all weekend long?"

"I just went shoppin' with my mother late Friday night."

"I hate this."

"Tell me about the shopping trip. How could you have slept all weekend long? Let's go, get writing, I shouldn't see anyone not writing."

The students fidgeted, and some wrote—tentatively at first, but then with greater interest, as though realizing that moving a pencil wouldn't hurt them. Mr. Andrews walked up the first row of desks, bending over papers. He smiled a lot and touched hesitant arms. Most were writing now.

I can't think of nothin'. . . . I can't think of nothin'. . . . I can't think of nothin'. . . . I can't think of nothin'. . . . I can't think of nothin'. . . . I can't think of nothin'. . . .

I went to my boyfriend's house. I can't tell you the rest.

Well yesterday night I didn't do nothing special but I was in my House with my brother and my friend Trevor talking About Girls and what we are going to do next weekend and when my friend left I just went to watch t.v. and at 11:30 PM I watch the fight It wasn't boarding Because when you are with your friend everything is not as bad as when you're alone. . . .

the End.

"José?" Mr. Andrews walked toward the back of the classroom. On the desk, José rested his head on folded arms. He was not sleeping. "José!"

José turned his head away from Mr. Andrews.

"Aren't you going to write? Aren't you going to do the assignment?" Mr. Andrews's stance revealed his frustration. His arms akimbo, he stared down at José. "Why don't you do the assignment like everyone else?"

José shrugged. Mr. Andrews walked away.

José did not speak English very well; his family was from Mexico, and they spoke only Spanish at home. One parent supported a handful of children. José worked after school, maybe even forty hours a week. Or maybe he didn't work; he went home to videogames. He disliked school, except to see his friends.

How was José going to be convinced to write, to learn? Did Mr. Andrews's Anglo face—demanding, cajoling, and pleading—shut this student off?

The next day in class, Mr. Andrews took a stack of lined paper and passed it out. Cutting off the students' resentful and angry retorts somewhere between the base of their throats and the tips of the tongues, he said: "We're going to do something fun today. Who has ever seen a movie in which a psychologist says a word to a patient and the patient is supposed to say the first word that comes to mind? Do you know what I'm talking about?"

A few students nodded, hesitant to acknowledge that they had been thrown off guard.

"Here's how it's going to work," Mr. Andrews said. "I'll give you a word, and you write down the first things that come into your heads, OK?"

"How many things do we have to write?" a student asked.

"Five," Mr. Andrews said, gaining confidence. The students were buying into it.

Mr. Andrews read the word *weekend,* and José wrote:

1. HBO
2. Basketball
3. GIRls
4. StrawBerry SHortcake
5. BEACH

Mr. Andrews then told the students to circle the one thing that they either enjoy the most or know the most about. "Now, write anything you know about what you circled. Tell me what you like about it. You're the expert; it's your subject." He stood and waited, his panic carefully, very carefully, hidden behind his somber eyes and slightly arched, expecting eyebrows.

"I wrote this much," a student told him.

"How much do we need to do?" another student asked.

"Done," another student breathed, visibly tired after writing two sentences.

José wrote:

This Girls in Central they sure got some nice Behnds. It is just Beutiful i look and it just so fresh this Girls Here make you feel so Good and they know that Boys like it when they ware tight pants that's why they ware them some of them are ugly but that's just the way life is they got to like it even if they can't want to this Girls here are the Best and they are not the Best just Because they are pretty is Because i'm in this school

Mr. Andrews was relieved. Something written is better than nothing. But what was José doing? Was he teasing? Challenging? Showing attitude? He wanted to comment, to continue the writing process and let José develop his piece. But should he let him stretch the limits of appropriateness?

QUESTIONS TO CONSIDER

1. What is your interpretation of José's motives in writing this piece?

2. If you were Mr. Andrews, how would you respond to this writing? Would you encourage José to develop this piece?

3. Would your decision be different if this teacher were female?

4. Should Mr. Andrews have steered José away from the subject of girls? What is your reasoning?

PART B

Mr. Andrews decided to encourage José's writing, even if it continued to test the limits of appropriateness. He handed back José's paper the next day:

> José,
>   What do the girls wear? What else about the girls makes them pretty? Tell me more about pretty girls and what makes them pretty. I want to hear about it. It's OK to write about girls.
>   —Mr. Andrews

Mr. Andrews passed out lined paper. His instructions poured out quickly—too quickly. He was nervous. "Think about telling a story with your words," he told them. "Give me details. Rewrite your first drafts, and tell me more about your topic."

"I'm not rewritin' nothin'," José said. He sat, doodling. Mr. Andrews glanced over, and their eyes met. Mr. Andrews shrugged, his body language telling José that he was expected to do the work. José looked down. He read. He began to write . . . a sentence . . . a few words . . . crumpled paper thrown toward the waste basket . . . a fixed stare. . . . "Mr. Andrews, can I get another piece of paper?"

> The Girls Here wear tight pants and short skirts and they fix their Hair Real nice and thats why when you look at them you see that then look so pretty. the way they are they way they talk to you everything Happends just like if they were practicing before they talk or act.
>   The way they are with people, and the way they talk to you. They really explain them self to you. so that you wont have no doubt or question to ask. They get all giddy around their friends. They get happy, and kind of sure of them self Because they got somebody they know, and that can help them react or talk. But what I don't like about these girls is that they cant tell you yes or no when they got too. They take it too slow. for example when some girl is going out with you and they dont want to go out with you no more thay cant just tell you, I dont want to go out with you no more. They just look for any excuse to tell you "that's it". But the rest is ok I think, and I guess that's about it. I guess I explain my self. ok.
>   I hope is ok Mr. Andrews and "thank you"
>   José

Mr. Andrews wanted even more from the next writing assignment. He wanted them to finish, to complete the work. They were to pair up and help edit each other's papers with the help of some questions that Mr. Andrews had put on the board: "Does the first word of the sentence start with a capital letter?" "Does the sentence have end punctuation?" "Does the sentence make sense?" "Does the sentence sound right to you?" He would take these final drafts, type them, and make copies. He wanted to show them that they could publish their writing and would be authors.

Mr. Andrews waited a few seconds for the conversations to die out so that he could give them today's instructions. David nudged Gloria, and Miguel whispered to Willy. They worked. Some students stared ahead in thought. They had not had that much practice editing, helping each other put words and sentences together. They needed time to think it through. Mr. Andrews walked systematically through the room, stopping at desks to encourage, to prod.

"Nice job. What about this person? What have you told us about him?"

"Mr. Andrews. Come over here."

"Elba, in English we only use one question mark, at the end of a sentence."

"Yeah, I know."

"Marlon, what do you do with the first word in the sentence?"

Some students told him to leave them alone. Others did what they had to and no more.

José edited his essay. It read:

The girls at Central are so nice and pretty. The girls here wear tight pants and short shirts and they fix their hair really nice. They are nice and friendly. The way they talk to you is really wild. When they talk to you, they explain themselves to you so you won't have any doubts or questions to ask. They talk to you straight, so you kind of get scare. What I like about them is that they get all giddy around their friends. They get happy, and kind of sure of them selfs because they got somebody they know, and that can help them react or talk. But—What I don't like about them is that these girls can't tell you yes or no when they have too. They take too long, for example when some girl is going out with you and they don't want to go out with you any more they can't tell you I don't want to go out with you any more. They just look for any excuse to tell you "that's it". But the rest is OK I think and I'm really glad that there is always somebody you could spend some time with, like my girlfriend. I hope you like it Mr. Martin and "thank you"
    by José Rosario

I do like your story, José, and you're most welcome. And, José, "Thank *you*."

QUESTIONS TO CONSIDER

1. Suppose José had responded to Mr. Andrews's questions "What do the girls wear? What else about the girls makes them pretty?" with more graphic writing about

"behinds" and other sexually explicit material. What would you advise Mr. Andrews to do?

2. Could José's essay reflect his cultural framework and not be an expression of attitude? How girls respond to José may be a large part of his life at this time, and in some cultures boys of his age may be expected to look over women in sexually evaluative terms. How could Mr. Andrews distinguish between students who are displaying attitude and those who are interpreting a situation through a cultural lens?

3. Teachers who want to enter into students' worlds take the risk of learning about "Susie's abortion" or "Johnnie's abusive parents." Such teachers must consider the boundaries of their invitations to students and must make those boundaries explicit. What boundaries should Mr. Andrews set? What should he say to the class?

ACTIVITIES

1. Invite an English teacher to address your class about methods of teaching reluctant students to write. What does the teacher do about sexual comments in writing? How does the teacher encourage students to let their thoughts and feelings flow on paper without discouraging them when they write about sexual or violent themes?

2. Imagine an alternative ending to this case, in which José writes about women's bodies in a threatening or pornographic way. How would you handle a paper containing such a theme? What if carrying guns or rough treatment of women is standard practice in José's neighborhood? Would you invite José to write about his world?

3. Brainstorm with other students about ways to motivate writers from inner-city schools. Interview teachers from such schools to learn how they motivate students. Put these ideas and teaching strategies together in a resource guide.

READINGS

Atwell, N. (1987). *In the middle: Writing, reading, and learning with adolescents.* Portsmouth, N.H.: Boynton/Cook.

Dorwick, K. (1993). Beyond politeness: Flaming and the realm of the violent. Paper presented at the annual meeting of the Conference on College Composition and Communication. San Diego.

Freedman, S. G. (1991). *Small victories: The real world of a teacher, her students and their high school.* New York: HarperPerennial.

Spaulding, C. L. (1989). Understanding ownership and the unmotivated writer. *Language Arts* 66 (4): 414–422.

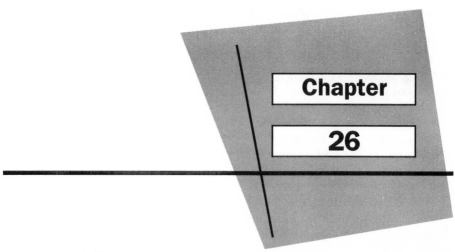

March in Minneapolis

Pat Hutchings

Pam Higgins needed to collect her thoughts for her 11 A.M. class, Critical Approaches to Literature, but she couldn't get her mind off the session of Elements of Literature that had just ended. What had happened, anyway? John Updike's short story "A&P" had always served her well as a practice ground for developing students' analytical skills. This time, somehow, discussion had slid into politics and away from literature. Maybe "A&P" was a bad choice, or maybe. . . . Well, Pam wasn't sure how she felt about what had happened.

Pam had been teaching Elements of Literature at Midwest College on and off for seven years now. The reading list had changed a bit, but the goals listed in this semester's syllabus looked much as they always had. Pam believed that literature was one of the best ways known to teach analysis and critical thinking, and she geared her teaching to that end. She was pleased if students developed a more personal appreciation for the stories chosen, but class activities were aimed at critical analysis, not the expression of personal feelings or (a word Pam couldn't abide) "sharing."

This first five-week unit on the short story, for instance, focused explicitly on the elements of fiction. In the first three weeks students had learned about plot, point of view, and theme. Pam's goal was for students to see how the author's choices about these formal elements combined to create the story's overall effect. And Updike's often-anthologized story "A&P" was one of her favorite pieces for this kind of analysis. It wasn't, admittedly, her favorite short story, but it was one of several short stories Pam had come to depend on in her introductory course as eminently *teachable:* A setting students found familiar, a narrator one could clearly distinguish from the author, a shapely plot that came to a nice clear conflict, and short enough for the kind of up-close reading that Pam believed should be at the heart of an introductory course like Elements of Literature.

Pam's attention to analysis was also part of the larger picture at Midwest College, where attempts were under way to teach writing and critical thinking across the curriculum. Pam felt lucky to have landed at this small liberal arts college for women. The faculty were good colleagues who put first emphasis on teaching and students; students themselves were the type that Pam believed she could really help.

Take Sue, for instance, who was arriving just as Pam walked into room 113. If there was a typical student at Midwest, Sue was it: late twenties, a single mother with a young child, the first in her family to go to college, and a bit surprised to be there. Pam liked her students: They were nice people—not brilliant, maybe, but very nice, and eager to learn to use their minds in new ways; "teachable," you might say.

Sue was just shrugging her coat off her shoulders as Pam came in. "Hi, Sue," Pam said cheerily. "Lousy weather, eh?" It was a gray day, the end of a long winter in the Minneapolis area. Pam was aware that if there were going to be any energy in the classroom today, she was going to have to supply it. Everyone was worn down by mid-March in this town.

The room quickly filled up. "Hi, Barbara. Hi, Stephanie." Pam greeted people while she organized her notes and material on the desk. She glanced up at the clock: Her classes always began on time.

"Well," said Pam, moving forward into the room. "We finished 'Young Goodman Brown' last time. I wonder if there are any last thoughts about Hawthorne before we turn to today's assignment, John Updike's 'A&P.'" She looked expectantly around the room. People were still getting settled. Pam waited, not minding a little silence.

"OK, then, let's forge ahead," Pam announced. "I know some of you found Hawthorne's world a strange place, but here we are in a setting we all know too well: the supermarket. I spent hours there just last night!" she laughed.

"But I bet you didn't see any girls in bikinis!" Janice was just the kind of student you pray for, Pam thought: always prepared, always ready to jump in and get the discussion rolling.

Pam grinned. "That's for sure—especially not around here in March! And those girls in bikinis are what get Updike's story rolling, aren't they? Let's read the opening passage where they come into the grocery store."

> In walks these three girls in nothing but bathing suits. I'm in the third checkout slot, with my back to the door, so I don't see them until they're over by the bread. The one that caught my eye first was the one in the plaid green two-piece. She was a chunky kid, with a good tan, and a sweet broad soft-looking can with those two crescents of white just under it, where the sun never seems to hit, at the top of the backs of her legs. I stood there with my hand on a box of HiHo crackers trying to remember if I rang it up or not. I ring it up again and the customer starts giving me hell. She's one of these cash-register-

watchers, a witch about fifty with rouge on her cheekbones and no eyebrows, and I know it made her day to trip me up. She'd been watching cash registers for fifty years and probably never seen a mistake before.

Pam believed in spending class time reading aloud. Moreover, she believed in doing this reading *herself*. It only made students uncomfortable to be called on to read, and the point after all wasn't to have them practice reading. It was to focus attention: to linger over the important details, to model the process of paying close attention to words.

"So," Pam said, "What's going on in this passage? What's important? What strikes you?" She paused and looked expectantly around the room. The low energy of March was palpable. "What's important in this passage?" she repeated. "What words should we look at? What choices has Updike made here that direct our reading?"

Sue raised her hand, and Pam nodded with a smile. "Well, one thing that strikes me is that I just can't believe these girls would go into a store like that. I'd feel ridiculous. They're just asking for it."

Pam pointed to Deirdre, who looked like she was about to break in. "I agree," she said. "But, you know, they *do* that in beach towns. Everything is a lot more relaxed. It's not fair to judge them by your standards."

Sue looked down.

"You both make good points," Pam replied, trying to smooth over the difference in views and get back on track. "One of the things this story is about—isn't it?—is standards and limits and deciding what's right: We see Sammy, the young grocery-store clerk who narrates the story, eventually having to choose between his job and the girls. But let's just stick to the words in front of us for a few minutes. What can we infer from this first paragraph, and especially from Updike's use of language?" Pam wrote on the board as students offered up their observations:

the setting is a grocery store
the narrator is male
he's a store employee
not very grammatical
probably about seventeen
girl-crazy
rebellious
very observing

"OK, good," she said, trying to give the rather-routine discussion—the smattering of words on the board—a kind of point and coherence. "We have now established quite a bit about our narrator. And in the first paragraph we actually have most of the plot in a nutshell version: Sammy intent on three girls in swimsuits and, as a consequence, getting into hot water with an older person—the cash-register watcher. Is there some foreshadowing here? How does this first episode relate to the larger story?" Pam looked across the twenty-four faces in front of her, hoping someone would point to the conclusion of the story, where Sammy has to decide whether to uphold store policy—no swimsuits allowed—or side with the girls and lose his job. No one spoke.

Pam smiled. "It's not so easy thinking about summer in a beach town on this gray day in Minneapolis, is it?" she said soothingly. "Let's try something else." This would be a good time, she thought, to vary the pace with some small-group work.

"What I'd like you to do for the next twenty minutes is to pull your chairs around in groups of four or five and analyze the *theme of the story*. We talked about theme last week, you remember, and how elements like point of view and setting and style contribute to our sense of the theme. So, what theme or themes do you see in 'A&P'? As always, you should be prepared to explain how passages in the story support your ideas."

The groups went to work, slowly at first, but with pages turning . . . just what Pam had hoped for. Several groups were beginning to buzz. The group by the window was leaning in toward Jane's text, which Jane was pointing to and reading from. "Too good to be true," Pam said to herself.

Pam drifted from group to group, just listening in, but asserting her presence, keeping people on task. The point was not to "share" at random but to analyze. Pam perched on the edge of the desk and picked some lint off her corduroy pants, listening all the while. When she heard one of the groups drift off into talk of part-time jobs (apparently someone in the group had once worked in a grocery store), she looked at the clock: 10:40. Only twenty minutes left; time to get rolling.

"Let's see what you came up with," she called out. "Hello!" she shouted to the group in the back. "Which group would be willing to start us off?"

A hand went up by the window. Jane was in her early twenties, single, more sure of herself than many of the students, and with definite opinions. Pam looked around for another hand, since Jane had a tendency to dominate the discussion, but the doldrums seemed to have settled back over the room. She nodded at Jane.

"My group thinks that the theme of this story is sexism," Jane announced. "You said to look for passages, and that's what we did. Listen to this: 'She had on a kind of dirty-pink—beige maybe, I don't know—bathing suit with a little nubble all over it and what got me, the straps were down. They were off her shoulders looped loose around the cool tops of her arms, and I guess as a result the suit had slipped a little on her, so all around the top of the cloth there was this shining rim. . . .' If this isn't a story about sexism . . ." Jane's voice trailed off.

Pam nodded slowly, giving herself a moment to think. "So, Jane, you're saying the theme is sexism," she repeated. "Hmmmm." Having taught the story repeatedly, Pam was not really surprised by Jane's answer; she felt as though she knew every twist and turn the discussion might take. But how to respond was always tricky—and all the talk about political correctness now made it trickier yet. "Hmmmm," she repeated, looking thoughtful, her mind scrambling for the best way to get the discussion back on track. Every face in the room seemed fastened on her. The best thing, she thought, is to let this run its course for a bit, then turn back to analysis. "Are there any reactions to Jane's comment?" she asked.

"It's not just mine," Jane said. "We all agree in my group." Others nodded. Nicole, seated next to Jane, added, "We talked about beer ads, always with girls in bikinis. Car ads. I'm just sick of it. And now here it is in class as well!" Other students agreed, and several made comments about an introductory sociology class where, Pam knew, the professor's feminist values were openly evident and eye-opening for many of the students from traditional families who were only beginning to think about their world more critically. Pam shared those views—completely—but her goals in this class demanded, she believed, a different tack.

Pam went to the board and slowly wrote *Theme* and *Point of View*, in big letters. "Jane's comment is a great way for us to think about the elements of fiction we've been talking about for the past few weeks. Let's review and then come back around to the issue of theme and where sexism fits in. Barbara: What *is* point of view?"

"Who is telling the story?" said Barbara. "Who is telling the story," Pam wrote on the board. "Are there other definitions we should capture?" The room was silent. "And who *is* telling this story? Janice?"

"It's in the first person," said Janice. "The grocery guy is telling the story."

"OK, yes. It's Sammy," said Pam. "And here we come to a crucial point in helping us deal with Jane's comment—Jane's group's comment—that the theme of the story is sexism. Is it the author or the narrator who's the sexist here, Jane?" Pam asked, starting to feel things falling back into place. (It was interesting, she mused to herself, how what seemed like a tangent could be used to bring the discussion back around, to make a point more forcefully.) "Remember what we said a couple weeks ago about distinguishing between the author's attitudes and those of the narrator?"

"But how do you know they're not the same?" Jane shot back. "I don't see how we can be so sure. We don't know anything about Updike. I don't see why we should give him the benefit of the doubt. Maybe sexism isn't the theme he *intended*, but it's sure the one that *I* get. Nine-tenths of the story is a kid drooling over three girls in swimsuits!"

Pam walked back to the board and underlined *Theme*. "We can call the narrator a sexist pig if we want to," she said, trying to lighten up a little, smiling. "But you make an important point when you say *nine-tenths of the story*. What about the final tenth? Something else is happening at the end, isn't it, and we need to get the whole plot in focus in order to make inferences about the theme." She underlined the word again. "Is it sexism that this story is finally about?"

Pam glanced up at the clock. It was 10:53. Only seven minutes to set things right. "Let's look at the end of the story. What has happened?"

"Sammy has to make a choice?" Sue responded.

"Yes, yes," said Pam encouragingly. "Keep going."

"Sammy has to decide whether to side with the girls when the manager embarrasses them or to quit his job," Sue continued. "He makes a mistake. He shouldn't have quit."

"Hmmm," said Pam. "Is that what Updike thinks, or is that your view?"

"It's mine?" Sue responded, sounding distinctly uncertain of her answer.

"And what about the rest of you?" Pam asked. "What hints do we have about what *Updike* thinks is important here at the end? Any quick thoughts about theme in the last couple minutes?"

No hands went up, and Pam glanced at her watch: three minutes left. "Let me ask you to do a little exercise we did last week as a way of figuring out where we've gotten today. On any old sheet of paper, write me a sentence explaining what you think the most important part of this class was, and—second—what we should start with next time, what you want to talk more about. You don't have to put your names on your papers if you don't want to."

Pam erased the board as students wrote. She had, she thought, made the most of a bad situation today, but sometimes fifty minutes just wasn't enough. It was hard keeping people on track, and any little tangent threatened to take things away from the goals that were most important for students like these—to think critically, not always to respond out of personal experience, to develop analytical tools that would stand them in good stead beyond this course.

"Just leave your comments on the chair by the door," she said in a voice as cheerful as she could muster. "I'll see you on Monday."

On the way down the hall Pam flipped through the students' comments:

Most important: Women are often treated unfairly in literature.
Next time: I don't want to waste any more time on this story.

Most important: Theme and point of view.
Next time: I don't really know.

Pam, I don't really understand why you would assign a story like this. It's insulting.   —Nicole Benson

Most important: You really have to know how to analyze to understand the stories we read in this class.
Next time: Maybe you could tell us something about Updike.

Most important: Theme.
Next time: I don't know if I really understand the theme.

Pam read over the entire stack when she got settled in her office. She was feeling a bit of mid-March weariness herself. Maybe "A&P" wasn't such a good match for her goals anymore. She needed, she knew, to talk with her colleagues and to think carefully about the syllabus for the course. But not right now. Her next class, Critical Approaches to Literature, began in twenty-five minutes.

QUESTIONS TO CONSIDER

1. What is your view of Pam Higgins's goals in teaching literature? Are her goals too rigid and formalist? Should she encourage her students' personal, political, and contextual responses to literature?

2. What cues should Pam Higgins take from the one-minute papers that she collects from students at the end of class? How should the responses affect Pam's decisions for the next class? For the course next semester?

3. Should Pam Higgins have taken time at the beginning of the semester to prepare students for some of the controversial teaching matter that they would be encountering in traditional literature? Should she explicitly discuss with students her own goals for the class, her purposes for choosing curricula and strategies, her rationale for book and story selection, and her teaching slant? What should she say?

4. Should Pam Higgins adapt her lessons to her students' concerns? How might she frame this literature for students? Can she adapt to her students' political concerns while being true to the goals and standards of the discipline?

ACTIVITIES

1. In small groups, discuss how you would create a book list for a course like this one. What literature would you choose? Why? How would you deal with charges of sexism in the content of the plays of Shakespeare or other well-known, widely read authors?

2. Create a lesson plan for teaching John Updike's story "A&P." If possible, teach a ten-minute lesson to a group of peers who have not read this case. What issues arise during your teaching? Do the students bring up sexism? After the lesson, debrief the students to uncover how they were thinking about the material.

3. Examine book lists from previous literature courses in college and high-school English departments. Identify books that would be considered politically incorrect by today's standards. Do you agree with this assessment? Consider books like Richard Wright's *Native Son*, a classic of African-American literature that could be considered extremely sexist in content. Would you include this book in a literature course? In a course on African-American literature? How would you deal with the sexist themes?

READINGS

Bernstein, R. (1990). The rising hegemony of the politically correct. *New York Times* (October 28): E1.

Hairston, M. (1992). Diversity, ideology, and teaching writing. *College Composition and Communication* 43 (2): 179–193.

Newkirk, T. (1984). Looking for trouble: A way to unmask our readings. *College English* 46 (6): 756–766.

About the Editors

JUDITH KLEINFELD received her bachelor's degree from Wellesley College and her doctoral degree from the Harvard Graduate School of Education. She pioneered a teacher education program based on studying real-world cases of teaching problems and dilemmas. Dr. Kleinfeld edits a case series, *Teaching Cases in Cross-Cultural Education,* and has published cases on gender equity and issues in subject-matter teaching. She has done research examining what teacher education students learn from studying and writing cases. Dr. Kleinfeld has published numerous books and articles and is also a newspaper columnist in education and the social sciences. She is currently professor of psychology and Director of the Northern Studies program at the University of Alaska. In 1993 she won the Emil Usibelli Award for Distinguished Research.

SUZANNE YERIAN earned her teaching certificate in secondary biology in 1982 and her MAT in 1986 from the University of Alaska Fairbanks. She taught in Fairbanks middle schools for seven years before joining the faculty at UAF in 1989 as teacher liaison with the local school district. Since 1991 she has been working on her Ph.D. at the University of Washington. Her research interests are in the field of teacher education and curriculum development. She was one of the organizers of the gender equity project at the University of Alaska Fairbanks, in 1990.

Index